Wide Angle

4A

GARY PATHARE

OXFORD
UNIVERSITY PRESS

OXFORD
UNIVERSITY PRESS

198 Madison Avenue
New York, NY 10016 USA

Great Clarendon Street, Oxford, OX2 6DP,
United Kingdom

Oxford University Press is a department of the University of Oxford. It furthers the University's objective of excellence in research, scholarship, and education by publishing worldwide. Oxford is a registered trade mark of Oxford University Press in the UK and in certain other countries

© Oxford University Press 2019

The moral rights of the author have been asserted

First published in 2019

2023 2022 2021 2020 2019

10 9 8 7 6 5 4 3 2

No unauthorized photocopying

All rights reserved. No part of this publication may be reproduced, stored in a retrieval system, or transmitted, in any form or by any means, without the prior permission in writing of Oxford University Press, or as expressly permitted by law, by licence or under terms agreed with the appropriate reprographics rights organization. Enquiries concerning reproduction outside the scope of the above should be sent to the ELT Rights Department, Oxford University Press, at the address above

You must not circulate this work in any other form and you must impose this same condition on any acquirer

Links to third party websites are provided by Oxford in good faith and for information only. Oxford disclaims any responsibility for the materials contained in any third party website referenced in this work

ISBN: 978 0 19 454693 5   4A Wide Angle American 4A SB W/OP Pack
ISBN: 978 0 19 454687 4   4A Wide Angle American 4A SB
ISBN: 978 0 19 454666 9   4 Wide Angle American 4 OP

Printed in China

This book is printed on paper from certified and well-managed sources

ACKNOWLEDGEMENTS

Back cover photograph: Oxford University Press building/David Fisher
Illustrations by: A. Richard Allen/Morgan Gaynin Inc pp. 7, 137; John Holcroft/Lindgren & Smith pp. 52, 145; Shaw Nielsen pp. 13, 25, 37, 49, 61, 73, 85, 97, 109, 121, 133, 145.
Video Stills, Mannic Productions: pp. 12, 24, 36, 48, 60, 72, 84, 96, 108, 120, 132, 144. Oxford University Press: pp. 40.
The Publishers would like to thank the following for their kind permission to reproduce photographs and other copyright material: **123rf:** pp.28 (ice/Galyna Andrushko), 40 (4/byrdyak), 45 (6/Dmitriy Shironosov), 64 (Levi Strauss label/Thodsapol Thongdeekhieo), 65 (shirt/Natallia Khlapushyna), 69 (doctor/racorn), 77 (minimalist living room/skdesign), 88 (VR set/Dinis Tolipov), 91 (movie streaming/georgejmclittle), (Vinyl record/Giuseppe Porzani), 94 (lecturer/Cathy Yeulet), 106 (Thai fusion dish/Mongkol Aphisuthisarn), 114 (computer code/Yusuke Saito), (hieroglyphics/Fedor Selivanov), 122 (a/Stefano Carocci), 151 (fire alarm/Pisit Khambubpha); **Alamy:** pp. 5 (running up bleachers/Blend Images), 7 (view looking down from Empire State Building/Ryan Deberardinis), 26 (hot air balloon/Johner Images), 28 (underground/Robbie Shone), 30 (Jacques Cousteau/Everett Collection Historical), (Matthew Henson/Granger Historical Picture Archive), 34 (asteroid mining/Stocktrek Images, Inc.), 45 (3/Kerry Elsworth), (5/Lasse Bolstad), 54 (3/tom pfeiffer), 65 (long sleeved/Westend61 GmbH), 68 (tech company interior/Tribune Content Agency LLC), 76 (cluttered room/Noel Yates), 78 (cave paiting/Hemis), (view from plane/Aurora Photos), 81 (bored tourists/Pierre Rochon photography), 91 (movie screen/EditorialByDarrellYoung), 94 (mail carrier/Ian Allenden), 100 (movie award/Mohamed Osama), 103 (Selexyz bookshop/Arcaid Images), 104 (Zagat restaurant guidebook/Patti McConville), 105 (restuarant/Bruce yuanyue Bi), 114 (Voynich manuscript/GL Archive), 116 (ancient manuscript/dpa picture alliance archive), 117 (Loch Ness Monster/Chronicle), (Oak Island Money Pit/gary corbett), 128 (woman watching plane/Anton Unguryanu), 133 (customer and salesperson/allesalltag), 139 (a/Ink Drop), 150 (Titanic/AF archive); **BLINK:** Cover, Quinn Ryan Mattingly, pp. 3 (young basketball players/Edu Bayer), 11 (Architect and designer Carmela Dacchille/Gianni Cipriano), 15 (Correfoc devils fireworks celebration/Edu Bayer), 18 (school girls read the paper/Krissiane Johnson), 27 (train passenger/Gianni Cipriano), 35 (Fucino Space Center/Nadia Shira Cohen), 39 (pottery factory/Quinn Ryan Mattingly), 47 (shoe designer/Gianni Cipriano), 51 (two woman walking/Krisanne Johnson), 56 (rescuing truck/Edu Bayer), 63 (women Gambia/Edu Bayer), 66 (groom bow tie/Edu Bayer), 75 (man infront of Abbey/Gianni Cipriano), 80 (valley/Quinn Ryan Mattingly), 87 (doctor with x-ray/Quinn Ryan Mattingly), 93 (computers/Edu Bayer), 99 (man In theatre/GIanni Cipriano), 107 (local vegetables on table/GIanni Cipriano), 111 (abandoned boat/Nadia Shira Cohen), 119 (misty road/Gianni Cipriano), 123 (Carneval celebration/Nadia Shira Cohen), 131 (man on computer/Edu Bayer), 135 (mother and child on train/Quinn Ryan Mattingly), 143 (physics lesson/Gianni Cipriano); **Bridgeman:** p. 30 (Amy Johnson/Capstack, John (1881-1967)/Private Collection/Prismatic Pictures), (Gertrude Bell/Pictures from History); **Getty:** pp. 6 (Gary Kasparov playing chess/JOSE JORDAN/Stringer), (Oprah Winfrey/Sunday Times/Contributor), 7 (view looking down from the Abraj Al-Bait Towers/AFP Contributor/Contributor), 19 (photographers/Andrew Hobbs), 21 (journalist/Jeff Greenberg/Contributor), 25 (girl and woman/Ariel Skelley), 30 (Tenzing Norgay/James Burke/Contributor), (Yuri Gagarin/Popperfoto/Contributor), 33 (space/WLADIMIR BULGAR/SCIENCE PHOTO LIBRARY), 45 (4/Tooga), 49 (students/Westend61), 54 (6/Joe Raedle/Staff), 59 (women talking/Tetra Images), 67 (man with baby/KidStock), 83 (happy tourist/Catherine Delahaye), 88 (driverless car/NOAH BERGER/Stringer), 90 (VR environment/da-kuk), 94 (futuristic automated workplace/gong hangxu), (trash collector/Blend Images - Don Mason), 101 (cinema/John Eder), 114 (Braille/Frederic Cirou), 117 (Antikythera Mechanism/LOUISA GOULIAMAKI/Stringer), (DB Cooper sketches/Time Life Pictures/Contributor), 122 (c/ Chicago Tribune/RSVP International Onion Goggles, patented), 124 (family/Amanda Edwards/Contributor), 127 (man painting/Troy House), 129 (Tim Berners-Lee/Andreas Rentz/Staff), 134 (a/Elena Segatini), (d/Steve Debenport), 136 (books/maurizio siani), 138 (old man and boy/Camille Tokerud), 139 (c/Credit:Fabrice LEROUGE), 141 (man on tablet/Hero Images), 146 (men drinking juice/Thomas Barwick), 156 (African plain/Vicki Jauron, Babylon and Beyond Photography); **Hugh Pryor:** p. 89 (GPS art/Hugh Pryor); **iStock:** p. xvi, (phone/lvcandy), (tablet/RekaReka); **OUP:** pp. 26 (snowboarding/Shutterstock/Nurlan Kalchinov), 54 (2/123rf/federicofoto), (4/Shutterstock/idiz), 88 (drone/Shutterstock/Maria Dryfhout), (GPS/Shutterstock/Pincasso), 94 (firefighter/Shutterstock/Toa55), 106 (beach/Shutterstock/Maria Dryfhout), 148 (radio mic/Shutterstock/Planner); **REX:** p. 65 (James Dean/Warner Bros/Kobal/REX/Shutterstock), 102 (Citizen Kane/Alex Kahle/RKO/Kobal/REX/Shutterstock); **Shutterstock:** pp. 7 (view looking down from Burj Khalifa/Stefano Carnevali), (view looking down from Eiffel Tower/Life In Pixels), (view looking down from the Tokyo tower/witaya ratanasirikulchai), 9 (pyramids/Dan Breckwoldt), 10 (woman on laptop/Andrey Bondarets), 16 (cartoon/humphrey), 22 (Burj Khalifa with fireworks/Naufal MQ), 26 (motorcyclist/eZeePics), (parasailing/Vadim Petrakov), (rock climbing/Vixit), (skydiving/Germanskydiver), 28 (moutains/Inu), (underwater/fenkieandreas), 29 (artificial intelligence/Lagarto Film), 29 (DNA/Media Whalestock), 29 (human mind /patrice6000), 40 (1/atdr), (2/Kostikova Natalia), (3/MicrostockStudi), 45 (1/Dutourdumonde Photography), (2/Nataliya Hora), 54 (1/Ivano de Santis), (5/anthony heflin), 57 (man/Jack Z Young), (woman/Monkey Business Images), 65 (cowboy boot /Evgeniya Porechenskaya), 65 (trousers/Di Studio), 77 (cozy living room/lenisecalleja.photography), 78 (building blending with nature/alionabirukova), 88 (smartphone/leungchopan), (x-ray/create jobs 51), 91 (disc/Early Spring), (music download/Archiwiz), (TV/Hadrian), 94 (office worker/Pressmaster), 98 (flying car/Peter Albrektsen), 106 (tropical paradise hotel/Vitaly Titov), 112 (mysterious place/Trent Alexander Maxwell), 113 (reading news/Ruslan Guzov), 117 (Easter Island/Anthony Booker), 122 (b/Kullanart), (d/FERNANDO BLANCO CALZADA), 124 (friends café/YAKOBCHUK VIACHESLAV), (man on phone/WAYHOME studio), (woman and docter/Monkey Business Images), (working hard/Stokkete), 126 (man with book/Borysevych.com), 134 (b/Subphoto), (c/Lucky Business), (e/David Tadevosian), (f/tharamust), 139 (b/sandsun), (d/Dean Drobot), (post it/Kindlena), 141 (healthy smoothie/LMproduction); **SPL:** p. 34 (space junk/CHRIS BUTLER).

Authentic Content Provided by Oxford Reference

The author and publisher are grateful to those who have given permission to reproduce the following extracts and adaptations or copyright material:

p.16 Laberge, Yves, John A. Lent, William M. Wisser, Char Simons, and Yves Laberge. "Journalism." In *Oxford Encyclopedia of the Modern World*. : Oxford University Press, 2008. http://www.oxfordreference.com/view/10.1093/acref/9780195176322.001.0001/acref-9780195176322-e-837

p.31 Gilmartin, Patricia. "Women Explorers." In *The Oxford Companion to World Exploration*. : Oxford University Press, 2007. http://www.oxfordreference.com/view/10.1093/acref/9780195149227.001.0001/acref-9780195149227-e-0698

p.43 "Film Technology." In *The Oxford Encyclopedia of the History of American Science, Medicine, and Technology*. : Oxford University Press, 2014. http://www.oxfordreference.com/view/10.1093/acref/9780199766666.001.0001/acref-9780199766666-e-163

p.55 Brady, Lisa M., Gregory H. Maddox, and Gregory Clancey. "Natural Disasters." In *Oxford Encyclopedia of the Modern World*. : Oxford University Press, 2008. http://www.oxfordreference.com/view/10.1093/acref/9780195176322.001.0001/acref-9780195176322-e-1093

pp.64 Roth, Marty. "Blue Jeans." In *Oxford Encyclopedia of the Modern World*. : Oxford University Press, 2008. http://www.oxfordreference.com/view/10.1093/acref/9780195176322.001.0001/acref-9780195176322-e-189

p.78 "Environmental Aesthetics." In *Encyclopedia of Aesthetics*. : Oxford University Press, 2014. http://www.oxfordreference.com/view/10.1093/acref/9780199747108.001.0001/acref-9780199747108-e-268

p.88 Littlefield, Melissa M., and Pauline Kusiak. "representation and technology." In *Science, Technology, and Society*. : Oxford University Press, 2005. http://www.oxfordreference.com/view/10.1093/acref/9780195141931.001.0001/acref-9780195141931-e-94

p.104 "Zagat, Tim." In *Savoring Gotham: A Food Lover's Companion to New York City*. : Oxford University Press, 2015. http://www.oxfordreference.com/view/10.1093/acref/9780199397020.001.0001/acref-9780199397020-e-677

p.114 "Voynich Manuscript." In *The Oxford Companion to the Book*. : Oxford University Press, 2010. http://www.oxfordreference.com/view/10.1093/acref/9780198606536.001.0001/acref-9780198606536-e-5129

p.129 "Berners-Lee, Sir Tim." In *A Dictionary of Computer Science*, edited by Butterfield, Andrew, and Gerard Ekembe Ngondi. : Oxford University Press, 2016. http://www.oxfordreference.com/view/10.1093/acref/9780199688975.001.0001/acref-9780199688975-e-6305

p.137 "Proverb." In *Concise Oxford Companion to the English Language*, edited by McArthur, Tom. : Oxford University Press, 1998. http://www.oxfordreference.com/view/10.1093/acref/9780192800619.001.0001/acref-9780192800619-e-997

p.147 "Pyramids of Giza." In *The Oxford Companion To Archaeology*. : Oxford University Press, 2012. http://www.oxfordreference.com/view/10.1093/acref/9780199735785.001.0001/acref-9780199735785-e-0363

p.147 "Bruce Springsteen." In *Oxford Essential Quotations*, edited by Ratcliffe, Susan. : Oxford University Press, http://www.oxfordreference.com/view/10.1093/acref/9780191843730.001.0001/q-oro-ed5-00010371

p.148 "Newspapers." In *Oxford Essential Quotations*, edited by Ratcliffe, Susan. : Oxford University Press, http://www.oxfordreference.com/view/10.1093/acref/9780191843730.001.0001/q-oro-ed5-00007862

p.149 "T. S. Eliot." In *The Oxford Dictionary of American Quotations*, edited by Rawson, Hugh, and Margaret Miner. : Oxford University Press, 2006. http://www.oxfordreference.com/view/10.1093/acref/9780195168235.001.0001/q-author-00008-00000509

p.150 "Andy Warhol." In *Oxford Dictionary of Quotations*, edited by Knowles, Elizabeth. : Oxford University Press, 2014. http://www.oxfordreference.com/view/10.1093/acref/9780199668700.001.0001/q-author-00010-00003350

p.151 "Martin Luther King." In *Oxford Dictionary of Political Quotations*, edited by Jay, Antony. : Oxford University Press, 2012. http://www.oxfordreference.com/view/10.1093/acref/9780199572687.001.0001/q-author-00002-00000883

p.152 "Coco Chanel." In *Oxford Essential Quotations*, edited by Ratcliffe, Susan. : Oxford University Press, http://www.oxfordreference.com/view/10.1093/acref/9780191843730.001.0001/q-oro-ed5-00012116

p.153 "The Mind." In *Oxford Dictionary of Humorous Quotations*, edited by Brandreth, Gyles. : Oxford University Press, 2013. http://www.oxfordreference.com/view/10.1093/acref/9780199681365.001.0001/q-subject-00008-00000195

p.154 "Andrew Grove." In *Oxford Dictionary of Quotations*, edited by Knowles, Elizabeth. : Oxford University Press, 2014. http://www.oxfordreference.com/view/10.1093/acref/9780199668700.001.0001/q-author-00010-00001449

p.155 "W. Somerset Maugham." In *Oxford Essential Quotations*, edited by Ratcliffe, Susan. : Oxford University Press, http://www.oxfordreference.com/view/10.1093/acref/9780191843730.001.0001/q-oro-ed5-00007179

p.156 "René Magritte." In *Oxford Essential Quotations*, edited by Ratcliffe, Susan. : Oxford University Press, http://www.oxfordreference.com/view/10.1093/acref/9780191843730.001.0001/q-oro-ed5-00012502

p.157 "Heraclitus." In *Oxford Essential Quotations*, edited by Ratcliffe, Susan. : Oxford University Press, http://www.oxfordreference.com/view/10.1093/acref/9780191843730.001.0001/q-oro-ed5-00005370

p.158 "Stephen Vincent Benét." In *Oxford Dictionary of Quotations*, edited by Knowles, Elizabeth. : Oxford University Press, 2014. http://www.oxfordreference.com/view/10.1093/acref/9780199668700.001.0001/q-author-00010-00000277

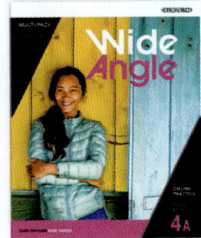

Cover photo by Quinn Ryan Mattingly.
Dalat, Vietnam, April 2017.
A portrait of Rolan Co Lieng, founder and owner of K'ho Coffee Company in Dalat, Vietnam. A member of the K'ho ethnic minority in Vietnam, her ancestors have been growing coffee in this region of Vietnam since the 1920s.

Contents

UNIT	READING	LISTENING	SPEAKING	WRITING
1 Achievements 3	Skimming and scanning *What makes a person an overachiever?*	Recognizing sentence stress and word boundaries ▶ The Empire State Building	Answering interview questions	Using appropriate language
2 News 15	Identifying topic sentences *The Development of Newspapers*	Recognizing linkers in fast speech	Describing an event	Using references and pronouns
3 Frontiers 27	Working out meaning from context *Discovering Explorers*	Recognizing rephrasing in a talk	Giving a presentation	Writing paragraphs and topic sentences
4 Processes 39	Classifying information from a text *Technology and the Big Screen*	Using visual information while listening ▶ Harris Tweed	Describing a process	Using examples and explanation linking words
5 Survival 51	Recognizing and understanding exemplification *The Great Lisbon Earthquake*	Interpreting changes in volume, speed, and pitch	Giving practical instructions	Using addition and contrast linking words
6 Trends 63	Using questions when reading *Blue Jeans*	Previewing using images	Talking about past habits	Note-taking while listening ▶ Lecture: Work habits

GRAMMAR FOCUS 159–164

ENGLISH FOR REAL	GRAMMAR	VOCABULARY	PRONUNCIATION	REVIEW
▶ Making inquiries	Simple present, present continuous, and present perfect State verbs *Each* and *every*	Personal development Collocations	Word stress in compound adjectives	see page 147
▶ Giving and reacting to news	Narrative tenses: simple past, past continuous, and past perfect *all, both, either* *was/were going to*	Taking action (verbs) Comment adverbs	Stressed auxiliary verbs and form of *be*	see page 148
▶ Interrupting and resuming	Verbs + *to* infinitive or *-ing* form Verbs + *-ing* form and verbs + *to* infinitive *so* and *such*	Exploration Suffixes for nouns	Shifting stress in suffix words	see page 149
▶ Asking for and giving clarification	Present passive and past passive Present passive with modal verbs Adjectives with prepositions	Production (verbs) Explaining a process	Chunking	see page 150
▶ Asking for and giving advice	Advice and warning with *should, ought to,* and *had better* Obligation with *must* and *have to* Intensifiers	Natural disasters (verbs) Extreme adjectives Phrasal verbs with *look*	Connected speech with words ending in /t/ or /d/	see page 151
▶ Asking for and giving opinions	Time expressions with the present perfect and simple past *used to* and *be/get used to* *do* for emphasis	Fashion (adjectives) Work Adverbs and phrases for emphasis	*used to*	see page 152

Acknowledgments

AUTHOR

Gary Pathare has a Master's in Education in TESOL from Newcastle University, England. He has been teaching English at the Higher Colleges of Technology in Dubai since 2001, after ten years teaching English and teacher training in Barcelona and Rome. Gary has spoken at international conferences on a wide range of topics, including spelling, literacy, writing, reading, grammar, metaphor, original uses of technology, memorization, materials writing, teacher training, and innovation in ELT.

SERIES CONSULTANTS

PRAGMATICS **Carsten Roever** is Associate Professor in Applied Linguistics at the University of Melbourne, Australia. He was trained as a TESOL teacher and holds a PhD in Second Language Acquisition from the University of Hawai'i at Manoa. His research interests include interlanguage pragmatics, language testing, and conversation analysis.

Naoko Taguchi is an Associate Professor of Japanese and Second Language Acquisition at the Dietrich College of Modern Languages at Carnegie Mellon University. She holds a PhD from Northern Arizona University. Her primary research interests include pragmatics in Second Language Acquisition, second language education, and classroom-based research.

PRONUNCIATION **Tamara Jones** is an instructor at the English Language Center at Howard Community College in Columbia, Maryland.

INCLUSIVITY & CRITICAL THINKING **Lara Ravitch** is a senior instructor and the Intensive English Program Coordinator of the American English Institute at the University of Oregon.

ENGLISH FOR REAL VIDEOS **Pamela Vittorio** acquired a BA in English/Theater from SUNY Geneseo and is an ABD PhD in Middle Eastern Studies with an MA in Middle Eastern Literature and Languages from NYU. She also designs ESL curriculum, materials, and English language assessment tools for publishing companies and academic institutions.

MIDDLE EAST ADVISORY BOARD **Amina Saif Al Hashami**, Nizwa College of Applied Sciences, Oman; **Karen Caldwell**, Higher Colleges of Technology, Ras Al Khaimah, UAE; **Chaker Ali Mhamdi**, Buraimi University College, Oman.

LATIN AMERICA ADVISORY BOARD **Reinaldo Hernández**, Duoc, Chile; **Mauricio Miraglia**, Universidad Tecnológica de Chile INACAP, Chile; **Aideé Damián Rodríguez**, Tecnológico de Monterrey, Mexico; **Adriana Recke Duhart**, Universidad Anáhuac, Mexico; **Inés Campos**, Centro de Idiomas, Cesar Vallejo University, Peru.

SPAIN ADVISORY BOARD **Alison Alonso**, EOI Luarca, Spain; **Juan Ramón Bautista Liébana**, EOI Rivas, Spain; **Ruth Pattison**, EOI, Spain; **David Silles McLaney**, EOI Majadahonda, Spain.

We would like to acknowledge the educators from around the world who participated in the development and review of this series:

ASIA **Ralph Baker**, Chuo University, Japan; **Elizabeth Belcour**, Chongshin University, South Korea; **Mark Benton**, Kobe Shoin Women's University, Japan; **Jon Berry**, Kyonggi University, South Korea; **Stephen Lyall Clarke**, Vietnam-US English Training Service Centers, Vietnam; **Edo Forsythe**, Hirosaki Gakuin University, Japan; **Clifford Gibson**, Dokkyo University, Japan; **Michelle Johnson**, Nihon University, Japan; **Stephan Johnson**, Rikkyo University, Japan; **Nicholas Kemp**, Kyushu International University, Japan; **Brendyn Lane**, Core Language School, Japan; **Annaliese Mackintosh**, Kyonggi University, South Korea; **Keith Milling**, Yonsei University, Korea; **Chau Ngoc Minh Nguyen**, Vietnam – USA Society English Training Service Center, Vietnam; **Yongjun Park**, Sangi University, South Korea; **Scott Schafer**, Inha University, South Korea; **Dennis Schumacher**, Cheongju University, South Korea; **Jenay Seymour**, Hongik University, South Korea; **Joseph Staples**, Shinshu University, Japan; **Greg Stapleton**, YBM Education Inc. – Adult Academies Division, South Korea; **Le Tuam Vu**, Tan True High School, Vietnam; **Ben Underwood**, Kugenuma High School, Japan; **Quyen Vuong**, VUS English Center, Vietnam

EUROPE **Marta Alonso Jerez**, Mainfor Formación, Spain; **Pilar Álvarez Polvorinos**, EOI San Blas, Spain; **Peter Anderson**, Anderson House, Italy; **Ana Anglés Esquinas**, First Class Idiomes i Formació, Spain; **Keith Appleby**, CET Services, Spain; **Isabel Arranz**, CULM Universidad de Zaragoza, Spain; **Jesus Baena**, EOI Alcalá de Guadaira, Spain; **José Gabriel Barbero Férnández**, EOI de Burgos, Spain; **Carlos Bibi Fernandez**, EIO de Madrid-Ciudad Lineal, Spain; **Alex Bishop**, IH Madrid, Spain; **Nathan Leopold Blackshaw**, CCI, Italy; **Olga Bel Blesa**, EOI, Spain; **Antoinette Breutel**, Academia Language School, Switzerland; **Angel Francisco Briones Barco**, EOI Fuenlabrada, Spain; **Ida Brucciani**, Pisa University, Italy; **Julie Bystrytska**, Profi-Lingua, Poland; **Raul Cabezali**, EOI Alcala de Guadaira, Spain; **Milena Cacko-Kozera**, Profi-Lingua, Poland; **Elena Calviño**, EOI Pontevedra, Spain; **Alex Cameron**, The English House, Spain; **Rosa Cano Vallese**, EOI Prat Llobregate, Spain; **Montse Cañada**, EOI Barcelona, Spain; **Elisabetta Carraro**, We.Co Translate, Italy; **Joaquim Andres Casamiquela**, Escola Oficial d'Idiomes – Guinardó, Spain; **Lara Ros Castillo**, Aula Campus, Spain; **Patricia Cervera Cottrell**, Centro de Idiomas White, Spain; **Sally Christopher**, Parkway S.I., Spain; **Marianne Clark**, The English Oak Tree Academy, Spain; **Helen Collins**, ELI, Spain; **María José Conde Torrado**, EOI Ferrol, Spain; **Ana Maria Costachi**, Centro de Estudios Ana Costachi S.I., Spain; **Michael Cotton**, Modern English Study Centre, Italy; **Pedro Cunado Placer**, English World, Spain; **Sarah Dague**, Universidad Carlos III, Spain; **María Pilar Delgado**, Big Ben School, Spain; **Ashley Renee Dentremont Matthäus**, Carl-Schurz Haus, Deutch-Amerikanisches-Institut Freiburg e.V., Germany; **Mary Dewhirst**, Cambridge English Systems, Spain; **Hanna Dobrzycka**, Advantage, Poland; **Laura Dolla**, E.F.E. Laura Dolla, Spain; **Paul Doncaster**, Taliesin Idiomes, Spain; **Marek Doskocz**, Lingwista Sp. z o.o., Poland; **Fiona Dunbar**, ELI Málaga, Spain; **Anna Dunin-Bzdak**, Military University of Technology, Poland; **Robin Evers**, l'Università di Modena e Reggio Emilia, Italy; **Yolanda Fernandez**, EOI, Spain; **Dolores Fernández Gavela**, EOI Gijón, Spain; **Mgr. Tomáš Fišer**, English Academy, Czech Republic; **Juan Fondón**, EOI de Langreo, Spain; **Carmen Forns**, Centro Universitario de Lenguas Modernas, Spain; **Ángela Fraga**, EOI de Ferrol, Spain; **Beatriz Freire**, Servicio de Idiomas FGULL, Spain; **Alena Fridrichova**, Palacky University in Olomouc, Faculty of Science, Department of Foreign Languages, Czech Republic, **Elena Friedrich**, Palacky University, **JM Galarza**, Iruñanko Hizkuntz Eskola, Spain; **Nancie Gantenbein**, TLC-IH, Switzerland; **Gema García**, EOI, Spain; **Maria Jose Garcia Ferrer**, EOI Moratalaz, Spain; **Josefa García González**, EOI Málaga, Spain; **Maria García Hermosa**, EOI, Spain; **Jane Gelder**, The British Institute of Florence, Italy; **Aleksandra Gelner**, ELC Katowice, Bankowa 14, Poland; **Marga Gesto**, EOI Ferrol, Spain; **Juan Gil**, EOI Maria Moliner, Spain; **Eva Gil Cepero**, EOI La Laguna, Spain; **Alan Giverin**, Today School, Spain; **Tomas Gomez**, EOI Segovia, Spain; **Mónica González**, EOI Carlos V, Spain; **Elena González Diaz**, EOI, Spain; **Steve Goodman**, Language Campus, Spain; **Katy Gorman**, Study Sulmona, Italy; **Edmund Green**, The British Institute of Florence, Italy; **Elvira Guerrero**, GO! English Granada, Spain; **Lauren Hale**, The British Institute of Florence, Italy; **Maria Jose Hernandez**, EOI de Salou, Spain; **Chris Hermann**, Hermann Brown English Language Centre, Spain; **Robert Holmes**, Holmes English, Czech Republic; **José Ramón Horrillo**, EOI de Aracena, Spain; **Laura Izquierdo**, Univeirsity of Zaragoza, Spain; **Marcin Jaśkiewicz**, British School Żoliborz, Poland; **Mojmír Jurák**, Albi – jazyková škola, Czech Republic; **Eva Kejdová**, BLC, Czech Republic; **Turlough Kelleher**, British Council, Callaghan School of English, Spain; **Janina Knight**, Advantage Learners, Spain; **Ewa Kowalik**, English Point Radom, Poland; **Monika Krawczuk**, Wyższa Szkoła Finansów i Zarządzania, Poland; **Milica Krisan**, Agentura Parole, Czech Republic; **Jędrzej Kucharski**, Profi-lingua, Poland; **V. Lagunilla**, EOI San Blas, Spain; **Antonio Lara Davila**, EOI La Laguna, Spain; **Ana Lecubarri**, EOI Aviles, Spain; **Lesley Lee**, Exit Language Center, Spain; **Jessica Lewis**, Lewis Academy, Spain; **Alice Llopas**, EOI Estepa, Spain; **Angela Lloyd**, SRH Hochschule Berlin, Germany; **Helena Lohrová**, University of South Bohemia, Faculty of Philosophy, Czech Republic; **Elena López Luengo**, EOI Alcalá de Henares, Spain; **Karen Lord**, Cambridge House, Spain; **Carmen Loriente Duran**, EOI Rio Vero, Spain; **Alfonso Luengo**, EOI Jesús Maestro Madrid, Spain; **Virginia Lyons**, VLEC, Spain; **Anna Łętowska-Mickiewicz**, University of Warsaw, Poland; **Ewa Malesa**, Uniwersytet SWPS, Poland; **Klara Małowiecka**, University of Warsaw, Poland; **Dott. Ssa Kim Manzi**, Università degli Studi della Tuscia – DISTU – Viterbo, Italy; **James Martin**, St. James Language Center, Spain; **Ana Martin Arista**, EOI Tarazona, Spain; **Irene Martín Gago**, NEC, Spain; **Marga Martínez**, ESIC Idiomas Valencia, Spain; **Kenny McDonnell**, McDonnell English Services S.I., Spain; **Anne Mellon**, EEOI Motilla del Palacar, Spain; **Miguel Ángel Meroño**, EOI Cartagena, Spain; **Joanna Merta**, Lingua Nova, Poland; **Victoria Mollejo**, EOI San Blas-Madrid, Spain; **Rebecca Moon**, La Janda Language Services, Spain; **Anna Morales Puigicerver**, EOI TERRASSA, Spain; **Jesús Moreno**, Centro de Lenguas Modernas, Universidad de Zaragoza, Spain;

Emilio Moreno Prieto, EOI Albacete, Spain; **Daniel Muñoz Bravo**, Big Ben Center, Spain; **Heike Mülder**, In-House Englishtraining, Germany; **Alexandra Netea**, Albany School of English, Cordoba, Spain; **Christine M. Neubert**, Intercultural Communication, Germany; **Ignasi Nuez**, The King's Corner, Spain; **Guadalupe Núñez Barredo**, EOI de Ponferrada, Spain; **Monika Olizarowicz-Strygner**, XXII LO z OD im. Jose Marti, Poland; **A. Panter**, Oxford School of English, Italy; **Vanessa Jayne Parvin**, British School Florence, Italy; **Rachel Payne**, Academia Caledonian, Cadiz, Spain; **Olga Pelaez**, EOI Palencia, Spain; **Claudia Pellegrini**, Klubschule Migros, Switzerland; **Arantxa Pérez**, EOI Tudela, Spain; **Montse Pérez**, EOI Zamora, Spain; **Esther Pérez**, EOI Soria, Spain; **Rubén Pérez Montesinos**, EOI San Fernando de Henares, Spain; **Joss Pinches**, Servicio de Lenguas Modernas, Universidad de Huelva, Spain; **Katerina Pitrova**, FLCM TBU in Zlin, Czech Republic; **Erica Pivesso**, Komalingua, Spain; **Eva Plechackova**, Langfor CZ, Czech Republic; **Jesús Porras Santana**, JPS English School, Spain; **Adolfo Prieto**, EOI Albacete, Spain; **Sara Prieto**, Universidad Católica de Murcia, Spain; **Penelope Prodromou**, Universitá Roma Tre, Italy; **Maria Jose Pueyo**, EOI Zaragoza, Spain; **Bruce Ratcliff**, Academia Caledonian, Spain; **Jolanta Rawska**, School of English "Super Grade," Poland; **Mar Rey**, EOI Del Prat, Spain; **Silke Riegler**, HAW Landshut, Germany; **Pauline Rios**, Rivers, Spain; **Laura Rivero**, EOI La Laguna, Spain; **Carmen Rizo**, EOI Torrevieja, Spain; **Antonio F. Rocha Canizares**, EOI Talavera de la Reina, Spain; **Eva Rodellas Fontiguell**, London English School; **Sara Rojo**, EOI Elche, Spain; **Elena Romea**, UNED, Spain; **Ann Ross**, Centro Linguistico di Ateneo, Italy; **Tyler Ross**, Ingliese for you, Italy; **Susan Royo**, EOI Utebo, Spain; **Asuncion Ruiz Astruga**, EOI Maria Molinar, Spain; **Tamara Ruiz Fernandez**, English Today, Spain; **Soledat Sabate**, FIAC, Spain; **Maria Justa Saenz de Tejad**, ECI Idiomas Bailen, Spain; **Sophia Salaman**, University of Florence, Centro Linguistico de ATENEO, Italy; **Elizabeth Schiller**, Schillers Sprachstudio, Germany; **Carmen Serrano Tierz**, CULM, Spain; **Elizabeth R. Sherman**, Lexis Language Centre, Italy; **Rocio Sierra**, EOI Maspalomas, Spain; **David Silles McLaney**, EOI Majadahonda, Spain; **Alison Slade**, British School Florence, Italy; **Rachael Smith**, Accademia Britannica Toscana, Italy; **Michael Smith**, The Cultural English Centre, Spain; **Sonia Sood**, Oxford School Treviso, Italy; **Monika Stawska**, SJO Pigmalion, Poland; **Izabela Stępniewska**, ZS nr 69, Warszawa / British School Otwock, Poland; **Rocío Stevenson**, R & B Academia, Spain; **Petra Stolinova**, Magic English s.r.o., Czech Republic; **Hana Szulczewska**, UNO (Studium Języków Obcych), Poland; **Tim T.**, STP, Spain; **Vera Tauchmanova**, Univerzita Hradec Kralove, Czech Republic; **Nina Terry**, Nina School of English, Spain; **Francesca R. Thompson**, British School of East, Italy; **Pilar Tizzard**, Docklands Idiomas, Spain; **Jessica Toro**, International House Zaragoza, Spain; **Christine Tracey**, Università Roma Tre, Italy; **Loredana Trocchi**, L'Aquila, Italy; **Richard Twiggl**, International House Milan, Italy; **Natàlia Verdalet**, EOI Figueres, Spain; **Sergio Viñals**, EOI San Javier, Spain; **Edith von Sundahl-Hiller**, Supernova Idiomas, Spain; **Vanda Vyslouzilova**, Academia, Czech Republic; **Helen Waldron**, ELC, Germany; **Leslie Wallace**, Academia Language School, Switzerland; **Monika Wąsowska-Polak**, Akademia Obrony Narodowej, Poland; **Melissa Weaver**, TLC-IH, Switzerland; **Maria Watton**, Centro Lingue Estere CC, Italy; **Dr. Otto Weihs**, IMC FH Krems, Austria; **Kate Williams**, Oxford House Barcelona, Spain; **June Winterflood**, Academia Language School, Switzerland; **Ailsa Wood**, Cooperativa Babel, Italy; **Irene Zamora**, www.speakwithirene.com, Spain; **Coro Zapata**, EOIP Pamplona, Spain; **Gloria Zaragoza**, Alicante University, Spain; **Cristina Zêzere**, EOI Torrelavega, Spain

LATIN AMERICA **Fernando Arcos**, Santo Tomás University, Chile; **Ricardo Barreto**, Bridge School, Brazil; **Beth Bartlett**, Centro Cultural Colombo Americano, Cali, Colombia; **Julie Patricia Benito Lugo**, Universidad Central, Colombia; **Ana Luisa Bley Soriano**, Universidad UCINF, Chile; **Gabriela Brun**, I.S.F.D N 129, Argentina; **Talita Burlamaqui**, UFAM, Brazil; **Lourdes Leonides Canta Lozano**, Fac. De Ciencias Biolgicas UANL, Mexico; **Claudia Castro**, Stratford Institute – Moreno-Bs.As, Argentina; **Fabrício Cruz**, Britanic, Brazil; **Lisa Davies**, British Council, Colombia; **Adriana de Blasis**, English Studio Ciudad de Mercedes, Argentina; **Nora Abraira de Lombardo**, Cultural Inglesa de Mercedes, Argentina; **Bronwyn Donohue**, British Council, Colombia; **Andrea C. Duran**, Universidad Externado de Colombia; **Phil Elias**, British Council, Colombia; **Silvia C. Enríquez**, Escuela de Lenguas. Universidad Nacional de La Plata, Argentina; **Freddy Espinoza**, Universidad UCINF, Chile; **Maria de Lourdes Fernandes Silva**, The First Steps School, Brazil; **Doris Flores**, Santo Tomás English Program, Chile; **Hilda Flor-Páez**, Universidad Catolica Santiago de Guayaquil, Ecuador; **Lauriston Freitas**, Cooplem Idiomas, Brazil; **Alma Delia Frias Puente**, UANL, Mexico; **Sandra Gacitua Matus**, Universidad de la Frontera, Chile; **Gloria Garcia**, IPI Ushuaia-Tierra del Fuego, Argentina; **Alma Delia Garcia Ensastegui**, UAEM, Mexico; **Karina Garcia Gonzalez**, Universidad Panamericana, Mexico; **Miguel García Rojas**, UNMSM, Peru; **Macarena González Mena**, Universidad Tecnológica de Chile, Inacap, Chile; **Diana Granado**, Advanced English, Colombia; **Paul Christopher Graves**, Universidad Mayor, Chile; **Mabel Gutierrez**, British Council, Colombia; **Niamh Harnett**, Universidad Externado de Colombia, Colombia; **Elsa Hernandez**, English Time Institute, Argentina; **Reinaldo Hernández Sordo**, DUOC UC, Chile; **Eduardo Icaza**, CEN, Ecuador; **Kenel Joseph**, Haitian-American Institute, Haiti; **Joel Kellogg**, British Council, Colombia; **Sherif Ebrahim Khakil**, Chapingo Universidad Autonoma Chapingo, Mexico; **Cynthia Marquez**, Instituto Guatemalteco Americano, Guatemala; **Aaron McCarroll**, Universidad Sergio Arboleda, Colombia; **Milagro Machado**, SISE Institute, Peru; **Marta de Faria e Cunha Monteiro**, Federal University of Amazonas – UFAM, Brazil; **Lucía Murillo Sardi**, Instituto Británico, Peru; **Ricardo A. Nausa**, Universidad de los Andes, Colombia; **Andrea Olmos Bernal**, Universidad de Guadalajara, Mexico; **M. Edu Lizzete Olvera Dominguez**, Universidad Autonoma de Baja California Sur, Mexico; **Blanca Ortecho**,

Universidad Cesar Vallejo Centro de Idiomas, Peru; **Jim Osorio**, Instituto Guatemalteco Americano, Guatemala; **Erika del Carmen Partida Velasco**, Univam, Mexico; **Mrs. Katterine Pavez**, Universidad de Atacama, Chile; **Sergio Peña**, Universidad de La Frontera, Chile; **Leonor Cristina Peñafort Camacho**, Universidad Autónoma de Occidente, Colombia; **Tom Rickman**, British Council, Colombia; **Olga Lucia Rivera**, Universidad Externado de Colombia, Colombia; **Maria-Eugenia Ruiz Brand**, DUOC UC, Chile; **Gabriela S. Eguiarte**, London School, Mexico; **Majid Safadaran**, Instituto Cultural Peruano Norteamericano, Peru; **María Ines Salinas**, UCASAL, Argentina; **Ruth Salomon-Barkmeyer**, UNILINGUAS – UNISINOS, Brazil; **Mario Castillo Sanchez Hidalgo**, Universidad Panamericana, Mexico; **Katrina J. Schmidt**, Universidad de Los Andes, Colombia; **Jacqueline Sedore**, The Language Company, Chile; **Lourdes Angelica Serrano Herrera**, Adler Schule, Mexico; **Antonio Diego Sousa de Oliveira**, Federal University of Amazonas, Brazil; **Padraig Sweeney**, Universidad Sergio Arboleda, Colombia; **Edith Urquiza Parra**, Centro Universitario México, Mexico; **Eduardo Vásquez**, Instituto Chileno Britanico de Cultura, Chile; **Patricia Villasante**, Idiomas Católica, Peru; **Malaika Wilson**, The Language Company, Chile; **Alejandra Zegpi-Pons**, Universidad Católica de Temuco, Chile; **Boris Zevallos**, Universidad Cesar Vallejo Centro de Idiomas, Peru; **Wilma Zurita Beltran**, Universidad Central del Ecuador, Ecuador

THE MIDDLE EAST **Chaker Ali Mhamdi**, Buraimi University College, Oman; **Salama Kamal Shohayb**, Al-Faisal International Academy, Saudi Arabia

TURKEY **M. Mine Bağ**, Sabanci University, School of Languages; **Suzanne Campion**, Istanbul University; **Daniel Chavez**, Istanbul University Language Center; **Asuman Cincioğlu**, Istanbul University; **Hatice Çelikkanat**, Istanbul Esenyurt University; **Güneş Yurdasiper Dal**, Maltepe University; **Angeliki Douri**, Istanbul University Language Center; **Zia Foley**, Istanbul University; **Frank Foroutan**, Istanbul University Language Center; **Nicola Frampton**, Istanbul University; **Merve Güler**, Istanbul University; **H. Ibrahim Karabulut**, Dumlupınar University; **Catherine McKimm**, Istanbul University; **Merve Oflaz**, Dogus University; **Burcu Özgül**, Istanbul University; **Yusuf Özmenekşe**, Istanbul University Language Center; **Lanlo Pinter**, Istanbul University Language Center; **Ahmet Rasim**, Amasya University; **Diana Maria Rios Hoyos**, Istanbul University Language Center; **Jose Rodrigues**, Istanbul University; **Dilek Eryılmaz Salkı**, Ozyegin University; **Merve Selcuk**, Istanbul Kemerburgaz University; **Mehdi Solhi Andarab**, Istanbul Medipol University; **Jennifer Stephens**, Istanbul University; **Özgür Şahan**, Bursa Technical University; **Fatih Yücel**, Beykent University

UNITED KINGDOM **Sarah Ali**, Nottingham Trent International College, Nottingham; **Rolf Donald**, Eastbourne School of English, Eastbourne, East Sussex; **Nadine Early**, ATC Language Schools, Dublin, Ireland; **Dr. Sarah Ekdawi**, Oxford School of English, Oxford; **Glynis Ferrer**, LAL Torbay, Paignton Devon; **Diarmuid Fogarty**, INTO Manchester, Manchester; **Ryan Hannan**, Hampstead School of English, London; **Neil Harris**, ELTS, Swansea University, Swansea; **Claire Hunter**, Edinburgh School of English, Edinburgh, Scotland; **Becky Ilk**, LAL Torbay, Paignton; **Kirsty Matthews**, Ealing, Hammersmith & West London's college, London; **Amanda Mollaghan**, British Study Centres London, London; **Shila Nadar**, Twin ECL, London; **Sue Owens**, Cambridge Academy of English, Girton, Cambridge; **Caroline Preston**, International House Newcastle, Newcastle upon Tyne; **Ruby Rennie**, University of Edinburgh, Edinburgh, Scotland; **Howard Smith**, Oxford House College, London; **Yijie Wang**, The University of Edinburgh, Scotland; **Alex Warren**, Eurotraining, Bournemouth

UNITED STATES **Christina H. Appel**, ELS Educational Services, Manhattan, NY; **Nicole Bollhalder**, Stafford House, Chicago, IL; **Rachel Bricker**, Arizona State University, Tempe, AZ; **Kristen Brown**, Massachusetts International Academy, Marlborough, MA; **Tracey Brown**, Parkland College, Champaign, IL; **Peter Campisi**, ELS Educational Services, Manhattan, NY; **Teresa Cheung**, North Shore Community College, Lynn, MA; **Tyler Clancy**, ASC English, Boston, MA; **Rachael David**, Talk International, Miami, FL; **Danielle De Koker**, ELS Educational Services, New York, NY; **Diana Djaboury**, Mesa Community College, Mesa, AZ; **Mark Elman**, Talk International, Miami, FL; **Dan Gauran**, EC English, Boston, MA; **Kerry Gilman**, ASC English, Boston, MA; **Heidi Guenther**, ELS Educational Services, Manhattan, NY; **Emily Herrick**, University of Nebraska-Lincoln, Lincoln, NE; **Kristin Homuth**, Language Center International, Southfield, MI; **Alexander Ingle**, ALPS Language School, Seattle, WA; **Eugenio Jimenez**, Lingua Language Center at Broward College, Miami, FL; **Mahalia Joeseph**, Lingua Language Center at Broward College, Miami, FL; **Melissa Kaufman**, ELS Educational Services, Manhattan, NY; **Kristin Kradolfer Espinar**, MILA, Miami, FL; **Larissa Long**, TALK International, Fort Lauderdale, FL; **Mercedes Martinez**, Global Language Institute, Minneapolis, MN; **Ann McCrory**, San Diego Continuing Education, San Diego, CA; **Simon McDonough**, ASC English, Boston, MA; **Dr. June Ohrnberger**, Suffolk County Community College, Brentwood, NY; **Fernanda Ortiz**, Center for English as a Second Language at the University of Arizona, Tuscon, AZ; **Roberto S. Quintans**, Talk International, Miami, FL; **Terri J. Rapoport**, ELS, Princeton, NJ; **Alex Sanchez Silva**, Talk International, Miami, FL; **Cary B. Sands**, Talk International, Miami, FL; **Joseph Santaella Vidal**, EC English, Boston, MA; **Angel Serrano**, Lingua Language Center at Broward College, Miami, FL; **Timothy Alan Shaw**, New England School of English, Boston, MA; **Devinder Singh**, The University of Tulsa, Tulsa, OK; **Daniel Stein**, Lingua Language Center at Broward College, Miami, FL; **Christine R. Stesau**, Lingua Language Center at Broward College, Miami, FL; **David Stock**, ELS Educational Services, Manhattan, NY; **Joshua Stone**, Approach International Student Center, Allston, MA; **Maria-Virginia Tanash**, EC English, Boston, MA; **Noraina Vazquez Huyke**, Talk International, Miami, FL

Overview

A REAL-WORLD VIEWPOINT

Whatever your goals and aspirations, *Wide Angle* helps you use English to connect with the world around you. It empowers you to join any conversation and say the right thing at the right time, with confidence.

3 Frontiers

UNIT SNAPSHOT

Who first got to the top of Mount Everest? 30
Who secretly traveled the world as a man? 32
What came first: lenses or printing presses? 38

Why do people go to new places?
Which areas have humans explored? How?
How do people feel when they cross a frontier?

BEHIND THE PHOTO

1 Answer the questions.

1 If you were going to explore an area of the world, where would you go and why?
I would go to New Zealand or somewhere else with lots of beautiful scenery. I love wild places and love going hiking in the mountains.
2 What are the benefits of exploring? Who benefits most?
3 What are the problems? Who faces them?

2 Discuss your answers with a partner. Do you have similar views?

REAL-WORLD GOAL
Visit somewhere you have never been before

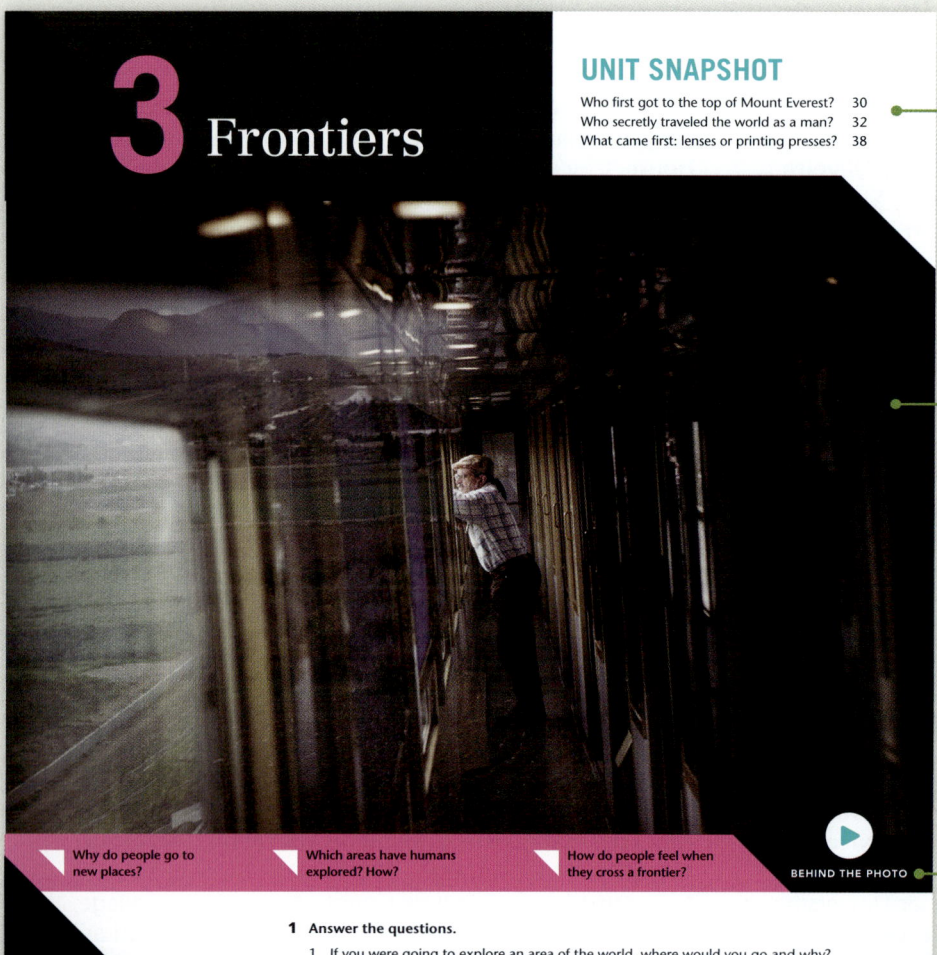

Start thinking about the topic with relevant, interesting **introduction questions.**

blink

Be inspired by the **vibrant unit opener images** from Blink photography. The international, award-winning photographers bring stories from around the world to life on the page.

Watch the **"Behind the Photo"** video from the photographer.

"People go to new places for a variety of reasons: to work, to study, to learn, relax, challenge themselves, or simply to discover something new. Travel is the ideal way to test yourself. It pushes people to their limits and gets them outside of their comfort zone."

Gianni Cipriano

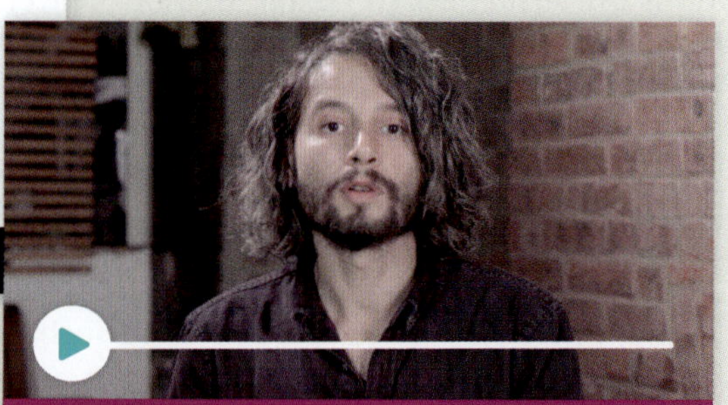

Apply learning to your own needs with **Real-World Goals**, instantly seeing the benefit of the English you are learning.

Enjoy learning with the huge variety of **up-to-date, inventive, and engaging audio and video**.

Understand what to say and how to say it with **English For Real**.

These lessons equip you to choose and adapt appropriate language to communicate effectively in any situation.

3.4 Excuse Me…

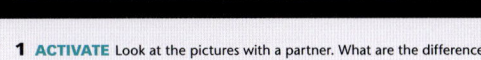

1 ACTIVATE Look at the pictures with a partner. What are the differences? Discuss the question in relation to the following.

location
situation
relationships between speakers

2 IDENTIFY Watch a conversation between Max, Andy, Phil, and Kevin about a lecture they have just attended. What do they keep doing?

3 ASSESS You are going to watch an extract of the lecture the friends were talking about in Exercise 2. Max wants to ask the speaker a question. What do you think Max's interruption will be like compared to the way the friends interrupted each other in their conversation? Why?

4 ANALYZE Watch the video and check your answers to Exercise 3.

REAL-WORLD ENGLISH Interrupting and resuming

Interrupting appropriately for the situation will get a better response from the speaker.

Sometimes it is necessary to interrupt a formal presentation to check understanding. You can raise your hand and then say you want to interrupt and why.

Excuse me for interrupting. Could I ask…?
I'm sorry to interrupt. Do you mind if…?
Excuse me for saying so, but I don't think…

With people you know in informal situations, you can use just one word like *but*, *so*, or *sorry* to show you want to say something.

So, why does…?
But what about…?
Sorry, but…?

When starting to speak again after an interruption, the speaker can use phrases to show it is their turn again.

Anyway, as I was saying…
Going back to what I was talking about…
So, where was I?

ENGLISH FOR REAL

5 IDENTIFY Watch the complete video and take notes on the different ways of interrupting and resuming in each situation. Include phrases and actions. Compare your notes with a partner.

	In the lecture hall	Outside the lecture hall
Speakers	Max and lecturer	Max, Andy, Kevin, and Phil
To interrupt		
To resume		

6 INTEGRATE Work in pairs. Rewrite the interruptions so that they can be used for a more formal situation (e.g., the lecture hall situation in the video). Then listen and compare your answers. Did you rewrite them in the same way as the sentences in the audio?

1 But what about the start time?
2 So, we can finish early?
3 Actually, that's not right.
4 Sorry, but I need to say something here.

7 INTERACT Work in a group of three (A, B, and C) to do a role play. Choose situation 1 or 2, and prepare what you will say. Then role play the situation. Discuss what worked well in your role play. Then swap roles and repeat.

Situation 1: You join two friends in a café. They are having a conversation about a documentary they both saw. You need to tell them about the plans for that evening.

Situation 2: You and two friends meet outside the movie theater. They immediately start talking about the party last night. The movie is starting in ten minutes, and there is a line for tickets. You don't want to miss the start of the movie.

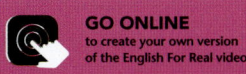
GO ONLINE to create your own version of the English For Real video.

Step into the course with **English For Real videos** that mimic real-life interactions. You can record your voice and respond in real time for out-of-class practice that is relevant to your life.

COMPREHENSIVE SYLLABUS

Ensure progress in all skills with a pedagogically consistent and appropriately leveled syllabus.

---

2 WHAT'S YOUR ANGLE? Imagine that you are on an exploration team. What skills do you have that would be useful?

3 VOCABULARY Complete the description of successful explorers with the words in the box.

independent	explore	quit	practical
survive	set off	keep going	flexible

 Oxford 3000™

Successful explorers…

- ¹ _____ to ² _____ with hope, energy, and positive feelings.
- know how to ³ _____ when things get tough.
- ⁴ _____ even when other people go back.
- don't like to ⁵ _____ but know that sometimes it is necessary.
- are ⁶ _____ and are not afraid of changing their plans.
- are ⁷ _____ —they listen to others, but they make their own decisions.
- are ⁸ _____ —they know how to take care of themselves and others.

LISTENING SKILL
Recognizing rephrasing in a talk

Speakers often use specific topic words and ideas that may not be familiar to the audience. They usually rephrase these to help the listener understand. Sometimes they do this immediately.

Would you make a good explorer? Do you want to find out about the world, push back frontiers, discover new places?

Sometimes they use signals to show they are rephrasing. Listen for these, for example:

*in other words   that is   by that I mean
to put it another way*

6 IDENTIFY The speaker rephrases the three key points in the first part of her presentation. Can you remember how she did this? Match the original phrases to the rephrasing signals and to the rephrasing. Then listen again and check.

	Rephrasing signal	Rephrasing words
1	make a commitment	to put it another way	take in everything… going on around

▼ VOCABULARY

The Oxford 3000™ is a word list containing the most important words to learn in English. The words are chosen based on frequency in the Oxford English Corpus and relevance to learners of English. Every word is aligned to the CEFR, guiding you on the words you should know at each level.

---

4 IDENTIFY Read the essay again. Find the topic sentence in each paragraph.

5 EXPAND Take notes of the supporting ideas and examples in paragraphs 2 and 3.

Paragraph 2:
_____

GRAMMAR IN CONTEXT *so* and *such*

We use *so* and *such* to emphasize what things are like.

so + adjective
so exciting

such (+ *a* / *an*) + adjective + noun
such a good idea

We don't need an adjective with *such* if the noun is something that is always good, bad, etc.
It was such a problem.

Also, we don't use *a* / *an* with *such* when the noun is uncountable.
It was such bad weather.

See Grammar focus on page 161.

7 IDENTIFY Find an example of *so* and *such* in the essay.

8 INTERACT Complete the sentences with *so*, *such*, or *such a / an*.
1. I understand why some people are _____ negative about space travel.
2. Space travel is _____ expensive activity. We should limit it.

▼ GRAMMAR

The carefully graded grammar syllabus ensures you encounter the most relevant language at the right point in your learning.

Discovering explorers

What do Christopher Columbus, Captain Cook, and Marco Polo have in common? Yes, they were all famous explorers—and they were all male explorers, as are most of the well-known ones. However, women have a significant
5   place in the history of **exploration**, and interest in female explorers has been rising since the 1980s. The very real achievements of female explorers, like Mary Kingsley, are finally getting the **recognition** they deserve.
Why have attitudes changed? One **explanation** is that
10 the women's **movement** of the 20th and 21st centuries has increased interest in women's **accomplishments**. Also, their journals provide fascinating stories; these women appeared to enjoy facing danger, showing a **willingness** to confront wild animals, extreme weather, hostile natives,
15 injury, and **illness**. Their **confidence** and **commitment** are an **inspiration** to today's women. It is often shocking to read about the attitudes they faced, especially in repressive Victorian Britain. For example, women were constantly denied recognition for their achievements. When the
20 Liverpool Geographical Society wanted to learn about Mary Kingsley's explorations in West Africa, her paper was read aloud by a man while she sat in the background, as the **organization** would not allow women to speak. Equally shocking is the fact that **membership** of the New York
25 Explorers' Club was male-only until 1981.

So, what were these women explorers like? Apart from having strong **personalities** and being intelligent and practical, they were usually middle-aged or beyond, having gained their **independence** after fulfilling family
30 **obligations**, such as looking after elderly parents. In fact, one **attraction** for many women was the **possibility** of escape from a lifetime of service. They were usually unmarried, as few husbands would consider giving permission for their wives to pursue such a profession.
35 They were also rich enough to afford to pay for their trips (**sponsorship** was usually not possible for women) and sufficiently educated and experienced to deal with the inevitable **complications** that arose. Mary Kingsley fits this profile. Unmarried, smart, and self-educated, Mary took
40 care of her family while her father went on explorations. Only when both her parents died and her brother moved away was Mary finally able to begin her own explorations.
Now that the **contributions** of these women are finally revealed, in the context of their gender their **achievements**
45 appear to be even more remarkable than those of their more famous male counterparts. While they didn't discover America, they made significant discoveries, but above all they showed that women can overcome impossible challenges to achieve **greatness**.

—adapted from *The Oxford Companion to World Exploration*, edited by David Buisseret

Oxford Reference is a trusted source of over two million authentic academic texts.

Free access to the Oxford Reference site is included with Student Books 4, 5, and 6.

Personalize the lesson topics and see how the language can work for you with **What's Your Angle?** activities.

3.1 End of the Road?

 mountains
 ice
 underwater
 underground

1 ACTIVATE What kind of people make good explorers? What are they like? What do they do?

2 WHAT'S YOUR ANGLE? Imagine that you are on an exploration team. What skills do you have that would be useful?

3 VOCABULARY Complete the description of successful explorers with the words in the box.

| independent | explore | quit | practical |
| survive | set off | keep going | flexible |

Oxford 3000™

Successful explorers…
- ¹_____ to ²_____ with hope, energy, and positive feelings.
- know how to ³_____ when things get tough.
- ⁴_____ even when other people go back.
- don't like to ⁵_____ but know that sometimes it is necessary.
- are ⁶_____ and are not afraid of changing their plans.
- are ⁷_____—they listen to others, but they make their own decisions.
- are ⁸_____—they know how to take care of themselves and others.

4 INTERACT Discuss the questions with a partner.
1 Which ideas from the description in Exercise 3 did you mention in Exercises 1 and 2?
2 Which three ideas about explorers do you most agree with?

5 INTEGRATE Listen to the first part of a talk about modern-day exploration. Which skills and qualities from Exercise 3 are mentioned?

> **LISTENING SKILL**
> Recognizing rephrasing in a talk
>
> Speakers often use specific topic words and ideas that may not be familiar to the audience. They usually rephrase these to help the listener understand. Sometimes they do this immediately.
> *Would you make a good explorer? Do you want to find out about the world, push back frontiers, discover new places?*
> Sometimes they use signals to show they are rephrasing. Listen for these, for example:
> *in other words   that is   by that I mean
> to put it another way*

6 IDENTIFY The speaker rephrases the three key points in the first part of her presentation. Can you remember how she did this? Match the original phrases to the rephrasing signals and to the rephrasing. Then listen again and check.

	Rephrasing signal	Rephrasing words
1 make a commitment	to put it another way	take in everything… going on around you…rather than just…looking ahead
2 be aware of your surroundings	by that I mean	the person to turn to…
3 be in control	in other words	make a decision…stick to it…get through the really bad times

7 INTEGRATE Review the key facts and predict the answers. Then listen to the rest of the talk and check.

> **Key facts**
> - Caves discovered in the world: about ¹___%
> - Earth's surface covered by ocean: about ²___%
> - Unexplored ocean: about ³___%
> - Life under Antarctic ice: up to ⁴___ million years old
> - Money spent on brain research in Europe per year: over €⁵___

> **GRAMMAR IN CONTEXT**
> Verbs + *to* infinitive or *-ing* form
>
> Some verbs can take the *-ing* form or the *to* infinitive with little or no change in meaning. For example: *attempt, begin, can't stand, continue, hate, like, love, prefer, start.*
> *Do you like to be in control? / Do you like being in control?*
> Other verbs can take both the *-ing* form or the *to* infinitive but with a clear difference in meaning. For example: *stop, forget, remember.*
> *Do you stop to look?* (Do you stop doing something because you want to look?)
> *Do you stop looking?* (Do you no longer look at what you were looking at before?)

See Grammar focus on page 161.

8 IDENTIFY Work in pairs. Is there a difference in meaning in the sentences in each pair? What is it?
1 He stopped to talk to me. / He stopped talking to me.
2 She forgot meeting them. / She forgot to meet them.
3 I prefer traveling alone. / I prefer to travel alone.
4 He remembered visiting the place. / He remembered to visit the place.
5 She began to explain. / She began explaining.

9 INTEGRATE Read the extracts from the talk. Choose the verb form the speaker used. Then listen and check.
1 …we need to stop *to worry / worrying* about being the first to go somewhere.
2 …they forgot *to look / looking* and *learn / learning* about where they were.
3 … people will continue *to explore / exploring* forever, inward and outward…
4 …we should remember *to leave / leaving* the place as we find it…

10 WHAT'S YOUR ANGLE? Look at the areas for exploration in the pictures in this lesson and answer the questions.
1 Which areas should we continue exploring? Why?
2 Which should we definitely stop exploring? Why?
3 What other areas should we start to explore? Why?

the human mind

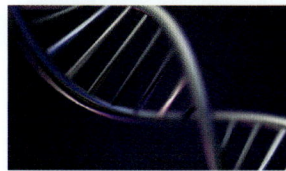
DNA

artificial intelligence

11 INTERACT Share your answers to the questions in Exercise 10 in a group. Try to agree on the top two areas for each answer.

READING AND LISTENING
Explicit reading and listening skills focus on helping you access and assimilate information confidently in this age of rapid information.

Build confidence with the **activation-presentation-practice-production** method, with activities moving from controlled to less controlled, with an increasing level of challenge.

> **WRITING SKILL**
> Writing paragraphs and topic sentences
>
> Paragraphs with strong topic sentences help the reader to understand the organization of the text and the main ideas. This means the reader can:
> - get a clear overview quickly.
> - find the information they want more easily.
> - understand the progression of the ideas.
>
> Paragraphs should have one main idea, and the topic sentence usually presents this. Examples and more detailed information in the rest of the paragraph should support the main idea.

to live.
However, space travel also has signi… especially financial ones. Each missio… dollars, and many people are unhappy money should be spent on problems … change, poverty, and disease. All of th… from the billions of dollars that are cur… travel. There is also an environmental … in space, as we burn rocket fuel, use u… materials, and leave behind litter in spa…
In conclusion, I feel there should be … question of space exploration because uses too many resources. In today's w… sure that our money and effort are dire… most needed.

> **SPEAKING** Giving a presentation
>
> The audience listens and learns more when a presentation is well organized and presented.
> Give a clear, engaging introduction that tells your audience what you are going to talk about.
> *Today, I'm going to talk about…
> First, I'll talk about…
> Then I'll outline…
> Finally, we will look at…
> There will be time for questions at the end.*
> Then use signpost phrases to show the audience where you are in the presentation and to highlight changes of topic.
> *So, first of all,…   Moving on to…   In this final part,…*

5 INTEGRATE Listen to the introduction again. Write a possible outline for the rest of the presentation.

6 ASSESS Listen to the opening parts for the other

5 relation—relationship
6 lazy—laziness

9 INTERACT Complete the noun a suffix, and mark the stress on thes check. Then listen again and repeat
1 I would like to look at other deve
2 …the simple lens gave us the pos
3 …of raising the level of human in
4 …the recogni_____ of the im
5 …this will be an explora_____ inventions…

10 PREPARE Choose an item you co three most important inventions for Write a list of reasons to support yo

11 DEVELOP Work in pairs. Review y invention and then together decide presentation.

WRITING
The writing syllabus focuses on the writing styles needed for today, using a **process writing approach** of **prepare-plan-draft-review-correct** to produce the best possible writing.

SPEAKING
Speaking and **pronunciation skills** build the functional language you need outside of class.

A BLENDED LEARNING APPROACH

Make the most of *Wide Angle* with opportunities for relevant, personalized learning outside of class.

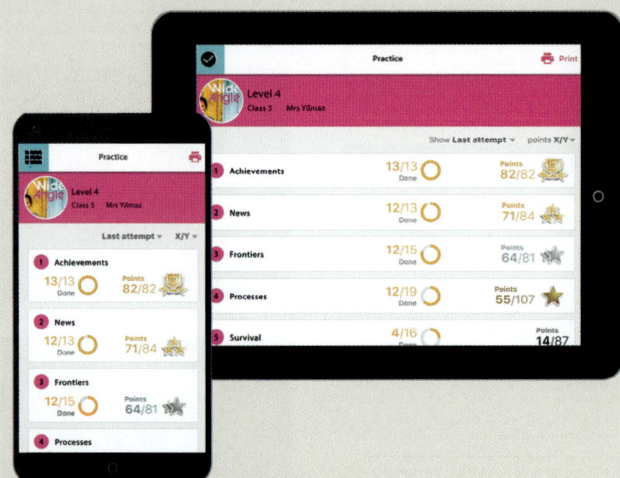

ONLINE PRACTICE

When you see this icon in your Student Book, go online to extend your learning.

With Online Practice you can:

- Review the skills taught in every lesson and get **instant feedback**.
- Practice grammar and vocabulary through **fun games**.
- Access **all audio and video** material. Use the Access Code in the front of this Student Book to log in for the first time at **wideangle.oxfordonlinepractice.com**.

WORKBOOK

Your Workbook provides additional practice for every unit of the Student Book.

Each unit includes:

- An entirely new reading with skill practice linked to **Oxford Reference**.
- Support for the **Discussion Board**, helping students to master online writing.
- Listening comprehension and skill practice using the **Unit Review Podcast**.
- Real-life English practice linked to the **English For Real** videos.
- **Grammar** and **vocabulary** exercises related to the unit topic.

Use your Workbook for homework or self-study.

FOCUS ON THE TEACHER

The Teacher's Resource Center at **wideangle.oxfordonlinepractice.com** saves teachers time by integrating and streamlining access to the following support:

- **Teacher's Guide**, including fun **More to Say** pronunciation activities and **professional development** materials.
- **Easy-to-use** learning management system for the student Online Practice, **answer keys**, **audio**, lots of **extra activities**, **videos**, and so much more.

The **Classroom Presentation Tool** brings the Student Book to life for heads-up lessons. Class audio, video, and answer keys, as well as teaching notes, are available online or offline and are updated across your devices.

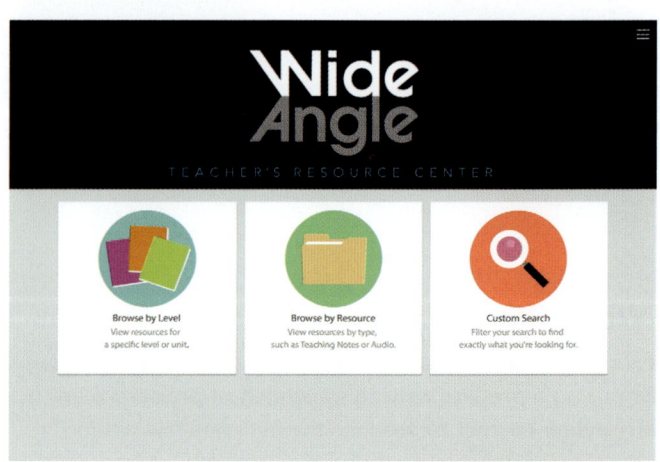

1 Achievements

UNIT SNAPSHOT

What are "overachievers" not afraid to admit? 4
Where is there a clock bigger than Big Ben? 7
Which TV star runs a company and marathons? 6

- What achievements do young people celebrate together?
- Why do people like to celebrate achievements together?
- Should achievements always be rewarded?

BEHIND THE PHOTO

REAL-WORLD GOAL
Watch a movie about a famous person

1 Which of these do you think is the greatest achievement? Put them in order. Add another achievement.

___ Quitting smoking
___ Raising a family
___ Forgiving yourself for a mistake
___ Doing a kind act without expecting reward
___ Finishing a marathon
___ Doing well on a test
___ Writing a novel
___ Other: _____

2 Share your ideas with a partner. Do you agree?

1.1 Getting to the Top

1 ACTIVATE Ask and answer the quiz questions with a partner. How similar are you? What do you think the quiz was trying to find out?

Do you…

1. write lists of things you want to achieve?   Yes   No
2. take classes to improve your skills?   Yes   No
3. finish everything that you start?   Yes   No
4. like people to tell you how good you are?   Yes   No
5. laugh when things go wrong?   Yes   No

READING SKILL Skimming and scanning

Readers approach texts in different ways to get the information they want quickly and effectively.

Skimming: To understand the general topic or "gist" of a text, look at the text quickly. Do not read every word. Instead, notice the title, headings, and pictures; the first sentences of paragraphs; and the repeated words, word families, and ideas. Skimming can help you decide if you want or need to read the complete text. It will also help you see how the text is organized and where to find information in it.

Scanning: To find specific information quickly, scan the text. Check what type of information you are looking for (e.g., a date or a name), and then scan for the correct form for the information (e.g., a number or a word starting with a capital letter).

2 IDENTIFY Skim the introduction to the blog article to find out what it is about.

| Home | About | Articles | Search |

Do you know any overachievers? My daughter Esmé does—Josh. Josh really annoys his classmates, including Esmé. According to her, Josh arrives each morning already knowing everything the teacher is about to present. Josh doesn't get A's, he gets A++'s. But will his early success continue? What qualities does he need to be an adult overachiever? I decided to find out, so this week's blog is all about people who overachieve as adults. Who are they, and what do they do?

1 _____
Overachievers take risks, but when things go wrong, they don't feel bad. They use humor to laugh at their mistakes. They also make sure they enjoy their successes—after all, they have achieved their goals, so why not have fun and make the most of the experience? Laughter helps us be more relaxed and realistic, and it makes us popular with others.

2 _____
Overachievers are not afraid to admit their own weak areas. They are, of course, certain that they have plenty of good points, too. But they never miss an opportunity to learn, train, and get experience to improve their skills.

3 _____
Overachievers are highly organized. Their desks (and minds) are usually tidy. By the time everyone else is just starting their day, overachievers have already made lists and set goals.

4 _____
Overachievers are very confident, and this helps them do their best even when things are difficult. But they also want people to notice and praise their hard work before they start on their next project. Around their desks, they like to display reminders of how they have made a difference in the world: photos, award certificates…anything that helps them stay motivated and also show the world how good they are.

5 _____
Overachievers know there will always be new ideas, but ideas on their own mean nothing—you have to do something with them. Overachievers take advantage of this. When they bring an idea (even someone else's) to life, it becomes their own achievement.

My daughter is reading this over my shoulder as I write. "Yes, yes, yes, yes, and yes," she is saying. "That's Josh." So, despite the fact that he annoys Esmé, it looks like Josh is developing the right skills for success in life.

3 **INTEGRATE** Skim the article, and match the article's subheadings to the sections.

A Organized and goal-driven
B Ready to turn ideas into action
C Confident but also need praise
D Have fun no matter what
E Know what they need to learn

4 **IDENTIFY** Review the subheadings in Exercise 3 and the words below. In which section of the article (1–5) do you think you will find each group of words (a–e)? Scan the article to check.

___ a   positive feedback / hard work
___ b   relaxed / popular
___ c   new ideas / own achievement
___ d   weak areas / good points
___ e   tidy / lists

5 **INTEGRATE** Read the article in detail to complete the sentences with *Josh* or *Esmé*.

1 Other students don't like _____.
2 _____ is the child of the writer.
3 _____ gets excellent grades.
4 _____ is next to the writer.
5 _____ agrees that _____ is an overachiever.
6 _____ will probably be a success later in life.

6 **WHAT'S YOUR ANGLE?** Work in pairs. Review your answers to the quiz in Exercise 1. Is either of you an overachiever? Why? Why not? What about when you were children?

7 **VOCABULARY** Complete the phrases with the correct verb. Scan the article in Exercise 2 to check your answers.

do	make	make	miss	take	take

1 *miss* an **opportunity**
2 _____ **risks**
3 _____ the most of something
4 _____ a **difference**
5 _____ your best
6 _____ **advantage** of something

⚷ Oxford 3000™

8 **BUILD** Complete the sentences with the correct phrase from Exercise 7.

1 People who _____ are more successful in life.
2 I want to volunteer this summer to _____ in my community.
3 Never _____ to try something new.
4 My teacher told me to just _____ on the test.
5 If you want to achieve more, _____ any opportunities that appear, even small ones. You never know what they might lead to!
6 We have one hour to complete the assignment. Let's _____ of it.

9 **INTEGRATE** Choose four of the phrases in Exercise 7. Write a definition or example for each one. Then share your ideas with your group.

> **GRAMMAR IN CONTEXT** Simple present, present continuous, and present perfect
>
> We use the simple present to talk about:
> - facts
>   Laughter _helps_ us be more relaxed.
> - things that happen regularly
>   Josh ¹ _____ A's.
>
> We use the present continuous to talk about:
> - things happening now or around now
>   My daughter ² _____ this over my shoulder.
> - things that are changing
>   Josh ³ _____ the right skills for success.
>
> We use the present perfect to talk about:
> - experiences up to now
>   They ⁴ _____ a difference in the world.
> - things that have already or just happened
>   They ⁵ _____ already _____ lists.

See Grammar focus on page 159.

10 **IDENTIFY** Scan the article for the Grammar in Context examples, and complete them in the box.

11 **APPLY** Choose the correct verb tenses to complete the profiles of these high achievers.

Garry Kasparov played his first game of chess at the age of six and won his first international tournament before he was 18. He ¹ *is holding / holds* the record for being number one in the world of chess for the most years, and many ² *are viewing / view* him as the best chess player of all time. Now middle-aged, he ³ *is still playing / has still played* chess with great success. He ⁴ *is recently playing / has recently played* against 30 chess players at the same time, winning all the games. He ⁵ *writes / has written* several books on chess.

Oprah Winfrey ⁶ *does / has done* many things over the years, including acting, hosting her own TV show, and running a company. She ⁷ *is even running / has even run* a marathon in under four and a half hours. Her childhood was difficult at times, but her experience ⁸ *shows / is showing* that difficulties can be overcome. The world is changing, and the number of women at the top of their profession ⁹ *increases / is increasing*. Many people say that Oprah ¹⁰ *has helped / helps* motivate many of these high-achieving women over the years.

12 **IDENTIFY** Find the sentences with incorrect verb forms, and correct them. There are four incorrect sentences.

1 I want to be a veterinarian ever since I visited my uncle's farm.
_____

2 I'm afraid it is getting harder to get into top colleges.
_____

3 Larry has exercised every morning to stay healthy and stress-free.
_____

4 Diana has currently written a book about her volunteer work in Africa.
_____

5 My sister is waiting for this promotion for more than a year.
_____

6 I usually work until late on weekdays.
_____

13 **INTERACT** Think of someone you know who has achieved a lot. Tell a partner about the person and their achievements. Do the people you both describe have the five qualities of overachievers described in the article in Exercise 2?

14 **WHAT'S YOUR ANGLE?** Complete the sentences with your own ideas. Then compare and discuss your sentences in a group. What can you learn from each other?

1 Taking risks makes life more…
 exciting. I love not knowing what's going to happen next!

2 I never miss an opportunity to…
_____

3 The best way to make a difference to other people is to…
_____

4 It is more important to do your best than…
_____

5 I have always made the most of…
_____

6 Try to take advantage of every opportunity when you…
_____

1.2 View from the Top

1 ACTIVATE Work in pairs. Complete the information about each structure with the cities and years in the box. Then match the structure to the view from its top (A–E).

| Tokyo | Paris | New York City | Mecca | Dubai | 2012 | 1931 | 1958 | 2010 | 1889 |

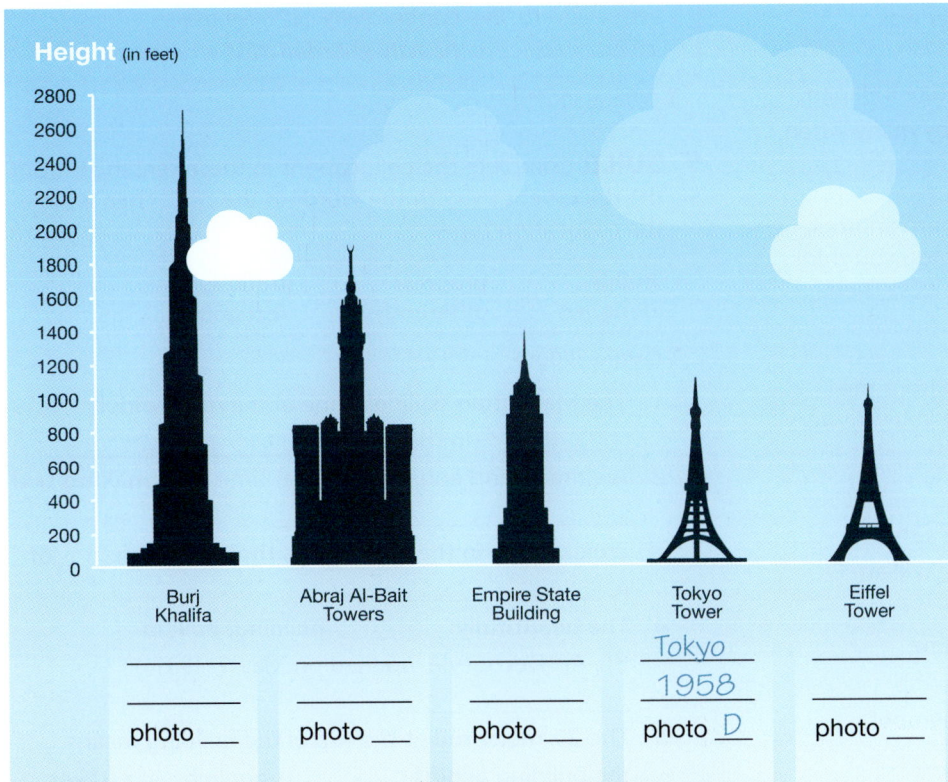

Burj Khalifa
_____
_____
photo ___

Abraj Al-Bait Towers
_____
_____
photo ___

Empire State Building
_____
_____
photo ___

Tokyo Tower
Tokyo
1958
photo D

Eiffel Tower
_____
_____
photo ___

2 ASSESS Now listen to part of a documentary about tall structures, and check your answers to Exercise 1.

3 WHAT'S YOUR ANGLE? Discuss the questions.
1. Have you or someone you know ever visited any of the towers mentioned in Exercise 2? When? Why? What did you or they do there?
2. Which towers would you like to visit? Put them in order of preference, and explain your reasons.

> **LISTENING SKILL Recognizing sentence stress and word boundaries**
>
> Speakers use sentence stress to make their message clearer. They stress the words that give the most important information. These words are often nouns, verbs, adjectives, and numbers.
>
> Unstressed words are not usually as clear and easy to hear, and this can make word boundaries (where words start and end) difficult to hear. However, unstressed words (e.g., articles, prepositions, auxiliary verbs, etc.) are less important for the meaning of the sentences.
>
> Sentence stress makes longer sentences sound shorter. The unstressed words between the important information are shortened. The number of stressed syllables usually indicates how long the sentence sounds.
>
> It is _still_ _one_ of the _tallest_ in _New York_.

4 IDENTIFY Listen and write the sentences you hear.

5 ◉ **ASSESS** Read the sentences from the documentary. Predict the main stressed words. Then listen and check.
1. New York's Empire State Building held the title of the "world's tallest building."
2. The Burj Khalifa in Dubai became the world's tallest man-made structure in 2010.
3. The tallest of the towers is the third-tallest building in the world.
4. The design of this orange-and-white tower was influenced by the Eiffel Tower.
5. Built in 1958, it is the second-tallest structure in Japan.
6. Though much loved now, it was disliked by many when first built.

6 ◉ **INTEGRATE** Listen to three sentences from another part of the documentary. Which tall building do you think it is about? Listen again, and write the sentences. Then listen and underline the stressed words.

7 ◉ **IDENTIFY** Listen to five more sentences from the documentary, and complete them. Compare your answers with a partner. Then listen again and check.
1. _____ Empire State Building _____ _____ midtown Manhattan _____ New York City,
2. _____ _____ designed _____ William F. Lamb.
3. _____ 1933, _____ building became _____ worldwide icon.
4. The _____ _____ _____ is a symbol of both _____ _____ and the _____ _____.
5. Its _____ was a _____ _____, and it has _____ many around the _____.

8 ▶ **INTEGRATE** Watch the documentary, and complete the notes with numbers and dates.

VOCABULARY DEVELOPMENT Collocations

The English language has many collocations. These are combinations of words that go together more frequently and naturally than other words. Using these correctly helps your speech sound more natural.

Collocations are made with combinations of different word types. For example:

verb + noun: **make contact** (NOT do contact)
verb + adverb: **live dangerously** (NOT live riskily)
adverb + adjective: **heavily guarded** (NOT strongly guarded)

⚿ Oxford 3000™

9 **BUILD** Complete the collocations in these sentences from the documentary with the words in the box. Then write the collocation types.

| highly | progress | trouble |
| designed | differently | recognized |

⚿ Oxford 3000™

1. The Manhattan skyline is one of the most **widely** _recognized_ in the world. _adverb + adjective_
2. Architects and engineers at that time were **making real** _____. _____
3. Professionals in the field always **thought** _____ of it. _____
4. The **beautifully** _____ building, built in the Art Deco style, opened on May 1, 1931. _____
5. The 20-meter rod at the top of the building means the building **avoids** _____ from lightning strikes. _____
6. It has motivated many around the world to **think** _____ about what they too can do. _____

The Empire State Building

Some basic facts
The location: Manhattan, New York
The year: 1931
The building: [1] ___ meters, [2] ___ floors
The people involved: William F. Lamb— the architect, more than [3] ___ workers
([4] ___ died)

Some interesting details
Construction: opened [5] ___ months ahead of schedule and [6] ___ million under budget.
Recognition: was world's tallest building for [7] ___ years. Ranked number [8] ___ on list by American Institute of Architects.
Movies: the movie King Kong used the building in [9] _____.
Tourists: [10] ___ million visit every year

10 🔊 **IDENTIFY** Choose the correct words to complete the collocations. Then listen and check.

1. Hard work does not *give / guarantee / take* success.
2. You should be *absolutely / obviously / heavily* certain you will succeed before you start.
3. Most people are *fully / perfectly / secretly* pleased when other people fail at something.
4. To achieve your academic goals, you have to take your studies *seriously / strongly / importantly*.
5. It is better to *make / find / acquire* knowledge rather than experience if you want to be successful.
6. We should stop worrying so much about achieving bigger and better things and learn to live *loosely / simply / easily*.

11 **WHAT'S YOUR ANGLE?** Explain which sentences from Exercise 10 you agree with and why.

> **GRAMMAR IN CONTEXT** State verbs
>
> Some verbs usually describe what we think, feel, experience, and possess. These are called state verbs, and we usually use them in simple tenses.
>
> *think: believe, agree, know, understand*
> Professionals always thought highly of it.
> ~~NOT Professionals were always thinking highly of it.~~
> *feel: like, love, hate, want*
> Tourists love the building.
> ~~NOT Tourists are loving the building.~~
> *experience: be, look, see, hear*
> Visitors see five different U.S. states.
> ~~NOT Visitors are seeing five different U.S. states.~~
> *possess: belong, have, own*
> The record belongs to an Australian.
> ~~NOT The record is belonging to an Australian.~~

See Grammar focus on page 159.

12 **IDENTIFY** Find the three sentences with state verb errors. Write the correct verbs.

1. The visitors love the design of the tower, but only two of them are wanting to go to the top. _____
2. More people are moving into tall buildings nowadays due to the rise in rents. _____
3. Some people are not believing it is healthy to live so high up. _____
4. The government wants to show how successful the country is by building the new tower. _____
5. Some companies like to rent office space in tall towers, but they aren't owning it. _____

13 **INTEGRATE** Complete the introduction to an article with the verbs in parentheses in the simple present, simple past, or present continuous.

The desire to build big is not new. The rulers of ancient Egypt ¹_____ (want) to construct pyramids that were bigger and better than those of their rivals. For example, the Great Pyramid of Giza ²_____ (reach) 148 meters into the sky and ³_____ (be) the tallest structure on earth for almost 4,000 years.

Over the past 200 years, more and more people have moved to cities. City planners ⁴_____ (know) from the start that the cheapest way to house all those people and the companies they worked in was to go upward. This ⁵_____ (lead) to many unsafe buildings and dark streets in the developing industrial cities.

Today's cities ⁶_____ (change) rapidly, but nowadays responsible planners ⁷_____ (understand) more about the safety of buildings and the happiness of the people who live in them. Who ⁸_____ (know) the design of our future buildings? Will they continue upward, or is there a new place for us to go, perhaps underground or even under the sea?

14 **WHAT'S YOUR ANGLE?** What do you think the next major engineering achievements will be? Write a list.

15 **INTERACT** Share your ideas from Exercise 14. Choose the two that are the most likely and tell the class.

1.3 Positive Impressions

1 ACTIVATE Read the job ad. What skills and experience would be useful for the job?

Project Planner
We are looking for a hardworking, well-organized person to manage a large project for our company. You will be responsible for planning the project, communicating with customers, and leading a team of twenty.

2 WHAT'S YOUR ANGLE? Would you apply for this job? Why or why not?

3 IDENTIFY Read the personal statement from an application for the job advertised in Exercise 1. Is the person right for the job? Why or why not?

Personal Statement

As an experienced team leader in a small international company, I have worked with several different teams, both within my department and in each of the company's international offices. Before entering the world of work, I studied business at the University of Michigan, graduating in 2015.

From my experience of planning and organizing demanding high-profile projects, I have developed strong skills in teamwork and people management. I can communicate effectively in English and Spanish, and I have used each language to build relationships and find solutions for customers on every project I have been involved with for the company.

My immediate goal is to gain a position in a larger company in which I can demonstrate and further develop my skills.

4 INTEGRATE Read the personal statement again, and check all the correct points in the checklist.

A personal statement…
- [ ] is a summary that goes with a job application or résumé.
- [ ] explains what is special about you.
- [ ] has clear sections focusing on different points.
- [ ] includes facts, experience, and future goals.
- [ ] can use *I* or *he / she*, but it must be consistent.
- [ ] should be about 100 to 150 words.

 WRITING SKILL Using appropriate language

Using appropriate language with the correct tone helps your message be understood correctly.

To create a positive tone in a personal statement, use positive structures and words. Avoid negatives. Write about:

1 who you are
   As an experienced…
2 what you can offer
   I have a lot of experience…
3 what you want to do
   My immediate goal…

5 IDENTIFY Match the three points from the Writing Skill box to the paragraphs in the personal statement in Exercise 3.

First paragraph: ___
Second paragraph: ___
Third paragraph: ___

6 INTEGRATE Match the positive words and phrases from the personal statement to the less positive phrases.

LESS POSITIVE	POSITIVE
1 not a beginner ___	a further develop my skills
2 difficult and stressful ___	b gain a position in a larger company
3 had to learn how to work in groups ___	c developed strong skills in teamwork
4 deal with problems ___	d find solutions for
5 not work in a small company anymore ___	e experienced
6 learn the things I don't know now ___	f demanding, high-profile

GRAMMAR IN CONTEXT *Each* and *every*

1 We use *every* + singular noun to talk about all the people or things in a group of three or more.
   Every job application *needs a personal statement.*

2 We use *each* + singular noun to talk about individual people or things in a group of two or more.
   Each application *needs a specially written personal statement.*

3 We also use *every one* / *each* + *of* + *the* + plural noun/ pronoun with the same meaning as *each*. (However, we only use *every one* with three or more items.)
   Each of the jobs *needs its own application.*
   Every one of them *needs its own application.*

See Grammar focus on page 159.

7 IDENTIFY Find three examples of *each* and *every* in the personal statement in Exercise 3. Match them to the Grammar in Context points.

8 INTERACT Choose the correct words to complete the sentences. Then find examples of positive phrases in the sentences.

1 I have worked for several companies and learned a lot from *every / each* of them.
2 The job is demanding, but I have successfully dealt with each *challenge / challenges*.
3 Every *team / teams* needs a strong leader, and I believe I am that person.
4 I have received extremely positive comments about *every one of / every* project.
5 Every one of *them / they* is connected with business skills.

9 PREPARE Work in pairs. Tell your partner about a job you would like to have. Discuss skills and experience people need for the job. Take notes in the table.

Skills	Experience

10 WRITE Write your personal statement for the job you would like to have. Use the checklist to help.

☐ Use positive language.
☐ Include three sections (who you are, what you can offer, what you want to do).
☐ Match the statement to the job requirements.
☐ Write 100–150 words.

11 IMPROVE Review your partner's personal statement. Does it match each point on the checklist?

12 WHAT'S YOUR ANGLE? Read other classmates' personal statements. Which make a positive impression on you? Why?

Workers in a design workshop in Palermo, Italy

1.4 Asking the Right Questions

1 **ACTIVATE** Look at the pictures. Guess the answers to the questions, and tell a partner.
   1 Is the setting private or public?
   2 Do the speakers know each other?
   3 What is each speaker doing?
   4 What is the purpose of the communication?

2 ▶ **IDENTIFY** Watch the video of an interaction at a career fair, and check your answers to Exercise 1. What information in the video did you use to check?

3 ▶ **ASSESS** Watch the video again, and take notes on what Kevin says to the company representative.

   information Kevin gives _____
   information Kevin inquires about _____

REAL-WORLD ENGLISH Making inquiries

We often make inquiries in a customer service or professional context. We usually don't know the other person in this situation. In these cases, we tend to use longer and more indirect ways of speaking than when talking to a friend. This is more polite and, therefore, more likely to get a good result.

I wonder if you could help.
Could / Can you help me please?
NOT ~~Help me.~~ / ~~I need help.~~

The person you are asking may also need background information. Clear, complete answers will make it easier for them to help you.

That's right. I'm a first-year student at Columbia University.
I'm a student, so I can only work evenings and weekends.

Be aware of the situation and the amount of time the inquiry is taking, especially if other people are waiting. Only ask the important questions, and go straight to the point.

Thanking the other person for their time ensures that you leave the person with a positive impression and more likely to follow up if necessary.

ENGLISH FOR REAL

4 ANALYZE Work in pairs. Read the questions and sentences. Match them to functions A–D. How will the person listening to the question or sentence react?

A Making an inquiry
B Asking for help
C Thanking
D Giving information

1 I wonder if you could help. ___
2 Do you know how I can apply? ___
3 Thanks for your time. ___
4 Sorry to bother you again, but could you tell me the location? ___
5 I'm sorry, but that's not possible. They like to speak to the interviewee by phone. ___
6 Could the person text me instead? ___

5 INTEGRATE Work in pairs. The following questions are directed to a close friend. Rewrite them, so they become inquiries in a professional setting directed to someone you don't know. Then listen and compare.

1 Where is the office?
2 What time is the interview?
3 Call me tomorrow?
4 How do I get there?

6 PREPARE Work in pairs. Take turns making inquiries about job interviews. Ask for details about the information in the box. After you get the answer, thank the person for their time.

location	interview time
things to bring to the interview	name of interviewer
number of jobs available	deadline for application

7 INTERACT Work in pairs (A and B) to do a role play. Choose situation 1 or 2, and prepare what you will say. Then role-play the situation. Swap roles and repeat.

Situation 1
Student A: You are job hunting. You want to find out about the jobs a company is offering. You approach a company representative at a career fair.
Student B: Your company is hiring. You are one of the company representatives at a career fair. You are dealing with inquiries about the available jobs.

Situation 2
Student A: You want to learn a language. You need some information about a language course. You call a language school and talk to the manager.
Student B: You are the manager of a language school. One of your roles is to deal with course inquiries over the phone.

8 ANALYZE Get together with another pair, and repeat the role play. Get feedback.

9 WHAT'S YOUR ANGLE? When did you last make an inquiry? What was it about, and was the person you spoke to helpful?

GO ONLINE to create your own version of the English For Real video.

1.5 A Successful Interview

1 ACTIVATE Tell your partner about the last interview you had for work or study. Can you remember any questions from the interview?

2 **IDENTIFY** Listen to the job interview, and number the questions in the order you hear them.

___ a What do you consider your greatest achievement?
___ b Can you tell me about yourself?
___ c Where do you see yourself in five years?
___ d Could you tell us about something you have done to overcome a problem at work?

SPEAKING Answering interview questions

Interviews are usually formal situations, so formal language is necessary. Listen carefully to the question, and use similar language in your answer.

What do you consider your greatest achievement?
I think, to date, my greatest achievement has been to create an award-winning training course.

Answers normally require details and specific examples. If necessary, pause before answering to give yourself time to think, so your answers are clear and your language (tenses, use of articles, vocabulary, etc.) is accurate.

3 **INTEGRATE** Listen again, and take notes on how the candidate answers these questions. Compare your notes with a partner.

Can you tell me about yourself?
_____

Could you tell us about something you have done to overcome a problem at work?
_____

Where do you see yourself in five years?
_____

PRONUNCIATION SKILL
Word stress in compound adjectives

Using the correct word stress with compound adjectives makes your English easier to understand and sound more natural.

Compound adjectives are usually stressed at the start when followed by a noun. When not followed by a noun, the stress is usually on the second part if the first word is an adverb or adjective.

He is a well-known person.   It is a full-time job.
He is well known.   The job is full-time.

4 IDENTIFY Find the stress on the compound adjectives in these sentences. Listen and check. Then listen again, and repeat the sentences.

1 I'd like to attend a part-time MBA program.
2 It's an award-winning course.
3 It's a five-hour session.
4 The company signed another two-year contract.
5 The clients were highly valued.

5 WHAT'S YOUR ANGLE? Use the compound adjectives in the box to make sentences about yourself. Remember to stress the words correctly.

part-time	full-time	hardworking
highly qualified	award-winning	open-minded
four-year	life-changing	

6 INTERACT Work in pairs. Listen to your partner's sentences from Exercise 5, and write the compound adjectives, marking the stress.

7 PREPARE Choose a job to interview for. Then review the questions in Exercise 2, and practice your answers. Think of two questions to ask the interviewer.

8 INTERACT Work in groups of three. Take turns playing the following roles.

A: You are the interviewer. Ask the four questions from Exercise 2. Then answer B's questions about the job.
B: You are the job candidate. Answer A's questions. Then ask two questions about the job.
C: Watch the interview and take notes of examples, numbers, success stories, and additional questions the candidate uses.

9 INTEGRATE In your group, share your notes on the interviews. Discuss the most successful answers.

What were they?
Why were they successful?

10 INTERACT Work with a new partner to do the interviews again. Which questions did you answer more successfully this time? Tell your partner.

Now go to page 147 for the Unit 1 Review.

2 News

UNIT SNAPSHOT

Who wrote for the newspapers in the 1840s?   16
What was heard first on August 31, 1920?   148
What exactly fits in a newspaper?   148

BEHIND THE PHOTO

▼ What makes a news story?
▼ Do you prefer to read, watch, or listen to the news?
▼ Is 24/7 news good or bad for us? Why?

REAL-WORLD GOAL

Find an interesting news story every day for a week

1 Which news do you follow most? Number the top three.
___ on my neighborhood
___ on my town or city
___ on my region of the country
___ on my country
___ on my continent
___ international
___ other: _____

2 Why do you find news interesting? Compare and discuss your answers from Exercise 1 with a partner.

2.1 Read All About It

1 ACTIVATE Discuss the questions with a partner.
1. Which of these sections would you read first in a newspaper or on a news site?
2. Are there any parts of a newspaper you would never read? Why?

A Main stories
Man Drowned in Boating Tragedy

B SPORTS
Giants Win State Championship

C CULTURE
Modern Art Exhibit to Open at City Gallery

D POLITICAL OPINION
Governor's Education Plan Falls Short

F FINANCE
Major Retail Chain to Close Stores

E Comic strips

G Lost and found

H Classified ads

2 IDENTIFY When do you think the sections in Exercise 1 first appeared in newspapers? Write A–H on the timeline. Then scan the article to check your answers.

1800   1900   2000

The development of newspapers

1 _____
Newspapers have changed the world. They have **brought down** governments, **announced** wars, and made people aware of issues like global warming. However, their reign may soon be over as sales fall and electronic news takes over. But how have they managed to be so important in our lives and for so long?

2 _____
The story of modern newspapers started in Western Europe in the late 17th century. Newspapers came out weekly and mostly consisted of opinion pieces and some brief news items. Lost-and-found features were popular since up until then the main way of finding lost property had been to trust in magic. Later in the 18th century, advertisements were added, usually written in the same format as the news items.

3 _____
Newspaper content, it seems, was initially fairly lightweight. However, at the time of the French Revolution at the end of the 18th century, newspaper content was becoming increasingly political. This **led to** a struggle between freedom and control. When they **realized** that newspapers were powerful and were forming opinion, governments acted by **preventing** radical and liberal journalists from expressing their political views. However, in the newly formed United States, cases such as John Peter Zenger's libel trial in 1735, after he had been in jail for almost a year, improved the freedom of the press. In France, the rulers **attempted** to stop newspapers from printing what they wanted, and this helped **lead to** the 1830 revolution in which journalists played an important part. Later, Karl Marx **launched** his career by writing newspaper articles in the 1840s, leading eventually to the Russian Revolution.

4 _____
In the late 19th century, when the world was full of bad news, the newspapers started printing more stories to **distract** their readers—sensational stories such as sightings of the Loch Ness Monster in Scotland. By then, visuals had become important, starting with drawings and then photographs. Newspapers also began to include sports columns and, in North America, comic strips. By the middle of the 20th century, newspapers were becoming more or less what they are today.

5 _____
But, in the era of multiple forms of media, will newspapers survive? It seems so. In fact, all the different forms of media seem to work together—we listen to the radio in the car, read a newspaper for more in-depth coverage, and watch television for dramatic pictures and light entertainment. Newspapers surely have a future even though they may be viewed on a screen rather than on paper.

—adapted from *Oxford Encyclopedia of the Modern World*, edited by Peter. N. Stearns

Oxford 3000™

> **READING SKILL** Identifying topic sentences
>
> The topic sentence indicates the main idea or point of a paragraph. Focusing on topic sentences first helps you understand the general theme and structure of the text more quickly. Then you can read for more detail.
>
> The topic sentence is often the first in the paragraph. However, sometimes it is the second or final sentence. The other sentences in the paragraph provide supporting details, explaining and developing the topic further.

3 IDENTIFY Find the topic sentence in the first paragraph. Explain to a partner how you decided.

4 EXPAND Find the topic sentences in the other paragraphs. Compare your answers with a partner.

5 INTEGRATE Match the headings to each paragraph by skimming the paragraphs and using the topic sentences to help. (There is one extra heading.)

A A move toward entertainment
B The growing interest in ideas
C The importance of the paper
D The work and the writers
E A changing but successful future
F The early story

6 BUILD Read the text again. Focus on the supporting details, explanations, and examples. Decide if these sentences are true (T) or false (F) or if the information is not given (NG).

1 Early newspapers were mostly read by rich people. ___
2 The first newspaper was French. ___
3 Before newspapers, people often used magic to look for things they had lost. ___
4 John Peter Zenger went to prison for two years. ___
5 Comic strips first came out in South America. ___
6 Many thought people would stop reading newspapers because of television. ___

7 WHAT'S YOUR ANGLE? Discuss the questions.

1 Where do you get your news?
2 Has this news medium changed over the past few years? How? Why?
3 Where do you think we will get our news in the future?

8 VOCABULARY Review the highlighted verbs in the article. Then match the verbs to their definitions below.

Verbs	Definitions	Synonyms
1	to cause something to happen	
2	to make somebody lose power	
3	to begin an activity	
4	to tell people about something	
5	to direct someone's attention to something different	
6	to try to do something	
7	to become aware of something	
8	to make sure something doesn't happen	

9 IDENTIFY Match the synonyms to the verbs and definitions in Exercise 8.

cause	defeat	make known
aim to	set in motion	entertain
stop	recognize	

10 INTEGRATE Choose the correct verb to complete each question. Then ask your partner the questions. Use the verbs and synonyms from Exercises 8 and 9 to explain.

1 Which newspaper stories have *brought down / led to / attempted* changes in your country?
2 Who has successfully *launched / prevented / realized* their career through the media in your country?
3 How long do you think it will be before all newspapers *announce / distract / launch* that they are ending their print edition?
4 Can you think of news stories that have *brought down / distracted / attempted* high-profile personalities?
5 Do you think social media *leads to / distracts / announces* the public from real news stories?

GRAMMAR IN CONTEXT Narrative tenses: Simple past, past continuous, and past perfect

We use the narrative verb tenses to tell a story or talk about events in the past.

1 Main events—simple past:
   *The story of newspapers **started** in Western Europe.*

2 Background events or longer actions interrupted by a shorter one— past continuous:
   *When they realized newspapers **were driving** opinion, governments acted.*

3 Events happening earlier than the main events—past perfect:
   *By then, visuals **had become** important.*

See Grammar focus on page 160.

11 IDENTIFY Match the narrative verb tense in bold in the extracts (a–c) with the rules (1–3) in the Grammar in Context box.

a ...by the middle of the 20th century, newspapers **were becoming** more or less what they are today. ___

b ...cases such as John Peter Zenger's libel trial in 1735, after he **had been** in jail for almost a year, established the freedom of the press. ___

c This **led** to a struggle between freedom and control. ___

12 EXPAND Find another example of each narrative tense in the article.

13 INTEGRATE Complete the story about someone hearing news for the first time. Use the correct form of the verb in parentheses. Then listen and check.

I ¹_____ (listen) to the radio in the kitchen. It was around seven, so I ²_____ (make) breakfast. I ³_____ (not sleep) well, so I was really tired, and I also remember that I ⁴_____ (be) really hungry. (Funny what you remember about these moments when you look back!) And that's when I ⁵_____ (hear) the news on the radio. I ⁶_____ (not look) at the newspaper yet, so it ⁷_____ (be) a total surprise. It's really strange because I ⁸_____ (see) him on TV the day before. Anyway, I ⁹_____ (make) my coffee and then ¹⁰_____ (sit) down to read the newspaper to find out more.

14 WHAT'S YOUR ANGLE? Think of an example for each of the following types of news.

A major change in your country
The death of a famous person
An event that affected other countries

15 INTERACT Work in pairs. Share your examples from Exercise 14. Use the questions to find out more about your partner's news stories.

- Where were you when you heard the news?
- What were you doing?
- What had happened just before that?
- What did you do next?

School girls read a newspaper in Mbabane, Swaziland

2.2 Filling In the Detail

1. **ACTIVATE** For what reasons do famous people appear in the news? Think of at least three.

2. **WHAT'S YOUR ANGLE?** Which type of news involving famous people do you read? Why?

3. **IDENTIFY** Read the news report and choose the best headline in your opinion.
   1. "We Are the Lucky Ones"
   2. Help Goes to Those in Need
   3. Billionaires to Give Away Fortunes

4. **EXPAND** Read the article again. Decide if the statements are True, False, or Not Given. Correct the false statements.
   1. Judd Boyle and Antonia Benares are famous for giving their money to charity.
      _____
   2. The couple has been traveling a lot to places that need help.
      _____
   3. The motivation for giving away some of their fortune comes from the recognition that they are very lucky to be wealthy.
      _____
   4. The couple intends to give lots of their money to hospitals because they have experience in the medical industry.
      _____
   5. The couple will continue to travel to make sure the money reaches its destination.
      _____

NEWS

Home | Top news | World | **Business** | Science | Health

They have famous names, but they will never be seen in the same way again. Judd Boyle and Antonia Benares, the Internet billionaires well known for their parties and lifestyle, have announced that they will give away at least 50 percent of their
5 fortune in the next ten years, starting in the next six months. Speaking at a news conference yesterday, they promised that the money would be spent on education or medicine. They said they are looking at either area in places that need the most help. Both billionaires have traveled a lot in the past year, visiting places in
10 need, so the news was not a complete surprise.

When it was announced, the news was obviously received with excitement by all the people present. However, there were a number of questions about it from the audience of selected journalists. When a member of this group asked why it had taken
15 them so long to decide to give away some of their huge fortune, neither billionaire was prepared to answer. However, when asked about why they were doing it—were they doing it in order to help others or to improve their images— Antonia made a statement that explained their aim. "We both understand that we are the lucky ones. We both believe in the power of passion, and we want to use this to help those who are less fortunate than we are. To be honest, neither of us cares too much about our image. We know who we are, we know why we are doing it, so people can
20 think whatever they like about us. It's really not important."

Boyle and Benares explained that they will give most of the money to projects in hospitals and schools. Either of these would be their first choice, but they are also thinking about helping local companies that work in these industries. The couple will also pay for the training of teachers and medical workers from local populations. Neither has experience in the medical or educational areas, so they are looking for experts to manage the work. However, the
25 billionaires said they would work with the experts themselves, staying closely connected to make sure their donation has a real effect. Both want to ensure that all the money reaches its destination without any problems.

5 INTEGRATE Read the news report again and complete the notes in the plan for the report.

Section 1

Who: _____ When: _____
What: _____ Where: _____

Section 2

Reaction from others: _____
Questions from others: _____
Aims of the project: _____

Section 3

The billionaires…
- will give money to _____
- are looking for _____
- will work with _____
- want _____

6 IDENTIFY Match the sections of the plan (1–3) in Exercise 5 to their content and purpose (a–c).

___ a Further information and closing—bringing the text to an end
___ b Reaction and quotes—helping readers to understand the context
___ c Lead information—the most important and interesting points

WRITING SKILL Using references and pronouns

Good writing avoids lots of repetition. Reference words and pronouns (e.g., *it, them, this, one*) help with this. Use these words to refer to nouns and phrases in the same sentence or other parts of the text.

Boyle and Benares explained that **they** will give the money to projects…

When **it** was announced, the news was obviously received with excitement.

…the Internet billionaires well known for **their** parties and lifestyle…

7 IDENTIFY Find the following words in the article. What do they refer to?

1. they (line 1) _____
2. either area (line 8) _____
3. it (line 13) _____
4. this (line 14) _____
5. us (line 20) _____

8 EXPAND Find the following nouns in the article. What other words are used to refer to these?

1. hospitals and schools (line 21) _____
2. the couple (line 23) _____
3. all the money (line 26) _____

GRAMMAR IN CONTEXT
all, both, either, neither

We use the quantifiers *all*, *both*, *either*, and *neither* to identify the number of people or things we are referring to.

all: everything in a group of three or more
*The news was obviously received with excitement by **all** the people.*

both: two things in a pair
***Both** billionaires have traveled a lot in the past year.*

either: one or the other in a pair
***Either** of these would be their first choice.*

neither: not one and not the other in a pair
***Neither** billionaire was prepared to answer.*

See Grammar focus on page 160.

9 IDENTIFY Find another example of each quantifier in the news report. What does each quantifier refer to? How many people or things does each refer to?

10 INTEGRATE Choose the correct quantifier for each sentence.

1. I enjoyed reading *both / either* news stories, but yesterday's was better.
2. Not many people read *neither / all* of the different sections in a newspaper.
3. I like online news sites and actual newspapers. I read *neither / either*—it depends where I am.
4. *Neither / Either* news report had much detail about the story.
5. I get the news from *all / both* types of media, including radio and print.

11 APPLY Complete the sentences with the correct quantifier.

1 Can I borrow today's newspaper from ___ of you?
2 ___ reporter was present during the news conference.
3 The article was read by ___ the people in the department before it was published.
4 ___ the *Times* and the *Post* reported the same details.
5 I can't find the information I need. ___ source is reliable.

12 PREPARE Work in pairs. Think of a recent story in the news. With your partner, complete a plan similar to the one in Exercise 5. Can you remember any quotes about the news or find them online? If not, imagine what people said about the news.

13 WRITE Work on your own. Write the news report. Use the checklist to help.

- ☐ Follow the plan.
- ☐ Include a headline.
- ☐ Write three paragraphs.
- ☐ Use references and pronouns.
- ☐ Use *all*, *both*, *either*, and *neither*.
- ☐ Write 200–300 words.

14 IMPROVE Review your partner's report. Does it follow the plan?

15 SHARE Read other classmates' news reports. Which kept you reading to the end? Why?

2.3 At the Scene

1 **ACTIVATE** Read the dictionary definition. What makes a news story newsworthy? List at least three things.

newsworthy
(ADJECTIVE)
interesting and important enough to be reported as news

2 **WHAT'S YOUR ANGLE?** Discuss the questions.
1 When was the last time you discussed something in the news with anyone?
2 What was the news?
3 Why did you talk about it?

3 **PREPARE** Read the words and phrases from a news report, and look at the picture. Then answer the questions.

| New Year's Eve | Dubai | tower |
| spectacular fireworks | flames and smoke | |

1 Do you remember the story?
2 What (do you think) happened?
3 What (do you think) made the story newsworthy?

LISTENING SKILL
Recognizing linkers in fast speech

Recognizing linkers (e.g., *but, and, so, or, while, as*) helps you understand the connections between the speaker's ideas.

Linking phrases and words are sometimes unstressed in fast speech. This can make them less clear. Listen carefully for how the ideas are joined.

…it started just before midnight while we were waiting…
…we had a table reservation, but our plans obviously changed.

4 **NOTICE** Read the extracts from a news report and predict which linker is used. Then listen to the extracts and choose the correct linker.
1 …they were shocked, *and / but / when* they realized they were looking at a…
2 …been a disaster, *but / as / then* the good news is that there were apparently no serious injuries…
3 …the fire services were able to clear the place *while / and / so* they put out the fire…
4 …we were waiting for the fireworks to begin, and it was then *that / so / but* we saw people pointing.

5 **EXPAND** Read these extracts from the news report, and predict which linker is used. Then listen and complete the extracts.
1 …out of the building and _____ we saw flames…
2 …we saw people pointing, _____ we looked across…
3 I was worried about different things, for example, the traffic _____ how I was going to get home.
4 We were just making little movies to show our friends _____ we were waiting…

6 **INTEGRATE** Listen to the news report, and complete each sentence with one or two words you hear.
1 People watching the fireworks show were shocked to see a _____.
2 Even though the building was very big, there were _____ injuries.
3 Rosa was waiting in a _____ to see the show.
4 Rosa was about _____ from the actual fire.
5 Ronald and his wife had a _____ at the hotel that evening.
6 Amir felt _____ about going to see the event.
7 Amir spent the time before the show making _____ for friends.

22

7 WHAT'S YOUR ANGLE? Have you ever seen a newsworthy event in real life? What happened?

GRAMMAR IN CONTEXT was / were going to

We can use *was / were going to* to talk about future events from a point of view in the past. The events may or may not actually happen.

They **were going to** see a fireworks display.

Using *but* shows the events definitely didn't happen.

We **were going to** go, but, in the end, we stayed home.

See Grammar focus on page 160.

8 🔊 **ASSESS** Read and listen to three extracts from the news report. Then answer the two questions for each extract.

A Yes, that's right…We were going to watch from inside the hotel because we had a table reservation, but our plans obviously changed…

B I wasn't going to come, you know…I was worried about different things, for example, the traffic and how I was going to get home, but, unfortunately, my friend persuaded me.

C Thousands of us had been waiting for hours at the site, knowing we were going to see something spectacular.

1 What was the original plan or idea?
2 Did it actually happen?

9 INTEGRATE Match the sentence parts. Did the event in the first part of each sentence happen or not? Or is it impossible to tell? Explain your answers to a partner.

1 The reporter was going to interview me, ___
2 The police were going to cancel the event ___
3 The hotel was going to be closed for a few months ___
4 Many people were planning to come later, ___
5 The hotel was going to have a big event the next day. ___

a to be redecorated.
b but they stayed home in the end.
c but she didn't have enough time.
d However, this was canceled.
e and send everyone home.

VOCABULARY DEVELOPMENT Comment adverbs

Comment adverbs give the speaker's point of view about an action or event. Other types of adverbs often describe the action or event itself. Compare the following:

Comment adverb: **Luckily**, there were no injuries.
Other types of adverb: Many people **usually** go to the event. / They put out the fire **quickly**.

Comment adverbs usually go at the start of sentences. They can sometimes go in the middle but less often at the end. They are usually separated from the sentence by commas or pauses.

*People, **apparently**, were making videos.*
*People were making videos, **apparently**.*

10 BUILD Read the sentences in each pair. Discuss with a partner the difference in their meaning.

1 **Unfortunately**, we were late. / **Luckily**, we were late.
2 **Naturally**, not many people went. / **Curiously**, not many people went.
3 **Surprisingly**, it was all over the news. / **Obviously**, it was all over the news.
4 **Apparently**, it cost a lot of money. / **Sadly**, it cost a lot of money.

🗝 Oxford 3000™

11 🔊 **IDENTIFY** Which adverb from Exercise 10 completes each of these extracts from the news report in Exercise 6? Listen and check.

1 There were, _____, no serious injuries.
2 _____, given the size of the building, the fire services were able to clear the place.
3 _____, we thought it was the fireworks.
4 It was scary, _____.
5 _____, everyone got out safely.
6 …but, _____, my friend persuaded me.

12 WHAT'S YOUR ANGLE? Rewrite each sentence with a comment adverb so that it shows your point of view. Use the correct punctuation.

1 We have 24/7 news coverage nowadays.
2 People are interested in finding out about famous people.
3 Most of the news we see is bad news.
4 People are more emotionally affected by local or national news.

13 INTERACT Compare your sentences from Exercise 12, and discuss your points of view with a partner.

2.4 You'll Never Guess What...

1 **ACTIVATE** Look at the pictures. Guess the answers to the questions and tell a partner.

  1 Do the speakers know each other?
  2 Is this a professional call or an informal call?
  3 Was the woman expecting the call?

2 ▶ **IDENTIFY** Watch the video and check your answers for Exercise 1. What clues (verbal or nonverbal) in the video helped you answer the questions?

3 ▶ **ANALYZE** Watch the video again. Take notes on the two pieces of news Andy gives Anna. Which news is good, and which is bad?

First piece of news: _____

_____

Second piece of news: _____

_____

REAL-WORLD ENGLISH Giving and reacting to news

How we share our news with people we know can depend on whether the news is good or bad. In both cases, we usually "set the scene" for the listener before we give the actual news.

Have you heard the good / bad news?
I've got to tell you something.

When the news is good, we often show our excitement to get the listener involved.

I've got some great news.
You'll never guess what… Something amazing has happened!

When the news is not good on a personal level, we may want to warn the person before giving the actual news. This can help to "soften" the bad news.

I'm afraid I've got some bad news.
I don't know how to say this, but…

When we react to news, we often start by showing our surprise and then follow with our reaction.

Reacting to good news: Really? That's great! / How exciting! / I'm so pleased for you.
Reacting to bad news: I don't believe it. How awful. / That's terrible. / I'm so sorry.

ENGLISH FOR REAL

4 ▶ **ANALYZE** Watch the video again. Write the phrases Andy and Anna use to do the following:

1. give the good news _____
2. react to good news _____
3. break the bad news _____
4. react to bad news _____

5 **INTEGRATE** Work in pairs. Take turns using the same phrases from Exercise 4 that Andy uses to give his news and Anna uses to react to the news.

6 **INTERACT** Work in pairs. Take turns giving the following news. You are good friends: one of you breaks the bad news; the other reacts appropriately.

Classes today are canceled.
You have won a lot of money.
Your friend failed the exam.
The apartment you share was robbed.
Another friend is joining you both on a weekend trip.
Someone wants to buy your friend's car.
You won a prize both you and your friend were competing for.

7 **PREPARE** Work in a new pair. Choose one of the situations from Exercise 6. Add more detail to the situation.

Decide:
- how long you have known each other
- how well you know each other
- how each of you feels about the situation (the same or different?)
- where you are when you share the news

8 **INTERACT** Work with another pair. Present the details of the situation you chose in Exercise 7, and do the role play while the other pair watches. Get feedback.

9 **WHAT'S YOUR ANGLE?** Think about the last piece of good news you received. What was it about, and who did it come from? How did you respond?

GO ONLINE to create your own version of the English For Real video.

2.5 What an Experience!

1 **ACTIVATE** Look at the pictures. Discuss the questions.
   1 Which of these activities have you done or would you like to do? Why?
   2 Which one are you least likely to do in the future? Why?

snowboarding    riding a motorcycle    hot-air ballooning

skydiving    parasailing    rock climbing

2 **IDENTIFY** Listen to someone describing an exciting experience. Which activity is she describing?

> **SPEAKING Describing an event**
>
> Different tenses are necessary to describe the background, details, and actions of an event. Use sequencing words to make the order of actions clear.
>
> For actions before the event, use past perfect.
> …but actually, they **had bought** me something.
>
> Use past simple for facts and feelings and to describe the events or actions.
> It **was** my graduation. Anyway, I **was** a little bit down…
> It **was** amazing…Once I **got over** feeling scared, the view **was** unbelievable.
>
> Use past continuous for events happening at the same time.
> My family **was watching** my reaction.

3 **IDENTIFY** Listen again and note down details of the speaker's experience.

4 **INTERACT** Work in pairs. Use your notes to retell the story to your partner. If you are listening, check your notes for missing details. Then change partners and change roles.

> **PRONUNCIATION SKILL**
> **Stressed auxiliary verbs and forms of be**
>
> Affirmative auxiliary verbs (e.g., be, do, have) are not usually stressed. However, we can stress them if we want to add to the meaning of the sentence, for example, to contradict or show surprise.
> *I thought she hadn't booked the trip, but I was wrong. She **had** booked it.*
>
> We can also add a stressed auxiliary where we don't usually use an auxiliary (e.g., in affirmative statements in the simple present or simple past) to make our point more clearly.
> *You're wrong. He **did** want to go on the trip.*
>
> And remember, we always stress auxiliary verbs or the verb be in short answers.
> Did you go?   Yes, I **did**.
> Was it exciting?   Yes, it **was**.

5 **IDENTIFY** Read and listen to extracts from the description in Exercise 2, and find the stressed auxiliary verbs or forms of be. Why is the speaker stressing them? Then listen again and repeat the sentences.
   1 It was my birthday…Sorry, no, it wasn't.
   2 I thought my family hadn't bought me a present to celebrate, but actually, they had bought something.
   3 I thought it would be difficult to relax. But I did manage to.
   4 Despite what people might say about the peace and quiet, it was noisy.
   5 My family didn't go on the trip with me, but they were watching my reaction on camera back home.

6 **PREPARE** Think of an interesting experience you or someone you know has had. Get ready to describe it to your group by making notes. Use the prompts to help.
   who/what/when/why/where
   surprising or unexpected
   adjectives

7 **INTERACT** Work in groups of three.
   Take turns describing your experience. Make your description interesting with details, adjectives, and effective use of stressed words.
   When it is your turn to listen, ask questions at the end to find out more detail and explore the person's feelings.

8 **WHAT'S YOUR ANGLE?** Did anyone have similar experiences? What was the most exciting/scary/funny experience?

Now go to page 148 for the Unit 2 Review.

3 Frontiers

UNIT SNAPSHOT

Who first got to the top of Mount Everest? 30
Who secretly traveled the world as a man? 32
What came first: lenses or printing presses? 38

▼ Why do people go to new places?

▼ Which areas have humans explored? How?

▼ How do people feel when they cross a frontier?

▶ BEHIND THE PHOTO

REAL-WORLD GOAL
Visit somewhere you have never been before

1 Answer the questions.

1 If you were going to explore an area of the world, where would you go and why?
I would go to New Zealand or somewhere else with lots of beautiful scenery. I love wild places and love going hiking in the mountains.

2 What are the benefits of exploring? Who benefits most?

3 What are the problems? Who faces them?

2 Discuss your answers with a partner. Do you have similar views?

3.1 End of the Road?

mountains   ice   underwater   underground

1 ACTIVATE What kind of people make good explorers? What are they like? What do they do?

2 WHAT'S YOUR ANGLE? Imagine that you are on an exploration team. What skills do you have that would be useful?

3 VOCABULARY Complete the description of successful explorers with the words in the box.

independent	explore	quit	practical
survive	set off	keep going	flexible

Oxford 3000™

Successful explorers…

- ¹_____ to ²_____ with hope, energy, and positive feelings.
- know how to ³_____ when things get tough.
- ⁴_____ even when other people go back.
- don't like to ⁵_____ but know that sometimes it is necessary.
- are ⁶_____ and are not afraid of changing their plans.
- are ⁷_____—they listen to others, but they make their own decisions.
- are ⁸_____—they know how to take care of themselves and others.

4 INTERACT Discuss the questions with a partner.
1 Which ideas from the description in Exercise 3 did you mention in Exercises 1 and 2?
2 Which three ideas about explorers do you most agree with?

5 🔊 INTEGRATE Listen to the first part of a talk about modern-day exploration. Which skills and qualities from Exercise 3 are mentioned?

> **LISTENING SKILL**
> **Recognizing rephrasing in a talk**
>
> Speakers often use specific topic words and ideas that may not be familiar to the audience. They usually rephrase these to help the listener understand. Sometimes they do this immediately.
>
> Would you make **a good explorer**? Do you want to **find out about the world, push back frontiers, discover new places**?
>
> Sometimes they use signals to show they are rephrasing. Listen for these, for example:
>
> in other words   that is   by that I mean
> to put it another way

6 🔊 IDENTIFY The speaker rephrases the three key points in the first part of her presentation. Can you remember how she did this? Match the original phrases to the rephrasing signals and to the rephrasing. Then listen again and check.

		Rephrasing signal	Rephrasing words
1	make a commitment	to put it another way	take in everything… going on around you…rather than just…looking ahead
2	be aware of your surroundings	by that I mean	the person to turn to…
3	be in control	in other words	make a decision…stick to it…get through the really bad times

7 🔊 **INTEGRATE** Review the key facts and predict the answers. Then listen to the rest of the talk and check.

> **! Key facts**
>
> › Caves discovered in the world: about [1] ___%
> › Earth's surface covered by ocean: about [2] ___%
> › Unexplored ocean: about [3] ___%
> › Life under Antarctic ice: up to [4] ___ million years old
> › Money spent on brain research in Europe per year: over € [5] ___

GRAMMAR IN CONTEXT
Verbs + *to* infinitive or *-ing* form

Some verbs can take the *-ing* form or the *to* infinitive with little or no change in meaning. For example: *attempt, begin, can't stand, continue, hate, like, love, prefer, start.*

Do you **like to be** in control? / Do you **like being** in control?

Other verbs can take both the *-ing* form or the *to* infinitive but with a clear difference in meaning. For example: *stop, forget, remember.*

Do you **stop to look**? *(Do you stop doing something because you want to look?)*

Do you **stop looking**? *(Do you no longer look at what you were looking at before?)*

See Grammar focus on page 161.

8 **IDENTIFY** Work in pairs. Is there a difference in meaning in the sentences in each pair? What is it?
1. He stopped to talk to me. / He stopped talking to me.
2. She forgot meeting them. / She forgot to meet them.
3. I prefer traveling alone. / I prefer to travel alone.
4. He remembered visiting the place. / He remembered to visit the place.
5. She began to explain. / She began explaining.

9 🔊 **INTEGRATE** Read the extracts from the talk. Choose the verb form the speaker used. Then listen and check.
1. …we need to stop *to worry / worrying* about being the first to go somewhere.
2. …they forgot *to look / looking* and *learn / learning* about where they were.
3. … people will continue *to explore / exploring* forever, inward and outward…
4. …we should remember *to leave / leaving* the place as we find it…

10 **WHAT'S YOUR ANGLE?** Look at the areas for exploration in the pictures in this lesson and answer the questions.
1. Which areas should we continue exploring? Why?
2. Which should we definitely stop exploring? Why?
3. What other areas should we start to explore? Why?

the human mind

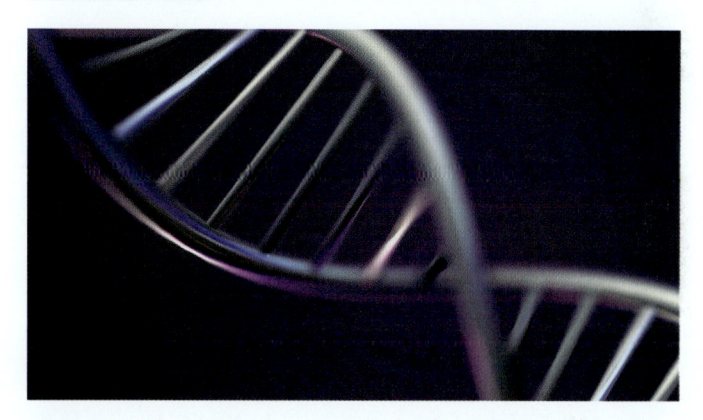

DNA

artificial intelligence

11 **INTERACT** Share your answers to the questions in Exercise 10 in a group. Try to agree on the top two areas for each answer.

3.2 Who Went Where?

1 ACTIVATE Match the dates, nationalities, and areas of exploration to the people shown in the pictures.

1934–1968	1903–1941	1910–1997
1868–1926	1866–1955	1914–1986
Soviet	British	French
American	British	Nepalese
desert	the Arctic	space
air	sea	mountains

1 Amy Johnson
   1903–1941
   British
   air

2 Jacques Cousteau
   _____
   _____
   _____

3 Matthew Henson
   _____
   _____
   _____

4 Yuri Gagarin
   _____
   _____
   _____

5 Tenzing Norgay
   _____
   _____
   _____

6 Gertrude Bell
   _____
   _____
   _____

2 IDENTIFY Work in pairs. Match the sentences (a–f) to the people in Exercise 1 (1–6). Then discuss the meaning of the words in bold.

a He was a **pioneer** in marine exploration and filmmaking, making the first French underwater film and helping to develop modern diving techniques. ___

b She was a brilliant **aviator**, being the first woman to fly solo from Britain to Australia. ___

c He was the first human to go into outer space and around the Earth, completing an **orbit** on April 12, 1961. ___

d She explored many areas of the Middle East, making friends and developing strong **bonds** with many leaders there. ___

e He made several **voyages** to the Arctic and was part of one of the first teams to reach the Geographic North Pole. ___

f He is one of the most famous climbers in history and the first person to reach the **summit** of Mount Everest. ___

> **READING SKILL**
> **Working out meaning from context**
>
> Knowing how to use context to deal with new words will help your reading become faster as you will need to look up words less often.
>
> Use the text around the new word to figure out its meaning. What is the topic of the sentence and the paragraph? What other words are linked to the new one?
>
> *He was a **pioneer** in marine exploration and filmmaking, <u>making the first</u> French underwater film and <u>helping to develop</u> modern diving techniques.*
>
> Use the word form and the grammar of the sentence to understand the function of the word. Does it have a prefix or suffix? Is it a verb, a noun, etc.?
>
> *She was a brilliant **aviator**.* (-or = noun suffix often indicating the noun is a person)
>
> Avoid using a dictionary to check the meaning of a lot of words, especially the first time you read. Use the context and improve your deduction skills. Check in a dictionary later to get a more precise definition.

3 EXPAND Review your answers to Exercise 2. Then use a dictionary to check the precise meaning of the words in bold.

4 WHAT'S YOUR ANGLE? From the facts in Exercise 2 and any information you know about the people in Exercise 1, which person would you most like to have been?

5 INTEGRATE Skim the topic sentences in the article below to help.

1. What kind of explorers is the article about?
2. What kinds of difficulties did these explorers face?

6 APPLY Work in pairs. Find the words in the box in the article. Then use the steps to figure out the meaning of each word.

fascinating (line 12)	obligations (line 30)
confront (line 14)	self-educated (line 39)
repressive (line 17)	

1. Read the sentences around the word, and decide on the topic and key words.
2. Identify the part of speech of the word and its use in the sentence.
3. Discuss the possible meaning of the word.
4. Check the precise meaning in a dictionary.

7 EXPAND Find three more words you do not know in the article. Use the steps in Exercise 6 to figure out their meaning.

8 INTEGRATE Read the article in detail, and write short answers to the questions.

1. What change has happened over the past 40 years?
2. What did the women's movement do?
3. What did the female explorers' journals show?
4. What were some practical ways in which women explorers were ignored?
5. What factors did many female explorers share?
6. What does the writer conclude about male and female explorers?

Discovering explorers

What do Christopher Columbus, Captain Cook, and Marco Polo have in common? Yes, they were all famous explorers—and they were all male explorers, as are most of the well-known ones. However, women have a significant place in the history of **exploration**, and interest in female explorers has been rising since the 1980s. The very real achievements of female explorers, like Mary Kingsley, are finally getting the recognition they deserve.

Why have attitudes changed? One explanation is that the women's movement of the 20th and 21st centuries has increased interest in women's **accomplishments**. Also, their journals provide fascinating stories; these women appeared to enjoy facing danger, showing a willingness to confront wild animals, extreme weather, hostile natives, injury, and illness. Their confidence and commitment are an **inspiration** to today's women. It is often shocking to read about the attitudes they faced, especially in repressive Victorian Britain. For example, women were constantly denied recognition for their achievements. When the Liverpool Geographical Society wanted to learn about Mary Kingsley's explorations in West Africa, her paper was read aloud by a man while she sat in the background, as the organization would not allow women to speak. Equally shocking is the fact that membership of the New York Explorers' Club was male-only until 1981.

So, what were these women explorers like? Apart from having strong personalities and being intelligent and practical, they were usually middle-aged or beyond, having gained their independence after fulfilling family obligations, such as looking after elderly parents. In fact, one attraction for many women was the possibility of escape from a lifetime of service. They were usually unmarried, as few husbands would consider giving permission for their wives to pursue such a profession. They were also rich enough to afford to pay for their trips (**sponsorship** was usually not possible for women) and sufficiently educated and experienced to deal with the inevitable **complications** that arose. Mary Kingsley fits this profile. Unmarried, smart, and self-educated, Mary took care of her family while her father went on explorations. Only when both her parents died and her brother moved away was Mary finally able to begin her own explorations.

Now that the contributions of these women are finally revealed, in the context of their gender their achievements appear to be even more remarkable than those of their more famous male counterparts. While they didn't discover America, they made significant discoveries, but above all they showed that women can overcome impossible challenges to achieve **greatness**.

—adapted from *The Oxford Companion to World Exploration,* edited by David Buisseret

Oxford 3000™

VOCABULARY DEVELOPMENT Suffixes for nouns

Recognizing suffixes can help you identify nouns and understand their meaning.

explora**tion**   personal**ity**   achieve**ment**
confid**ence**   member**ship**   willing**ness**

Using suffixes to make nouns will increase your vocabulary by allowing you to create new words from the basic ones you know (such as verbs and adjectives).

*However, women have a significant place in the history of **exploration**, and interest in female **explorers** has been rising since the 1980s.*

9 IDENTIFY Find all the examples of nouns with these suffixes in the article. Which suffixes are mainly added to verbs? Which to adjectives? Which to other nouns?

1 -tion: _____
   mainly added to _____
2 -ment: _____
   mainly added to _____
3 -ness: _____
   mainly added to _____
4 -ence: _____
   mainly added to _____
5 -ity: _____
   mainly added to _____
6 -ship: _____
   mainly added to _____

10 BUILD Add suffixes to the words in the box, and complete the sentences with the best word.

contribute	different	encourage

1 With _____, everyone can achieve their goals.
2 We all want to be recognized for our _____ to the world.
3 The ways we are the same are more important than our _____.

happy	friend	secure

4 We should focus on safety and _____, not adventure and exploration.
5 Family and _____ are more important than money and fame.
6 To have _____ we must have freedom.

11 WHAT'S YOUR ANGLE? Which sentences from Exercise 10 do you agree with? Why?

GRAMMAR IN CONTEXT
Verbs + -ing form and verbs + to infinitive

We use the *-ing* form only after certain verbs, for example:

admit, avoid, consider, deny, finish, practice, suggest
*Few husbands would **consider giving** permission for their wives to do this.*

We use the *-ing* form after verbs that talk about likes and dislikes, for example:

can't stand, enjoy, hate, like, (don't / doesn't) mind, prefer
*These women appeared to **enjoy facing** danger.*

We can also use the *to* infinitive with some of these verbs, for example:

like, hate, love
*She **liked to travel** to new places.*

We use the *to* infinitive after other verbs, for example:

afford, agree, aim, allow, choose, decide, demand, expect, hope, manage, need, offer, plan, want
*They were also rich enough to **afford to pay** for their trips.*

See Grammar focus on page 161.

12 INTEGRATE Complete the article about a female explorer with the correct forms of the verbs in parentheses.

Jeanne Baret (1740–1807)

Jeanne Baret managed [1] _____ (do) something no woman had done before: she completed a voyage around the world. However, she did this dressed as a man since no women were allowed [2] _____ (travel) on French Navy ships in those days. So, to avoid [3] _____ (be) thrown off the ship, Baret put on men's clothes and became Jean instead of Jeanne. It is not clear when Baret's true identify was discovered and whether she admitted [4] _____ (be) a woman or others on the ship had become suspicious and demanded [5] _____ (know). However, it is clear that she chose [6] _____ (live) life on her own terms and will forever have a place in the history books.

13 IDENTIFY Find the sentences with incorrect verb forms and correct them.

1 I really enjoy to visit new countries.
2 I can't stand traveling to places I have been before.
3 I hope visiting every continent in my lifetime.
4 I avoid to go to crowded travel destinations.
5 I have a list of travel destinations that I aim to visit in the next few years.
6 I'm planning going on an unusual trip soon.

14 WHAT'S YOUR ANGLE? Which sentences in Exercise 13 are true for you? Compare with a partner and explain your answers.

3.3 Inner or Outer Space?

1 ACTIVATE Work in pairs. Write a list of pros and cons of exploring space.

Pros	Cons

2 WHAT'S YOUR ANGLE? Decide whether you are for or against space exploration. Explain your view to your group. Who has the most similar view to yours?

3 INTEGRATE Read the essay. Are any of your ideas from Exercise 1 included?

> ### WRITING SKILL
> ### Writing paragraphs and topic sentences
>
> Paragraphs with strong topic sentences help the reader to understand the organization of the text and the main ideas. This means the reader can:
>
> - get a clear overview quickly.
> - find the information they want more easily.
> - understand the progression of the ideas.
>
> Paragraphs should have one main idea, and the topic sentence usually presents this. Examples and more detailed information in the rest of the paragraph should support the main idea.

Although it has been more than four decades since the last manned moon landing, humankind has not stopped exploring space. Almost daily we read reports of new rocket launches and landings on Mars, each costing millions of dollars. Many people do not agree with this; they say we need the money for solutions to problems on our own planet. In this essay, I will discuss the benefits and drawbacks of space exploration.

Starting with the benefits, there are several general advantages. The first is that space exploration helps to improve technology. This improvement eventually reaches consumers on earth. Many people also believe that humans are designed to explore and expand our knowledge, and space is the ultimate place to do this. This is such a strong argument that many governments are happy to fund projects with little short-term benefit. There are also some practical benefits, for example, the discovery of new resources in space or the possible discovery of a new place for humans to live.

However, space travel also has significant disadvantages, especially financial ones. Each mission costs millions of dollars, and many people are unhappy with this. They say the money should be spent on problems we face, like climate change, poverty, and disease. All of these would benefit from the billions of dollars that are currently spent on space travel. There is also an environmental cost both on earth and in space, as we burn rocket fuel, use up expensive and rare materials, and leave behind litter in space.

In conclusion, I feel there should be more discussion on the question of space exploration because it is so expensive and uses too many resources. In today's world, we need to make sure that our money and effort are directed where they are most needed.

4 **IDENTIFY** Read the essay again. Find the topic sentence in each paragraph.

5 **EXPAND** Take notes of the supporting ideas and examples in paragraphs 2 and 3.

Paragraph 2:
_____
_____
_____

Paragraph 3:
_____
_____
_____

6 **WHAT'S YOUR ANGLE?** Review the essay. Has it changed your mind about space exploration? Why or why not?

> **GRAMMAR IN CONTEXT** *so* and *such*
>
> We use *so* and *such* to emphasize what things are like.
>
> *so* + adjective
> *so exciting*
>
> *such* (+ *a / an*) + adjective + noun
> *such a good idea*
>
> We don't need an adjective with *such* if the noun is something that is always good, bad, etc.
> It was **such** a problem.
>
> Also, we don't use *a / an* with *such* when the noun is uncountable.
> It was **such** bad weather.

See Grammar focus on page 161.

7 **IDENTIFY** Find an example of *so* and *such* in the essay.

8 **INTERACT** Complete the sentences with *so*, *such*, or *such a / an*.
   1 I understand why some people are _____ negative about space travel.
   2 Space travel is _____ expensive activity. We should limit it.
   3 We should focus on the problems on earth only because they are _____ serious.
   4 Finding enough money for every issue is _____ challenge for most governments.
   5 We shouldn't stop space exploration because it gives us _____ good knowledge.
   6 Space travel is _____ opportunity for a country to show its scientific and technology skills.

9 **INTEGRATE** Rewrite the sentences to replace *so* with *such*, or *such* with *so*.
   1 It is such an expensive program that some people think it should be shut down.
      <u>The program is so expensive that some people think it should be shut down.</u>
   2 The university was so interested in his research that they decided to hire him.
      _____
   3 His discoveries were so valuable that many study his contributions today.
      _____
   4 You have such a strong argument in favor of space exploration.
      _____
   5 She has such a unique perspective on the issue.
      _____

10 **WHAT'S YOUR ANGLE?** Discuss the statements in Exercise 8. Which do you agree with?

11 **PREPARE** Choose one of the topics to write a for-and-against essay about. Should we spend money on the research into these areas nowadays? Write your notes in the table.

oceans	the human mind	underground
cures for diseases	the North or South Pole	
artificial intelligence	DNA	

Topic	
Arguments for/ advantages	
Arguments against/ disadvantages	
Conclusion	

12 **WRITE** Write a for-and-against essay of up to 300 words. Include an introduction, a paragraph "for," a paragraph "against," and a conclusion. Remember to use strong topic sentences and clear supporting details and examples.

13 **IMPROVE** Review your partner's essay.

Does the essay…
- include four paragraphs with strong topic sentences?
- include clear supporting ideas and examples?
- use *so* and *such* correctly?

14 **SHARE** Read other classmates' essays. Which have arguments you hadn't thought of before?

Satellite antennas on the grounds of the Fucino Space Center in Abruzzo, Italy

3.4 Excuse Me…

1 **ACTIVATE** Look at the pictures with a partner. What are the differences? Discuss the question in relation to the following.

location

situation

relationships between speakers

2 ▶ **IDENTIFY** Watch a conversation between Max, Andy, Phil, and Kevin about a lecture they have just attended. What do they keep doing?

3 **ASSESS** You are going to watch an extract of the lecture the friends were talking about in Exercise 2. Max wants to ask the speaker a question. What do you think Max's interruption will be like compared to the way the friends interrupted each other in their conversation? Why?

4 ▶ **ANALYZE** Watch the video and check your answers to Exercise 3.

REAL-WORLD ENGLISH Interrupting and resuming

Interrupting appropriately for the situation will get a better response from the speaker.

Sometimes it is necessary to interrupt a formal presentation to check understanding. You can raise your hand and then say you want to interrupt and why.

Excuse me for interrupting. Could I ask…?
I'm sorry to interrupt. Do you mind if…?
Excuse me for saying so, but I don't think…

With people you know in informal situations, you can use just one word like *but*, *so*, or *sorry* to show you want to say something.

So, why does…?
But what about…?
Sorry, but…?

When starting to speak again after an interruption, the speaker can use phrases to show it is their turn again.

Anyway, as I was saying…
Going back to what I was talking about…
So, where was I?

5 ▶ **IDENTIFY** Watch the complete video and take notes on the different ways of interrupting and resuming in each situation. Include phrases and actions. Compare your notes with a partner.

	In the classroom	Outside the classroom
Speakers	Max and lecturer	Max, Andy, Kevin, and Phil
To interrupt		
To resume		

6 🔊 **INTEGRATE** Work in pairs. Rewrite the interruptions so that they can be used for a more formal situation (e.g., the classroom situation in the video). Then listen and compare your answers. Did you rewrite them in the same way as the sentences in the audio?

1 But what about the start time?
2 So, we can finish early?
3 Actually, that's not right.
4 Sorry, but I need to say something here.

7 INTERACT Work in a group of three (A, B, and C) to do a role play. Choose situation 1 or 2, and prepare what you will say. Then role-play the situation. Discuss what worked well in your role play. Then swap roles and repeat.

Situation 1: You join two friends in a café. They are having a conversation about a documentary they both saw. You need to tell them about the plans for that evening.

Situation 2: You and two friends meet outside the movie theater. They immediately start talking about the party last night. The movie is starting in ten minutes, and there is a line for tickets. You don't want to miss the start of the movie.

8 INTERACT Now work in pairs (A and B). Review situations 3 and 4. How do they differ from situations 1 and 2 in Exercise 7? Choose situation 3 or 4. Decide on the details, and prepare what you will say. Then role-play the situation.

Situation 3: The lecturer is talking to a large group about the assignment that is due next week. You have some questions about it. Decide on course name, type of assignment, and so on.

Situation 4: It is your first day at work. You and ten other new people are in a training session with the manager. She hasn't answered your questions about the new job. Decide on the type of company, new job title, and so on.

9 ANALYZE Discuss what worked well in your role play in Exercise 8. How could you make your language more appropriate? Then swap roles and repeat.

10 WHAT'S YOUR ANGLE? Have you ever wanted to interrupt but didn't? Why not?

GO ONLINE to create your own version of the English For Real video.

3.5 Moving On

1 ACTIVATE Discuss the questions.
1. Which of these things have you used or benefited from this week?
2. How important is each one in your life?

compass	printing press	airplane
Internet	telephone	corrective eye lenses
paper money	mechanical clock	

2 ASSESS Answer the questions.
1. In which century were the items in Exercise 1 probably invented?
2. Which have been the most important in the development of human knowledge? Choose your top three.

3 INTERACT Discuss your answers in Exercise 2 in a group. Decide on the top three inventions.

4 🔊 IDENTIFY Listen to the start of a presentation. Which of the items from Exercise 1 is the speaker going to talk about?

> **SPEAKING Giving a presentation**
>
> The audience listens and learns more when a presentation is well organized and presented.
>
> Give a clear, engaging introduction that tells your audience what you are going to talk about.
> *Today, I'm going to talk about…*
> *First, I'll talk about…*
> *Then I'll outline…*
> *Finally, we will look at…*
> *There will be time for questions at the end.*
>
> Then use signpost phrases to show the audience where you are in the presentation and to highlight changes of topic.
> *So, first of all,…   Moving on to…   In this final part,…*

5 🔊 INTEGRATE Listen to the introduction again. Write a possible outline for the rest of the presentation.

6 🔊 ASSESS Listen to the opening parts for the other sections of the presentation, and check your answers to Exercise 5.

7 🔊 IDENTIFY Listen again and complete the phrases used to introduce or change the topic.
1. So, _____, the question is how…
2. _____ the history of…
3. In _____, I would like to look at…
4. _____ questions…

> **PRONUNCIATION SKILL**
> **Shifting stress in suffix words**
>
> Correct word stress helps the listener understand key nouns.
>
> When certain suffixes are added to adjectives or verbs to form nouns, the stress moves to a different syllable in the noun. For example, with the suffixes *-ity* and *-tion*, the stress moves to the syllable before the suffix.
>
> per**son**al—perso**nal**ity   ad**mire**—admi**ra**tion
>
> Some suffixes don't affect the stress when they are added, for example: *-ment*, *-ness*, *-ship*, and *-ence*.
>
> a**chieve**—a**chieve**ment   **hap**py—**hap**piness
> **mem**ber—**mem**bership   **con**fident—**con**fidence

8 🔊 IDENTIFY Notice the stress in the first word. Then identify the suffix in the noun form, and find the main stress. Listen and check.
1. disappoint—disappointment
2. available—availability
3. differ—difference
4. apply—application
5. relation—relationship
6. lazy—laziness

9 🔊 INTERACT Complete the nouns in the extracts with a suffix, and mark the stress on these nouns. Listen and check. Then listen again and repeat the extracts.
1. I would like to look at other develop_____s…
2. …the simple lens gave us the possibil_____…
3. …of raising the level of human intellig_____…
4. …the recogni_____ of the importance of this item…
5. …this will be an explora_____ of important inventions…

10 PREPARE Choose an item you consider to be in the top three most important inventions for human knowledge. Write a list of reasons to support your view.

11 DEVELOP Work in pairs. Review your partner's choice of invention and then together decide how to organize each presentation.

12 IMPROVE Practice your presentation. Ask your partner for feedback on the organization and delivery.

13 SHARE Give your presentation to a group. Answer questions from other students at the end of the presentation.

14 WHAT'S YOUR ANGLE? After listening to the other speakers in your group, have you changed your choice of important invention? Why or why not?

Now go to page 149 for the Unit 3 Review.

4 Processes

UNIT SNAPSHOT

What is made on an island in Scotland? 41
Which art depends entirely on technology? 43
Which movie end was changed to be sadder? 150

What kind of work requires processes?

Why are processes important?

What can happen if we don't follow a process?

BEHIND THE PHOTO

REAL-WORLD GOAL

Learn a new process from an online video

1   In which of these areas of life do you think we use these processes? Write A, B, or C next to each process. Then compare your answers with a partner. Do you agree?

A. work   B. leisure   C. education

Applying for a job ___   Preparing for a sports competition ___
Learning a skill ___   Preparing for a party ___
Learning a sport ___   Planning a wedding ___
Redecorating a room ___   Teaching someone a skill ___
Preparing for an exam ___   Applying for college ___

2   In pairs, choose two of the processes from Exercise 1. How many steps can you think of for each?

4.1 Proudly Made

1 **ACTIVATE** Complete each picture label with a verb and a noun from the box.

| cake | wool scarf | paper plane | clay pot | knit | fold | mold | bake |

1 _____ a _____   2 _____ a _____   3 _____ a _____   4 _____ a _____

2 **WHAT'S YOUR ANGLE?** Look at the photos in Exercise 1. Answer the questions.

1 Which of the items can you make?
2 Which would you like to be able to make? Why?

VOCABULARY DEVELOPMENT
Explaining a process

Ordinal numbers and signpost words and phrases can be used to make the steps of a process clear.

The first / second / third **stage is**…
Firstly,… / *Secondly,*…

These signposts usually come at the beginning of the sentence to make the step immediately clear. Make sure you understand the part of speech of the word or phrase and check that it fits with the grammar and punctuation of the sentence.

Following that, knit two more rows in blue wool.
Finally, pour the mixture into a cake tin.
Once the cake is cooked, remove it from the oven.
The last step is to sew the sides of the hat together.

Oxford 3000™

3 **IDENTIFY** Which of the things in Exercise 1 is the person making? Number the steps in the correct order.

___ a The last step is to decorate it.
___ b Once it is the right shape, make the bottom flat.
___ c Then make a hole in the ball with your thumb.
___ d After that, mold the sides into the correct shape.
___ e The first stage is to make a ball of clay.

4 🔊 **INTEGRATE** Listen and check your answers to Exercise 3. Underline the phrases in Exercise 3 that show the stages.

LISTENING SKILL
Using visual information while listening

Visual information can help you better understand what you are listening to. It can help you understand more complex language as well as learn new language.

Before you listen, review any images that accompany the listening. Look for items in the images that you know the words for. Check the vocabulary for items shown in the images that you don't know the words for.

While listening, use the images to follow what the speaker is saying and to support your understanding. Do this by focusing on sections of images highlighted by the speaker, considering how images shown relate to what is being said, and listening carefully for language you know that refer to elements in the image.

Listen a second time and make a note of unknown language you hear or see on any images used. Use a dictionary to check their meaning afterward.

5 **IDENTIFY** You are going to watch a video of people making a special type of fabric called Harris Tweed. Look at these images from the video. Label the items you know in English.

shades of blue

6 ▶ **NOTICE** Watch the video. Choose the phrases you hear.

- [ ] a   dyed a few different colors
- [ ] b   mix the base colors
- [ ] c   complicated colors and shades
- [ ] d   Chinese textile company
- [ ] e   highly skilled weavers
- [ ] f   the fabric and the patterns
- [ ] g   old-style foot-operated looms
- [ ] h   woven by hand
- [ ] i   small industry
- [ ] j   high-quality
- [ ] k   stamped
- [ ] l   Orb Mark trademark
- [ ] m   traditional brand
- [ ] n   modernized its operations

7 **IDENTIFY** Discuss the meaning of the words and phrases in Exercise 6 with a partner. Use the images from Exercise 5 and a dictionary to find out the meaning of any words you don't know. Which can you guess from the visuals?

8 ▶ **INTEGRATE** Watch the description of the process of making Harris Tweed, and match the two parts of the sentences.

1 The first stage of ___
2 The result of this ___
3 Following that, ___
4 During this stage, ___
5 The last step is for ___
6 Once ___

a old-style foot-operated looms are used, and the tweed is woven by hand.
b making the tweed is to mix the base colors of the wool to a specific recipe.
c the weavers create the fabric and the patterns.
d they're happy that it is high quality, the material is stamped with the Orb Mark trademark.
e the Harris Tweed Authority to inspect the material.
f more complicated colors and shades.

9 ▶ **INTEGRATE** Watch the complete video and answer the questions.

1 Who made and still makes the cloth?
2 Which material gets the special Orb Mark trademark?
3 What kind of wool do the mills use?
4 How does the tweed get its color?
5 What kinds of things are made of Harris Tweed nowadays?
6 Where do people buy the cloth?
7 Which country has invested in the production of this cloth?
8 Where does the wool come from nowadays?

GRAMMAR IN CONTEXT
Present passive and past passive

We use the passive form to focus on what happens to someone or something rather than who or what does the action. We make the passive with a form of *be* and the past participle of the verb.

active: The worker **stamps** the material.
passive: The material **is stamped**.

To change the time we are talking about, we change the tense of *be*.

*Cloth **was** developed.*

We use *by* + noun if we want to include who or what did the action.

*Harris Tweed was handmade **by people from the islands**.*

We often use the passive to continue talking about a particular thing.

Harris Tweed has been one of the most famous names in the British textile industry for more than 150 years, and it **is** now **known** all over the world.

See Grammar focus on page 162.

10 **IDENTIFY** Complete the sentences from the video with the correct passive form of the verb in parentheses.

1 Harris Tweed _____ (make) in the Outer Hebrides.
2 This quality cloth _____ first _____ (export) in the 1840s.
3 The Orb Mark trademark _____ (develop) to protect the brand.
5 Three mills _____ (license) to produce Harris Tweed.
6 Three years ago, half a million meters of Harris Tweed _____ (produce) every year.

11 **INTEGRATE** Rewrite the answers to Exercise 9 in the passive. (Use the questions to help you.)

1 The cloth was made and is still made by people from the islands.

12 🔊 **APPLY** Rewrite the sentences using the passive. Then listen to the extract from a cooking show and check.

1 We chose this week's recipe from a traditional cookbook.
2 In the past, people served this cake on special occasions.
3 People eat it at any time nowadays.
4 You combine all the ingredients in a large bowl.
5 You mix the eggs separately at first.
6 You bake the cake for 40 minutes.

13 **WHAT'S YOUR ANGLE?** What was the last thing you made / cooked / painted / grew / created?

4.2 Making It to the Big Screen

1 ACTIVATE Complete the information about movies with the numbers in the box.

| 11 | 38.6 | 71 | 245 | 718 | 164,000 |

In 2016:
- The global box office for all movies released in each country around the world reached $___ billion.
- Movie theater screens increased to ___ worldwide.
- ___ movies were released in the United States and Canada.
- ___% of U.S. and Canadian populations (about ___ million people) went to the movies at least once. ___% went at least once a month.

2 WHAT'S YOUR ANGLE? Answer the questions.
1 How often do you go to the movies? Why?
2 How often do you watch movies at home?

3 VOCABULARY Review the process for making a movie in *Got a Good Idea for a Film*. Complete the process with the correct form of the verbs in the box.

| film | promote | produce | select |
| design | solve | revise | create |

🔑 Oxford 3000™

4 WHAT'S YOUR ANGLE? Look at the process in *Got a Good Idea for a Film*. Answer the questions.
1 Which do you think is the most difficult stage of making a movie? Explain your reasons.
2 Which stage would you like to be involved in? Why?

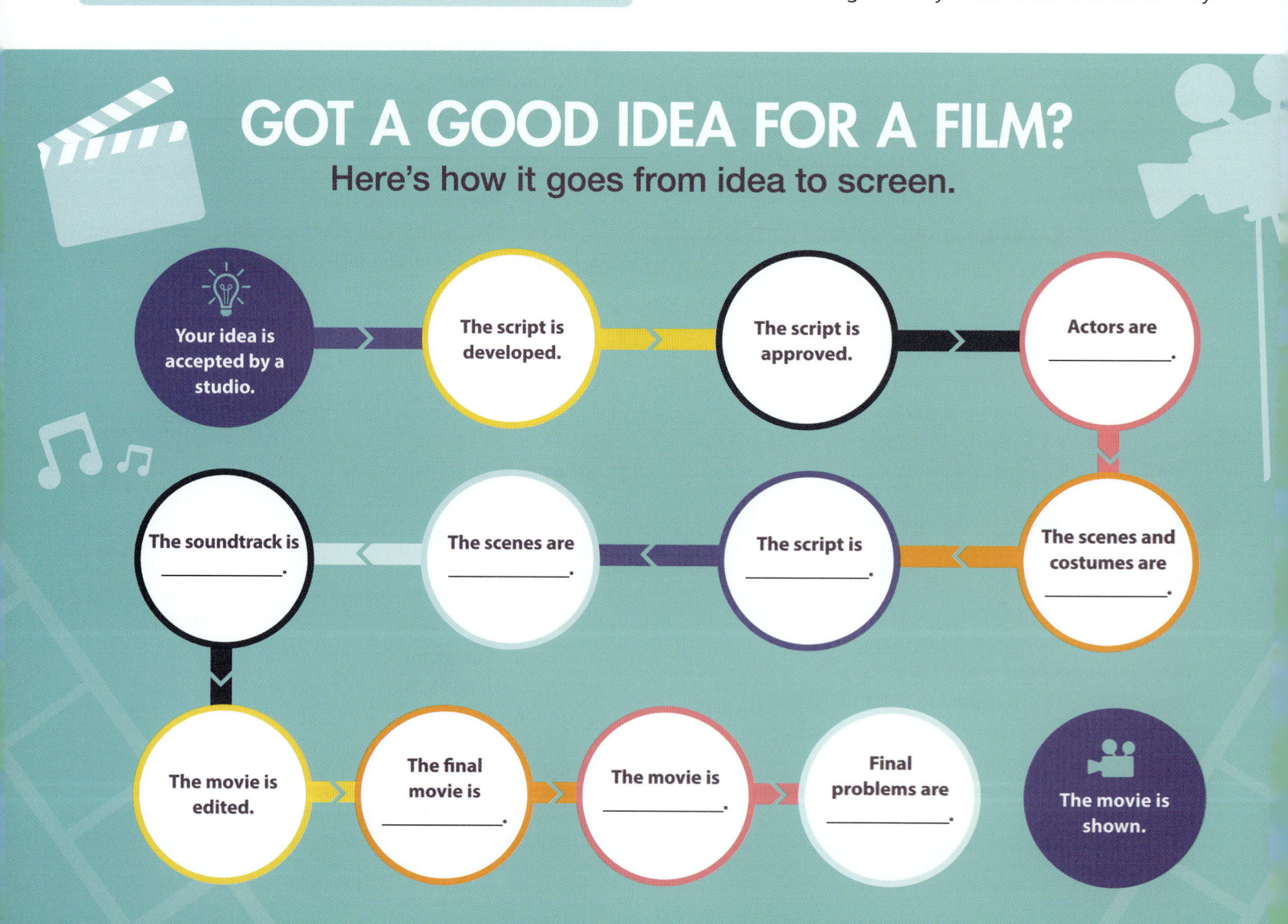

GOT A GOOD IDEA FOR A FILM?
Here's how it goes from idea to screen.

- Your idea is accepted by a studio.
- The script is developed.
- The script is approved.
- Actors are _____.
- The scenes and costumes are _____.
- The script is _____.
- The scenes are _____.
- The soundtrack is _____.
- The movie is edited.
- The final movie is _____.
- The movie is _____.
- Final problems are _____.
- The movie is shown.

5 ASSESS You are going to read an article about the history of the movies. Number these in the order you think they happened.

___ a   the first 3D movie process
___ b   U.S. weekly attendance fell from 90 to 51 million
___ c   Audion vacuum tube invented
___ d   *Toy Story* movie
___ e   first movies with sound and color
___ f   start of electrical recording
___ g   problems with color solved
___ h   *Avatar* movie
___ i   the increased use of computer-generated images (CGI)
___ j   *The Lord of the Rings* movies

> **READING SKILL**
> **Classifying information from a text**
>
> We can use diagrams to develop reading skills. Selecting and classifying information helps the reader understand the content and organization of a text. Diagrams are also useful for summarizing information, so they are good review tools.
>
> Flow charts show steps in a process.
>
> Step 1 ⟶ Step 2 ⟶ Step 3
>
> Timelines show when events happened.
>
> 1850   1900   1950   2000
>
> Mind maps show connections between ideas.

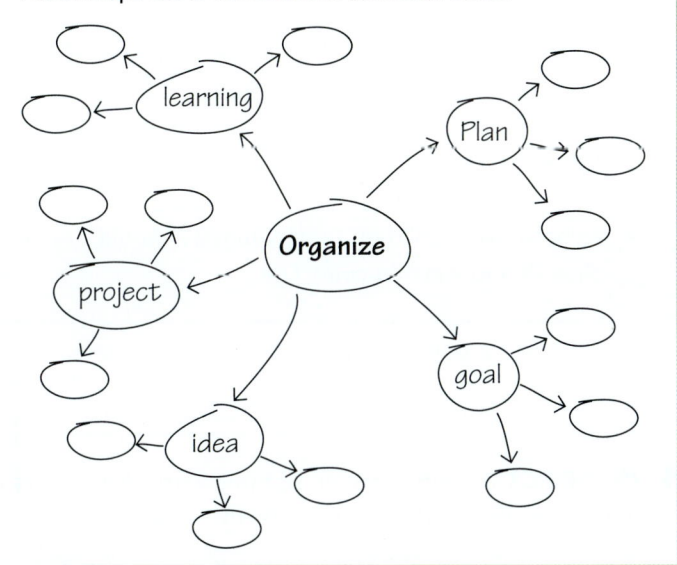

Technology and the big screen

When we watch a movie at the theater, unlike with many other arts, we see a pure product of technology. Without technology, no movie can be created since no sound can be recorded and no moving images filmed. However, for more than a hundred years, the development of motion picture technology has been a slow and irregular process.

The development of cinematic technology dates back to the late 19th century, and even though it took another century to evolve, many of the ideas were already in place in the early years. In the 1890s, for example, the initial movies were already made with sound and color, although it must be noted that these were very basic. British inventor William Friese-Greene even designed a 3D film process back in 1893.

The technology behind sound progressed quickly with the invention of the Audion vacuum tube in 1906, which enabled the amplification of sound, and the first electrical recordings around 1924. The technology behind color developed more slowly. It wasn't until the 1950s, for example, that complex technical problems in getting true color were solved by Kodak Eastman's new Eastmancolor process.

Movie technology accelerated in the middle to late 20th century. One reason was that between 1948 and 1952, the average weekly attendance at U.S. movie theaters fell from 90 to 51 million, largely because many people started preferring more active leisure activities, such as playing golf and traveling. For passive entertainment, they now had television. In response, the movie industry decided that moviegoers should be made to feel that they were actually participating in the movie action, so they developed technologies such as curved screens, which made the audience feel surrounded by the images, and powerful sound systems.

In recent times, digital technology dominates mainstream production, including the widespread use of 3D filming. In 1995, *Toy Story* was the first movie that showed that digital technology can be used to produce entire films. By the end of that decade, digital cameras were already used to film authentic-looking battle scenes, like those in the *Star Wars* episode *The Phantom Menace* in 1999.

In the 21st century, studios believe that audiences must be treated to amazing computer-generated special effects if they are to attend in mass numbers. In the past few decades, the studios have used them to produce spectacular blockbusters like *The Lord of the Rings* trilogy (2001–2003) and *Avatar* (2009). However, it should be remembered that there has been over a century of development to arrive at this point.

—adapted from *The Oxford Encyclopedia of the History of American Science, Medicine, and Technology*, edited by Hugh Richard Slotten

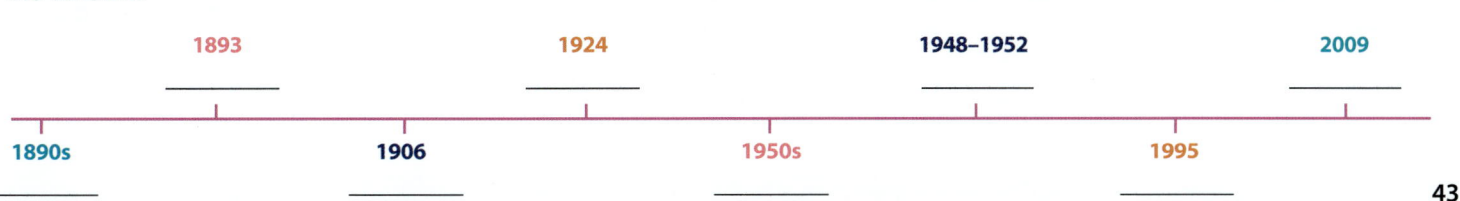

6 IDENTIFY Scan the article to find when the events in Exercise 5 happened. Write them in the correct place on the timeline.

| 1893 | 1924 | 1948–1952 | 2009 |
| ___ | ___ | ___ | ___ |

| 1890s | 1906 | 1950s | 1995 |
| ___ | ___ | ___ | ___ |

7 INTEGRATE Use the article and the words in the box to complete mind map blanks 1–8.

color   entertaining   images   leisure activities   screens   sound   sound systems   television

Technology
- early developments
  - quick: 1 _____
  - slow: 2 _____
- late developments
  - completion from 3 _____ + 4 _____
  - needed to be more 5 _____
  - improved
    - 6 _____
    - 7 _____
    - 8 _____
- current trends

8 EXPAND Add information about current trends to the mind map. Use ideas from the article and your own.

> **GRAMMAR IN CONTEXT**
> **Present passive with modal verbs**
>
> We can use the passive with modal verbs such as *can*, *could*, *might*, *should*, *must*, and so on.
>
> Subject + modal verb + *be* + past participle
> …no sound **can be recorded**…
> It **must be noted** that…

See Grammar focus on page 162.

9 IDENTIFY Find more examples of the present passive with modal verbs in the article. For each example, discuss with a partner who or what does the action.

10 APPLY Put the words in the correct order to make sentences in the present passive with a modal verb.

1 have to / nowadays, audiences / entertained / by more and more special effects / be
   _____

2 shouldn't / replaced / real actors / by digital avatars / be
   _____

3 be / more money / could / making movie theaters better / spent on / to attract bigger audiences
   _____

4 to be active, / children / encouraged / should / rather than sit and watch movies / be
   _____

5 banned / should / cell phones / be / from movie theaters
   _____

11 INTERACT Do you agree or disagree with the sentences in Exercise 10? Discuss your views with a partner.

12 WHAT'S YOUR ANGLE? Imagine you have a good idea for a movie. Answer the questions in a group.

1 Who would you select to act in it?
2 Who would you want to develop the script and direct it?
3 Where would you want it filmed?
4 Who would create the soundtrack?

4.3 What's the Difference?

1 ACTIVATE Discuss the items and match the words to the pictures. More than one may be possible for each picture.

handmade   machine-made   homemade   store-bought

2 WHAT'S YOUR ANGLE? What's your first choice for each of the following? Would you prefer them to be handmade, homemade, machine-made, or store-bought?

a birthday card   a cake   a special outfit   a car   a bag

3 **IDENTIFY** Read the introduction to the essay. Which two types of products are compared and contrasted?

4 **ASSESS** Read the essay. Complete the diagram with the information about handmade and machine-made products. Which information applies to each type of product? Which information applies to both?

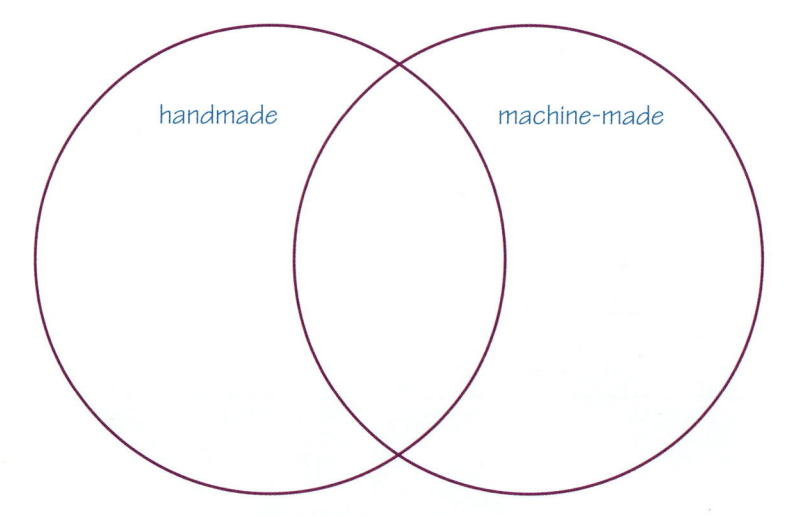

handmade — machine-made

> We live in an age of shopping. One aspect that separates the thousands of available items to buy is how they are produced—in general, things can be made by hand or by machine. In this essay, I will compare and contrast the two types of products.
>
> Starting with the similarities between the two types of products, the first point is that a good-quality item can be produced by either method. Actually, for many buyers, the fact that one item is made by hand and another by machine may not be important, especially if their quality is considered similar. For instance, most people are not interested in learning about how their washing machine was made—only if it works well. Most modern factories use machines to make excellent products, and customers, in general, are satisfied with such machine-made products. Another point in common is that both types of product are actually often made by highly skilled people. For instance, machine-made electrical equipment is frequently made by people who are very good at operating machines. This is the same for handmade items; in other words, items made by hand or by machine are typically made by workers who are excellent at their job.
>
> However, there are also differences between the two types of items. The main difference is the level of quality. Handmade products are usually made more slowly and carefully. For example, many people consider that a handmade car, such as a McLaren, is finished to a higher quality than a mass-produced car like a Toyota. Secondly, handmade products are made in smaller numbers. This smaller production means that these items are usually more expensive since they cost more to produce in this way. Finally, a handmade item is seen to be better than a mass-produced one, which also increases the price. That is to say, people are often prepared to pay extra for a handmade item because it makes them feel special.
>
> In conclusion, when we compare and contrast handmade and machine-made products, we can see that some things are the same and some are different. The quality of most machine-made products is excellent, and it is usually good enough for most people. However, there will always be a market for quality handmade products.

WRITING SKILL
Using example and explanation linking words

To help the reader, use examples and explanation to make your points clear. Use signpost words and phrases to show the reader you are doing this.

To introduce examples:

for instance,   for example,   such as   like
For instance, most people are not interested in learning about how their washing machine was made.

To introduce explanations:

this means,   that is (to say),   in other words,   to put it another way,
That is to say, people are often prepared to pay extra for a handmade item because it makes them feel special.

5 **INTEGRATE** Match the points to the examples, and add the linking words used in the essay.

1 difference between machine-made and handmade is not important _for instance_
2 both types are made by highly skilled people _____
3 handmade products take more time and care to make _____
4 a handmade car _____
5 not a handmade car _____

a machine-made equipment is made by people who are good at operating machines
b many people think that handmade cars are better quality than machine-made ones
c a Toyota
d people are not interested in how washing machines are made
e a McLaren

6 **IDENTIFY** Find the two linking phrases for explanations in the essay. Identify the point that is explained and the explanation that is given.

GRAMMAR IN CONTEXT
Adjectives with prepositions

We use prepositions after adjectives to talk about feelings, abilities, etc.

surprised by   bad at   bored with   pleased about
1 _____   2 _____   3 _____   4 _____

We can use an *-ing* form after some prepositions.
Most people are interested in learning about…
5 _____

See Grammar focus on page 162.

7 INTEGRATE Use a preposition and a phrase from the box to complete the sentences.

| baking | their response | my performance |
| people finding out | the bad quality | |

1 My cousin is good _____ homemade desserts.
2 I'm fed up _____ of mass-produced clothes.
3 My teacher was pleased _____ this semester.
4 I was surprised _____ to my speech.
5 Kate was worried _____ it was a store-bought dish.

8 IDENTIFY Complete the Grammar in Context box with more examples from the text.

9 WHAT'S YOUR ANGLE? Answer the questions. Explain your answers to your partner, giving explanations and examples to help.

What are you…
- good at?
- interested in?
- pleased about?
- surprised by?

10 PREPARE Work in pairs. Choose one of these topics for a compare-and-contrast essay. Complete a diagram for the two items you are comparing.
- a hand-painted picture and a photograph
- a store-bought gift and a handmade gift
- a homemade meal and a takeout meal

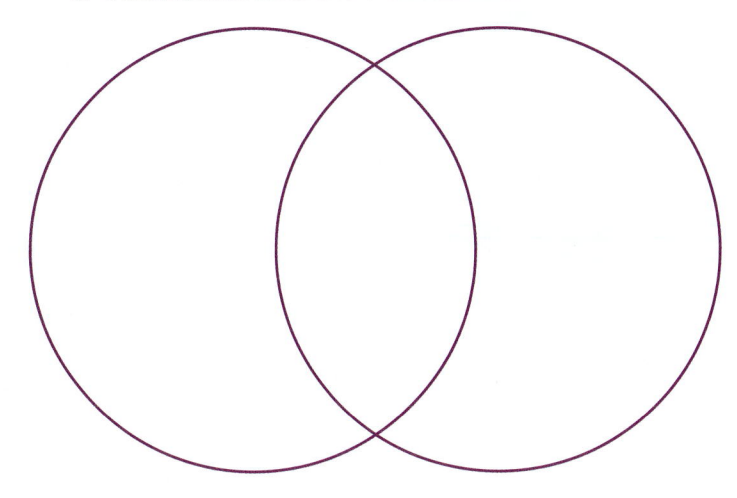

11 WRITE Write a compare-and-contrast essay individually. Use the checklist to help.

- [ ] Include an introduction explaining what you are comparing/contrasting.
- [ ] Include similarities and differences.
- [ ] Include explanations.
- [ ] Include examples.
- [ ] Use adjectives with prepositions.
- [ ] End with a conclusion.
- [ ] Write 200–300 words.

12 IMPROVE Compare your essay with your partner's. Do both essays match each point on the checklist?

13 SHARE Read other classmates' essays. Make a note of any new ideas and arguments you strongly agree or disagree with.

A technician shows the various designing steps in the creation of a Tod's shoe, at the Tod's headquarters in Sant'Elpidio a Mare, Italy

4.4 I Get It Now!

1 ▶ **ACTIVATE** Watch the first part of the video and answer the questions. What information in the video helped you answer them?

1. Where are Andy, Max, and Sarah from?
2. Where are the people in the movie that Andy and Max watched from?
3. Who is not sure about things in the movie?

REAL-WORLD ENGLISH Asking for and giving clarification

In conversation, we sometimes need to ask for clarification. This can be for different reasons; for example, we may not understand the information, we can't hear the person clearly, or we may not understand the language used.

Could you say that again? I didn't understand the part about… What do you mean by…?

When you ask for clarification,

- say what point you are asking about.
    Could you explain the part about…? What exactly is…?
- indicate when you understand.
    I get it now. OK, that makes sense.

When giving clarification, you can repeat the information in a different way or give examples to help the person understand.

I mean that… / It means that… To give you an example… Let me explain. It's when you…

2 ▶ **ASSESS** What did Max ask for clarification about? What do you think Sarah will say? Watch and check.

3 ▶ **IDENTIFY** Watch the complete video. What else is Max confused about? How do Sarah and Andy respond?

ENGLISH FOR REAL

4 ANALYZE Review the phrases from the video and decide if they are asking for clarification (1), indicating understanding (2), or giving clarification (3).

_1_ I didn't get some of the jokes.
___ I never saw a scarf!
___ Why was he the best?
___ OK, let me explain.
___ I get it now.
___ A muffler is part of a car.
___ Why is that funny?

5 EXPAND Work in pairs. Take turns asking for and giving clarification about these things mentioned in the video.

| a "best boy" | a silencer | a muffler | a scarf |

I didn't understand the part about a "best boy."
OK, let me explain. A "best boy"…

6 INTERACT Work in pairs and decide who is Student A and who is Student B. Read the situation and make notes on your role. Then act out the situation with your partner.

You had a different teacher for English class last week. There are some things you aren't clear about. Ask your partner for clarification and answer their questions.

Student A: You aren't sure what the homework was or how to spell the new teacher's name, but you know the topic of the test for the next class and what time you need to be in class.

Student B: You understood the homework, and you wrote down the new teacher's name, so you're confident you know how to spell it, but you're confused about the test in the next class. You don't know what the topic is or what time you need to be in class.

7 WHAT'S YOUR ANGLE? Think about two times you asked for or gave clarification. What were the situations? What language did you use? Why?

GO ONLINE to create your own version of the English For Real video.

4.5 It's Quite Simple, Really

1 **ACTIVATE** Discuss the questions.
   1. What kinds of games are popular in your country?
   2. What makes a good game?

2 **WHAT'S YOUR ANGLE?** What's your favorite board game? Tell your partner how to play it.

> **SPEAKING Describing a process**
>
> Start with an outline of the process. In this outline, you can include what the process is for and the number of steps or main stages.
>
> *I'm going to explain how to…*
> *There are three main stages…*
>
> When you describe the process, you can use ordinal numbers and signpost words and phrases to identify the different stages.
>
> *The first stage is to…   First of all,…*
> *After that,…*

3 **ASSESS** Review the steps for making a board game. Which stage of making a game does each step belong to? Which order would you put the steps in?

Making a board game	Initial concept	Developing the first version	Making the final version
___ make a simple version	☐	☐	☐
___ choose the basic design	☐	☐	☐
___ try the game	☐	☐	☐
___ decide on number of players	☐	☐	☐
___ identify the goals of the game	☐	☐	☐
___ choose the level of difficulty	☐	☐	☐
___ make the final game	☐	☐	☐
___ decide how players will interact or move	☐	☐	☐

4 **IDENTIFY** Listen to someone describing how to make a board game, and check the order of the steps in Exercise 3. Does it match the order you suggested?

> **PRONUNCIATION SKILL Chunking**
>
> Speech can be difficult to understand when the speaker doesn't use natural chunks.
>
> *OK, so I'm going to explain how to make a board game.*
>
> We use pauses between groups of words—or "chunks"— to help our listener understand our message.
>
> *OK, | so I'm going to explain | how to make a board game.*
>
> We use longer pauses between sentences and stages in a talk.
>
> *OK, | so I'm going to explain | how to make a board game. | You might think | it's going to be complicated, | but it's quite simple, really.*
> *So, | there are three main stages…*

5 **NOTICE** Listen to parts of the talk again, and mark the shorter and longer pauses.
   1. So, there are three main stages of making a game, and each has a number of steps. The first stage is to plan the game. First of all, the basic design must be chosen.
   2. And finally, will it be a difficult game or an easy game for all ages? And how long will a game take? At some point during this first stage of development, you also need to identify the main goal of the game.
   3. See how long it lasts, and look out for problems. Then, when you are sure it works, you are ready to plan the final product. So, the last stage is to make that final version.

6 **INTEGRATE** Work in pairs. Listen to your partner give parts of the talk from Exercise 5, and check the pauses.

7 **PREPARE** Choose an activity. Write a list of the main stages and individual steps needed to make or do it. Prepare your description, and identify the chunks and pauses.

8 **INTERACT** Work in pairs. Listen to your partner describe how to do the activity. Use the checklist to assess the instructions.
   - ☐ Are the main stages clear?
   - ☐ Are the steps clear?
   - ☐ Were the pauses and chunks helpful?

9 **IMPROVE** Get feedback from your partner on your description. Can you improve it?

10 **SHARE** Work in a group. Listen to each other's descriptions. What new information did you learn?

5 Survival

UNIT SNAPSHOT
What event changed the weather in 1883? 55
What do people say about a "problem shared"? 57
What uses wheels, tubes, and air to move? 62

- What problems do people encounter in this environment?
- What do they do to survive?
- In what other environments is it difficult for people to survive?

BEHIND THE PHOTO

REAL-WORLD GOAL
Help someone with an everyday disaster

1 Answer the questions.

1 How do friends and family help each other survive everyday difficult situations?
Friends and family can offer advice and emotional support. They can do things for each other and spend time together.
2 How do countries work together when natural disasters occur?
3 Why do many people want to help when they hear about problems?

2 Discuss your answers with a partner. Think of reasons and examples to support your opinions.

5.1 Everyday Disasters

1 ACTIVATE Look at the problems. Discuss the questions.
1. Which of these things have you ever done?
2. Which would be the worst thing for you to do?
3. Which would you know how to deal with?

sent a message to the wrong person

locked yourself out

forgotten where you parked the car

missed an important deadline

spilled a drink on a carpet

had a child repeat something bad you said

2 ASSESS Listen to the start of a radio show. Which problems from Exercise 1 do you think each expert could deal with?

3 IDENTIFY Listen to the show. Identify the three problems from Exercise 1.

> **LISTENING SKILL**
> **Interpreting changes in volume, speed, and pitch**
>
> Our words give information, but our voices also change according to what we are trying to communicate. We often change the volume, speed, and pitch (up and down). Listen for these changes and stressed words to understand the speaker better.
>
> Stressing words or slowing them down tells the listener how important particular ideas are and how strongly the speaker feels about them. For example, when:
>
> - giving advice:
>   I **really** think you should do that.
>
> - feeling frustrated:
>   I **reeeeeally** need to get rid of it before my parents see it.
>
> The intonation going down at the end of a sentence can show that the speaker is sure. For example, when:
>
> - giving a warning:
>   People never enjoy the result of that.
>
> Slowing speech can show that the speaker wants you to listen carefully or that the speaker is thinking carefully while speaking. For example, when:
>
> - realizing something as you say it:
>   But if you do that—then—we—will—lose.

4 IDENTIFY Listen to and read the extracts from the show. Decide what the speaker is doing: warning (W), realizing (R), or giving advice (A).
1. But the most important thing is not to lie to her. People never like that. ___
2. You really should look out when you have any kind of food or drink and white carpets… ___
3. Yes, there was. Uh…does that matter? ___

5 APPLY Listen again. Mark the stresses, speed, and pitch changes. Compare with a partner.

6 IDENTIFY Listen to more extracts, and decide what the speaker is doing.

1. _____   3. _____   5. _____
2. _____   4. _____   6. _____

7 INTEGRATE Complete the notes for the three everyday disasters and the advice Tom and Penny gave. Then listen again, and check your notes.

Caller	Everyday disaster	Advice
Chloe	What?	
	When?	
Lana	What?	
	When?	
Phil	What?	
	When?	

8 WHAT'S YOUR ANGLE? Look at your notes in Exercise 7. Answer the questions.

1 Do you have any more advice for Chloe and Lana?
2 What advice would you give Phil?

GRAMMAR IN CONTEXT Advice and warning with *should*, *ought to*, and *had better*

We use *should*, *ought to*, and *had better* to give and ask for advice.

We can use *should* in statements and questions.
*You **should** always listen.*
*He **shouldn't** say anything.*
***Should** I do that? Yes, you **should**. / No, you **shouldn't**.*

Ought to is more formal. We generally don't use *ought to* with *not* or in questions.
*You **ought to** try.*

Had better gives a stronger warning. We don't usually use it in questions.
*He**'d better** say something.*
*You**'d better** not do that.*

See Grammar focus on page 163.

9 APPLY Discuss these extracts from the radio show with a partner. Complete them with a form of *should*, *ought to*, or *had better*. Then listen and check.

1 _____ I try again?
2 You _____ give up yet.
3 You _____ tell her the truth as soon as possible.
4 Any parents listening out there _____ remember this.

VOCABULARY DEVELOPMENT Phrasal verbs with *look*

We can use *look* in many phrasal verbs. For example:

look into   look forward to   look up from   look out

1 Sometimes the meaning of the phrasal verb can be easily inferred from the individual meaning of its parts.
look around somewhere—visit all different parts of a place

2 Sometimes the meaning of the phrasal verb is less clear from its parts.
look after something—make sure that something is safe

🔑 Oxford 3000™

10 INTEGRATE Review the definitions below for the phrasal verbs from group 2 in the Vocabulary Development box. Then listen to the extracts from the radio show, and complete the phrasal verbs.

1 look _____ something—to take care of something
2 look _____—be careful
3 look _____ something—to examine something
4 look something _____—to look for information in a book or on the computer
5 look _____ somebody—respect somebody

11 INTEGRATE Complete the sentences with the correct words from the boxes.

| around | up from | through | forward |

1 I often look _____ my home to check on safety.
2 I always look _____ the safety instructions when I get on a plane.
3 The fire alarm goes off so often at work that I don't look _____ my computer now.
4 I look _____ things going wrong because I love helping to fix things.

| out | up to | into | after | up |

5 If I hear a strange noise at night, I get out of bed and look _____ the situation immediately.
6 When I have a practical problem, I look _____ the solution on the Internet.
7 I look _____ my phone and wallet very carefully when I'm in a big city.
8 When I'm out with friends, I'm always the one looking _____ for everyone else.
9 I look _____ to people who are very good at dealing with practical problems.

12 WHAT'S YOUR ANGLE? Which sentences in Exercise 11 are true for you?

5.2 Unexpected Consequences

1

earthquake
crack

2

3

4

5

6

1 ACTIVATE Match the words in the box to the pictures of natural disasters. Then write four key words related to each picture. Use a dictionary to help.

| earthquake | drought | hurricane |
| volcanic eruption | wildfire | flood |

2 WHAT'S YOUR ANGLE? Which of the natural disasters in Exercise 1 have you seen on the news recently?

3 ASSESS Match the years to the four natural disasters. What do you know about these disasters? Then scan the article to check the dates.

1 Great Lisbon Earthquake ___ a 1918
2 Eruption of volcano Krakatoa ___ b 1976
3 Spanish flu epidemic ___ c 1883
4 Great Tangshan Earthquake in China ___ d 1755

The Great Lisbon Earthquake

A natural disaster with unnatural consequences

Natural disasters, such as earthquakes, hurricanes, floods, drought, and fires, are natural events that destroy large areas, often cause loss of life, and have a major economic impact.

One way of assessing the impact of a natural disaster is to look at how many people died and how much property was destroyed. Of the hundreds of natural disasters that have happened in modern times, a few are more famous for the extent of the destruction they caused. The eruption of the volcano Krakatoa in 1883 changed the weather of the northern hemisphere for a while and destroyed more than 300 communities. Similarly, the Spanish flu epidemic of 1918 killed about 30 million people. However, the impact of a disaster sometimes is not measured only in terms of loss of life and property—history can be affected as well.

One of the most important natural disasters to shake the course of history was the Great Lisbon Earthquake of 1755. Its center was about 200 miles from the coast of Portugal, and its effects were felt far and wide—the shock destroyed parts of Spain, Morocco, and Algeria. However, it was Portugal that suffered the most losses. About 30,000 people died from the earthquake and up to 70,000 more from floods and fires. In addition, the Portuguese capital was almost completely destroyed.

Although the Lisbon earthquake is still considered one of the most powerful and destructive in European history, it is so important not because of its physical effects—the Great Tangshan Earthquake in China in 1976 killed more than 240,000 people—but because it changed the way we view and respond to such events. After the Lisbon earthquake, thinkers such as the French philosopher Voltaire started to question—and eventually gave up—the belief that such natural disasters had metaphysical causes and started looking for scientific explanations. Seismology, the study of earthquakes, became popular, as scientists and governments realized that they had to learn to forecast earthquakes. They developed the idea that to protect a place, people must prepare rather than react. In addition, the Lisbon earthquake had a major effect on politics. The terrible financial and human losses probably contributed to the end of Portugal as a great global power, leading to changes in the world order.

As a result of the Lisbon earthquake, we now recognize that we can't only assess natural disasters for their physical effects; they can change human thought and society, too.

—adapted from the *Oxford Encyclopedia of the Modern World*, edited by Peter N. Stearns

READING SKILL
Recognizing and understanding exemplification

The writer often give examples to help readers understand the points they are making.

Sometimes writers use signpost phrases for this:

Natural disasters, **such as** *earthquakes, hurricanes, floods, drought, and fires*, are natural events that destroy large areas.

However, sometimes readers need to recognize the relationship without a signpost phrase. This often involves making connections across sentences: sentences expressing a more general idea are sometimes followed by sentences or phrases providing more specific or detailed information or examples.

Of the hundreds of natural disasters that have happened in modern times, a few are more famous for the extent of the destruction they caused. **The eruption of the volcano Krakatoa** *in 1883…*

4 IDENTIFY Find examples of each of these things in the text.

1 where the effects of the Great Lisbon Earthquake were felt
2 the losses that Portugal suffered
3 an earthquake that had a greater physical impact than the Lisbon one
4 a philosopher that changed his way of thinking after the Lisbon earthquake
5 a change in people's view of natural disasters
6 a change in politics after the earthquake

5 INTEGRATE Read the article again. How was the Great Lisbon Earthquake different from other disasters?

GRAMMAR IN CONTEXT
Obligation with *must* and *have to*

We use *must* or *have to* to say that something is necessary.

We often use *must* to talk about the feelings and wishes of the speaker.

…people **must** prepare…

We usually use *have to* to talk about rules that come from someone else. We also usually use *have to* in questions.

…scientists **have to** look at all the potential causes of a disaster…
Do they **have to**…?

We use *can't* to say it is necessary not to do something.

…we **can't** only assess natural disasters for their physical effects…

We use *don't have to* to say that something isn't necessary.

…scientists **don't have to** feel the ground shake to know that an earthquake is starting…

Must doesn't have a past tense form, so we use *had to* instead.

…they **had to** learn to forecast earthquakes.

See Grammar focus on page 163.

6 APPLY Complete the sentences, so they reflect views from the article. Use *must*, *can't*, or the correct form of *have to*.

1 We _____ think about people, buildings, and history when studying natural disasters.
2 For natural disasters to be on worldwide news, there _____ be extensive damage.
3 We _____ only think about earthquakes after they happen. We _____ prepare for them.
4 Designers _____ think about natural disasters when planning new cities.
5 We _____ feel we are powerless against natural disasters. We can plan and prepare.

7 VOCABULARY Find the verbs in the article. Then match them to the definitions.

destroy	react	affect
forecast	protect	prepare

Oxford 3000™

1 _____: to do or say something because of something that happened
2 _____: to say something will happen in the future using information you have now
3 _____: to damage something very badly so it doesn't work or exist anymore
4 _____: to make sure something is safe
5 _____: to get ready for something
6 _____: to produce a change in something

8 EXPAND Use your own ideas to answer the questions.

1 What types of buildings are often **destroyed** in earthquakes?
2 What can be done to **protect** people after a natural disaster?
3 If a natural disaster, like a hurricane, is **forecast**, how can people prepare?
4 How do natural disasters **affect** decisions governments make?
5 How do people usually **react** when they see natural disasters on the news?

9 WHAT'S YOUR ANGLE? Complete the sentences, so they show your views about natural disasters.

1 We have to protect…
2 These types of disasters mostly affect…
3 We must prepare for…
4 Governments must spend more money on forecasting…
5 We must react quickly when…

10 INTERACT Tell a partner your sentences from Exercise 9. Does your partner agree with your views?

Neighbors help rescue a car which went off the road in Valls d'Aguilar, Catalonia, Spain

5.3 Absolutely Essential

1 **ACTIVATE** What are the advantages and disadvantages of getting advice from these different people and places?

family	online discussion boards
colleagues	friends
professional advisers	magazine advice columns

2 **WHAT'S YOUR ANGLE?** What people and places do you go to for advice on the following topics?

money   career   relationships   travel

3 **INTEGRATE** Read the online advice column. Summarize the problem in a sentence. Then summarize the advice in a list of steps.

AdviceZone

Home | About | Advice | News | Sign in

A problem shared…

The problem:

Life is so busy right now. I am moving to another apartment next week, I just got a promotion and a whole new team to work with, and my exams for my business course start next month. And although I'm absolutely exhausted the whole time, I can't sleep at night. What should I do to survive the next few months?
—Ana

The advice:

Thank you for writing in with your problem. I'm extremely pleased you have decided to get help at this time when things are a little difficult. Remember: a problem shared is a problem halved.

Your basic problem is time—like many people, you see it as your enemy, not your friend. However, that is not the case. So, as well as helping you, I hope this answer will help many of our readers.

First of all, it is absolutely essential that you change the way you think about time. There is always enough time if we use it in the right way. Right now, you should make time to sit down and write a list of things you have to do. In addition to helping you get organized, this will help you relax. Get the problems out of your head and on paper.

Next, look through your list and congratulate yourself. Many of the things you have listed are really good—a promotion, a lovely new home, finishing your business course. Yes, you have to do some work to get there, but you will manage.

Now you need to write A, B, or C next to each thing on the list: A is for very important, B for fairly important, and C for things that are hardly important at all. At this point, you shouldn't feel you have to keep everything on the list. Besides, you might not actually be the best person to do them. For example, yes, you need to move your things to your new home. However, perhaps a team with a van would do a better job than you and your very small car.

The final step is to decide the order to do the A things. You will find there is plenty of time as well as a natural order. The B and C things will follow naturally.

Comments:

cityboy123
You really should try this. I use this solution all the time. And the absolutely amazing thing about C things is that they often disappear by the time you get to them!

happytohelp
In addition to this advice, you should make sure you are eating well and exercising. You say you're really tired but can't sleep—that's a sign that you need to take care of yourself. It's hard to deal with problems when you're feeling absolutely awful.

> **WRITING SKILL**
> **Using addition and contrast linking words**
>
> Use linking words to show the relationship between parts of your writing.
>
> Addition linking words show when you are adding more information.
>
> in addition (to)   as well as   besides
> **In addition to** helping you get organized, <u>this will help you relax</u>.
>
> Contrasting linking words show when you are presenting different, sometimes opposing, ideas.
>
> but   however   although
> You see it as your enemy, not your friend. **However**, <u>that is not the case</u>.

4 IDENTIFY Find each idea from the first column in the text. Then write the linking word used in the text, and match the idea to the connected one from the second column.

1 Ana can't sleep, _although_   _e_
2 The advice will help Ana _____ ___
3 The advice will help Ana organize _____ ___
4 It is going to be hard work, _____ ___
5 Ana doesn't have to do everything. _____, ___
6 Ana needs to move her things. _____, ___

a a group of people might be better.
b there might be someone else better.
c help other people.
d helping her relax.
e she is very tired.
f she will be able to do it.

5 APPLY Rewrite these sentences, adding the best word from the parentheses and changing the grammar and punctuation as necessary.

1 He advised me to stop. I didn't want to. (as well as / however)
2 I need help with the project. I need help with my assignment. (as well as / but)
3 You shouldn't try to do everything. You should try to do as much as you can. (besides / although)
4 You don't have to offer to help. They may not want any help. (besides / however)
5 It will be difficult. That shouldn't stop you from trying. (as well as / but)
6 They worked very well together. They gave an amazing presentation. (although / in addition to)

6 VOCABULARY Match the adjectives in the first column to the ones with similar meanings in the second column. There may be more than one possibility for some of them.

1	tired	_d_	a	amazing
2	bad	___	b	huge
3	small	___	c	terrified
4	afraid	___	d	exhausted
5	good	___	e	freezing
6	pleased	___	f	extraordinary
7	surprising	___	g	awful
8	important	___	h	tiny
9	special	___	i	terrible
10	silly	___	j	delighted
11	big	___	k	essential
12	cold	___	l	ridiculous

Oxford 3000™

> **GRAMMAR IN CONTEXT Intensifiers**
>
> We can use an adverb before an adjective to make the adjective stronger or weaker.
>
> I'm **extremely** pleased.
> Things are **a little** difficult.
>
> Some adjectives are "ungradable." They often express perfection or its opposite. We use *absolutely* with ungradable adjectives only.
>
> I'm **absolutely** exhausted.
> ~~I'm very exhausted.~~
> ~~I'm absolutely tired.~~

See Grammar focus on page 163.

7 EXPAND Find nine more adverb + adjective pairs in the text. Complete the table.

Adverb	Gradable adjective	Ungradable adjective
absolutely		exhausted
extremely	pleased	

8 ASSESS Review the text, and write the adverbs from Exercise 7 on the scale showing how the adverb changes the adjective.

↑ to the highest degree _____

to a high degree _____
_____
_____

to some degree _____

to a low degree _____

to a very low degree _____

9 PREPARE Choose one of these problems to give advice on, or use your own idea. Then discuss your ideas with a partner, and make notes of any additional ideas.

You sent a text message to the wrong friend. In the message, you (correctly) complained about them. Now this friend won't speak to you.

Your boss doesn't recognize the good work you do. Instead, she praises another team member and thinks that person is responsible for your team's success.

Your new neighbor makes a lot of noise at night. You get up early in the morning, so you like to be asleep by 9:30 p.m. You haven't said anything yet, but the situation is getting worse.

10 WRITE Write a response of up to 300 words giving advice on the problem. Use intensifiers and ungradable adjectives.

11 IMPROVE Review your partner's advice with the checklist.

Did your partner…
- give clear and helpful advice?
- include additional and different ideas?
- use intensifiers with adjectives?
- write up to 300 words?

12 WHAT'S YOUR ANGLE? Read the advice from some of your other classmates. Do you have any additional or different ideas? Add comments.

5.4 What's the Problem?

1 **ACTIVATE** Look at the pictures. What do you think the problem is?

2 ▶ **IDENTIFY** Watch the first part of the video. Answer the questions with a partner.
   1 What is Kevin's problem?
   2 How does Andy respond to Kevin?

3 ▶ **ANALYZE** Watch the second part of the video. Choose the things that happen.
   ☐ a Max tells Andy about Kevin.
   ☐ b Andy explains the problem to Max.
   ☐ c Max calls Kevin to give him advice.
   ☐ d Andy asks Max for advice.
   ☐ e Max makes some suggestions.

> **REAL-WORLD ENGLISH** Asking for and giving advice
>
> When you ask for advice, give background information, so the person understands the situation.
> *Well, the problem is I missed the assignment deadline… What do you think I should do?*
>
> You can use modal verbs to ask for advice.
> *What would you do if you were me? What should I do?*
>
> Effective advice is often in the form of suggestions rather than instructions for what to do. Use modal verbs and phrases like *I think*.
> *I think you should…   You could…   Maybe you can…*
>
> Imperatives are stronger, and so is *had better*. They might sound more like instructions. Avoid these in more formal and delicate situations.
> *Speak to him.   Just tell him…   You'd better call.*
>
> When we give advice, we often show we are thinking from the other person's point of view.
> *If I were you, I would…   It's up to you, but I think…*
>
> The language used to ask for and give advice is different when the situation is more serious, if the context is more formal, or if the speakers don't know each other, for example, between a doctor and patient or in a professional context such as an employee speaking to their manager. In these situations, the language is less direct.
> *I'm trying to lose weight. Can you advise on what kind of diet I should follow?*
> *I'd recommend that you try to… It might be a good idea to…*

4 ▶ **ANALYZE** Watch the second part of the video again, and answer the questions. Then discuss the answers with a partner.

1. What is Max's suggestion? How does he express it the first time?
2. Did Andy accept the suggestion? Why or why not?
3. What does Max think is the problem with Kevin staying?
4. How does Max express his suggestion the second time? How is it different from the first time?

5 🔊 **IDENTIFY** Listen to extracts from the video, and complete the phrases for asking for and giving advice.

Asking for advice	Giving advice
1 What _____ do?	3 I think _____ call Phil.
2 _____ invite him to stay?	5 _____ invite him.
4 What _____ do if you were me?	6 _____ call Phil.

6 **WHAT'S YOUR ANGLE?** What would you do in Andy's situation?

7 **INTERACT** Work in pairs. Use the phrases in the Real-world English box and in Exercise 5 to ask for and give advice on the following situations.

an argument with a friend
not getting a good grade
what to wear on a night out
buying a new phone
trying to get fit

8 **PREPARE** Work in pairs. Review the problem. Discuss different advice to give.

A friend wants to borrow $30. You have the cash, but your friend hasn't paid you back $20 from last month. You ask your roommate for advice.

9 **INTERACT** Work with a new partner. Decide on your roles. Prepare what you will say. Then role-play the situation.

10 **ASSESS** How helpful was the advice? Did you accept or decline it? Why? What will you do?

11 **INTERACT** Change roles. Follow the same steps with the problem below.

A good friend is having some problems and needs somewhere to stay for a month. You have important exams coming up, and you are not supposed to have anyone to stay in your dorm room for longer than two nights. You ask another friend for advice.

GO ONLINE to create your own version of the English For Real video.

5.5 Don't Panic!

1 **ACTIVATE** If you had to do the following things, how would you find out what to do? Discuss your ideas with a partner. Use the list below to help.

rescue your phone from water	change a tire
find your keys	change an electric plug
get nail polish off the furniture	

Watch an online video.
Call a friend.
Read instructions in the manual or online.
Try to figure it out for yourself.
Something different.

2 **IDENTIFY** Listen to someone starting to give instructions. Answer the questions.
 1 What will the instructions be for?
 2 What problems does Dan have?

3 **ASSESS** Work in pairs. Number the steps in order to make instructions for changing a bicycle tire.
 ___ new tube in and tire on
 ___ air in new tire
 ___ bike upside down
 ___ wheel back on bike
 ___ wheel off bike
 ___ tube and tire off wheel

4 **IDENTIFY** Listen to the instructions.
 1 Is the order the same as yours?
 2 Do you agree with the instructions, or would you suggest something different?

> **SPEAKING Giving practical instructions**
>
> Instructions need to be clear and easy to follow.
> Use imperatives and simple sentences.
> *First, turn the bike upside down.*
> Use signposting phrases to show the order.
> *After that, you put the tube in.*
> *Finally, put the wheel back on.*
> If you're face-to-face with the person, you can use *this*, *that*, *here*, and *there* with gestures to show what you mean.
> *Look, hold this part here. Then turn that handle.*

5 **IDENTIFY** Listen and complete the extracts from the instructions with verbs and sequencing expressions.
 1 So, _____, _____ the bike upside down.
 2 _____ _____, _____ the levers.
 3 _____ _____ the tire and the tube off.
 4 And, _____, _____ the wheel back on.

> **PRONUNCIATION SKILL**
> **Connected speech with words ending in /t/ or /d/**
>
> Sounds can change in connected speech. We often miss /t/ and /d/ at the end of words when the next word starts with a consonant sound.
> *aroun(d) the*   *firs(t) turn*
> However, when the next word starts with a vowel sound, we hear /t/ and /d/ more clearly at the start of that word.
> *outside edge* → *outsi dedge*
> *flat tire* → *fla tire*

6 **INTEGRATE** Identify the words ending in /t/ and /d/ in these instructions, and predict how to say them in connected speech. Listen and check. Then practice.
 1 …turn the bike upside down.
 2 After that, turn the levers…
 3 Then take the tire and the tube off.
 4 …you're going to put the new tube in…
 5 …it's hard work, but if you keep trying…
 6 And, finally, put the wheel back on…
 7 …the opposite way from how you took it off.
 8 …call me if you get stuck…

7 **IDENTIFY** Listen to the summary of the instructions, and complete it. Then identify the words ending with /t/ and /d/, and predict how to say them. Listen again and check. Then practice.
 Don't panic. You can do it! Just remember the steps—
 ¹ _____ the bike upside down, ² _____ the wheel off, ³ _____ the tire off, ⁴ _____ the tube, ⁵ _____ the tire, ⁶ _____ the wheel back on.
 It's not hard at all.

8 **PREPARE** Work in pairs. Make a list of everyday disasters. Then choose a disaster from your list or from Exercise 1, and plan instructions for how to deal with it.

9 **IMPROVE** Practice giving your instructions. When you listen to your partner, use the checklist to give feedback.
 ☐ Are the instructions clear and easy to follow?
 ☐ Is there enough (but not too much) detail?
 ☐ Does your partner use imperatives and signposts?
 ☐ Are the instructions summarized at the end?

10 **INTERACT** Give your instructions to a group. Did they find them clear and easy to follow?

11 **WHAT'S YOUR ANGLE?** What's the most useful thing you learned from your group's instructions?

Now go to page 151 for the Unit 5 Review.

6 Trends

UNIT SNAPSHOT

How much is the jeans industry worth now? 65
Do people work more or less nowadays? 67
What was a popular diet drink in 1820? 69

- What is the appeal of tradition?
- How do traditions change to reflect the times?
- Why do people follow fashion?

BEHIND THE PHOTO

REAL-WORLD GOAL
Read a fashion blog

1. Work in pairs. What do you think will be the biggest trend in each of the following areas in the next 20 years?

   clothes   food   buildings   transportation   education

   I think sustainable fashion will be the biggest trend in clothes. People will buy fewer clothes, but they will last longer, and they will be made from environmentally-friendly materials.

2. Share your ideas with another pair, and choose the most likely trend.

6.1 Always in Fashion

1 **ACTIVATE** Discuss these questions with a partner.
   1. What's your favorite piece of clothing?
   2. Where did you get it?
   3. When do you wear it?
   4. How do you feel when you wear it?

> **READING SKILL Using questions when reading**
>
> Before you read, review the title, pictures, and general layout of the text. Ask yourself questions about the source, genre, and topic of the text and what you already know about it. This will help focus your mind on the topic and activate your knowledge of it.
>
> *Where is the text from?*
> *What do I already know about this topic?*
>
> Then read the introduction and think about the questions the text might answer.
>
> *Who…? What…? Where…? When…? Why…? How…?*
>
> As you read, look for answers to these questions. These will help you understand the main ideas and facts in the text as well as the author's attitude and point of view.
>
> After you finish reading, use the questions to summarize the main ideas. This will help you recall and retain the information better. If there is a question you can't answer, go back to the text and read more carefully.
>
> *What were the main points?*
> *What events or actions were described?*

2 **IDENTIFY** Look at the title, pictures, and layout of the text. Then discuss the questions with a partner.
   1. Where do you think the text is from—a blog, an encyclopedia, a magazine for teenagers, or a newspaper?
   2. What can you see in the pictures?
   3. What do you know about the topic of the text (facts, history, etc.)?

3 **ASSESS** Read the introduction, and write three questions you think the rest of the text might answer. Then compare your questions with a partner. Which three questions do you both think the article is most likely to answer?

4 **IDENTIFY** Read the text. Are any of your questions answered?

Blue jeans

Blue jeans are the most famous item of clothing ever invented and one of the world's most long-lasting trends. They have been fashionable for more than 50 years. Not only that, as they have traveled around the world, jeans have spread ideas about America as the land of the free and independent—not bad for what started out as cheap work pants.

The story of jeans began about 170 years ago when people went to California to look for gold in the desert. In 1853, Levi Strauss, a 24-year-old from far-off Bavaria, traveled to California to join his family in their San Francisco store. There they sold goods, including tents made of strong canvas, to workers in the gold fields.

Levi saw an opportunity; he had the idea of using the tents to make cheap, tough pants. Later, he changed the material to denim, and he dyed it blue so that dirt marks wouldn't show. Twenty years after this, Jacob Davis, a Latvian tailor, added metal rivets at places where the jeans needed to be stronger, such as by the pockets where the men put the heavy rocks containing gold. The red label on the left back pocket was created in 1936 to identify Levi jeans at a distance since there were now many other makers of jeans, like Lee and Wrangler.

Movies in the 1950s led to jeans becoming fashionable. These films showed exciting young actors, like James Dean, refusing to follow the normal rules of society. The actors and their uniform of tight jeans became symbols of change for younger people. The look was very different from the unfashionable loose pants that their parents wore then, and young people around the world started copying it. In 1957, *Jailhouse Rock*, starring Elvis Presley, spread the trend further, and hippie culture, rock and roll, and hip-hop have all added to it.

Jeans are now worn all over the world. Comfortable and long-lasting, they can be both casual and elegant depending on what they are worn with. They are, however, not always cheap—jeans designed in Milan and Paris are worn as high-fashion items by women in stylish high heels and expensive tops and jewelry.

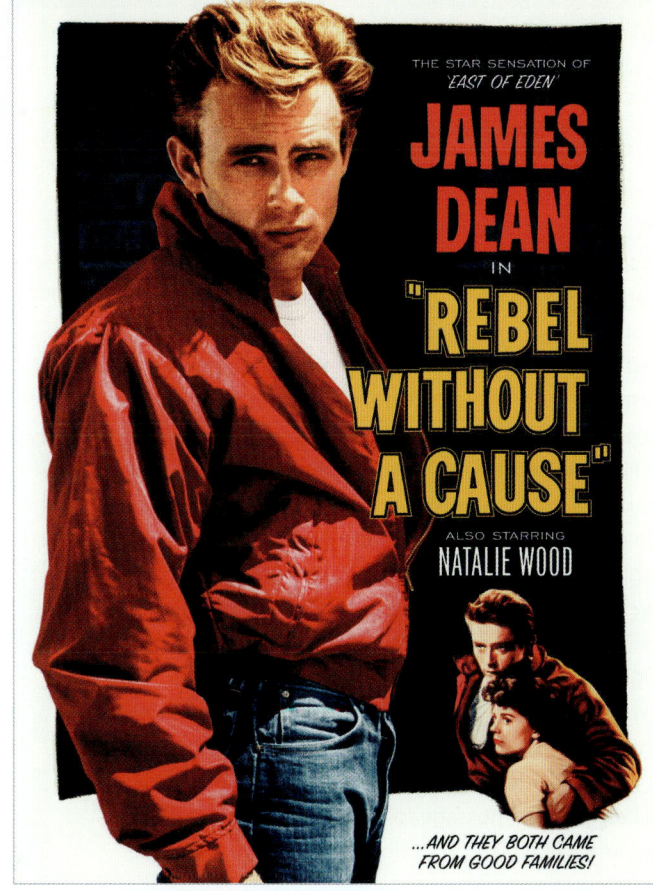

In 1986, *Life* magazine reported that 13 pairs of jeans were bought every second. Since its small beginnings, the jeans industry has grown to now be worth more than $700 billion, with almost all production happening at low cost in countries like India and Brazil. Levi Strauss, the young man who made it all happen, would be amazed to see how his practical, unfashionable working pants have become a global trend in fashion.

Glossary:
canvas: a strong heavy material for making tents and for painting on
tailor: a person whose job is to make clothes for individual customers
rivet: a metal pin used to put two pieces of strong material together

—adapted from *Oxford Encyclopedia of the Modern World*, edited by P. Stearns

5 INTEGRATE Review this information from the text. Write the question for each answer.

1 <u>What have jeans helped to spread</u>?
ideas about America
2 _____?
in San Francisco
3 _____?
so that the dirt didn't show
4 _____?
to make the pockets stronger
5 _____?
movies in the 1950s
6 _____?
all over the world
7 _____?
in countries like India and Brazil

6 EXPAND Work with a partner. Write three more questions about the text. Then exchange questions with another pair and answer them.

7 VOCABULARY Match the adjectives to their opposites.

casual	**classic**	unfashionable	**tight**
stylish	**loose**	**formal**	trendy

♂ Oxford 3000™

8 IDENTIFY Which adjectives from Exercise 7 are used to describe wearable items in the article? Scan paragraphs 4 and 5 to check.

9 INTEGRATE Label the pictures with the words. Then discuss the questions with a partner.

collar   heel   leg   pants   sleeve   top

1 _____   2 _____
3 _____   5 _____
4 _____   6 _____

1 Which of the words from Exercise 7 can be used to describe each picture?
2 What type of each item do you prefer?

GRAMMAR IN CONTEXT Time expressions with the present perfect and simple past

We usually use the present perfect with time expressions that indicate unfinished time periods.

*Jeans have been fashionable **for more than 50 years**.*
***Over the past few years**, jeans have become more popular.*

We usually use the simple past with time expressions that indicate finished time periods.

*The story of jeans began **about 170 years ago**.*
*Movies **in the 1950s** led to jeans becoming fashionable.*

Note that some time expressions can refer to either unfinished or finished periods.

***Have you talked** to the tailor **this morning**? (It is still morning.)*
***Did you talk** to the tailor **this morning**? (It is now afternoon or evening.)*

See Grammar focus on page 164.

10 IDENTIFY Identify the sentences in the text that help you decide if these sentences are true or false. Then discuss your answers with a partner.

1 Jeans are not fashionable now.
2 Jeans are usually made from canvas now.
3 Parents of teenagers have worn loose pants for the past 70 years.
4 More than 30 years ago, *Life* magazine reported on the number of jeans bought.
5 The jeans industry makes more money now than at the start.

A groom gets ready for his wedding in Upstate New York, the United States

11 APPLY Read the blog post, and complete it with the best form, present perfect or past simple, of the verbs in parentheses.

Dangerous trends

Home | About | Articles | News

Beware! Doctors give skinny jeans a "health warning."

In 2015, a 35-year-old Australian woman ¹_____ (spend) the morning cleaning out her closets while wearing tight jeans. By the end of the morning, her legs ²_____ (be) as big as balloons, so she ³_____ (go) to the hospital. The medical staff ⁴_____ (have to) cut her out of the skinny jeans. They ⁵_____ (be) so tight that they were pressing on the main nerves in her legs!

However, it's not only skinny jeans that cause problems for the stylish—other fashionable clothes can also be dangerous. Over the years, many men with tight collars ⁶_____ (complain) of neck pain, but few ⁷_____ (be) aware that those collars might also increase the pressure to their eyeballs and the risk of glaucoma. Similarly, millions of women ⁸_____ (experience) pain in their feet and legs after spending too long in shoes with very high heels, and some ⁹_____ (develop) serious back problems too.

Perhaps the message for the super-stylish is don't become a real fashion victim…

12 WHAT'S YOUR ANGLE? Discuss the questions in a group.

1 What kind of jeans do you have?
2 How long have you had them?
3 When do you wear them?
4 What kind of jeans did you wear ten years ago?
5 What kind of jeans would you never buy?
6 Have you ever been a "fashion victim"?

6.2 Working Trends

1 ACTIVATE Discuss the questions in a group.
1. Do you feel busier now than you did in the past? Why or why not?
2. Do you or people you know work more hours than in the past? Why or why not?

2 ▶ IDENTIFY Watch the start of a lecture, and answer the questions.
1. What question is the lecture about?
2. What is the lecturer going to discuss?

> **WRITING SKILL** Note-taking while listening
>
> Making notes when you listen will help you use the information later.
>
> Use the speaker's signpost phrases to help organize your notes.
>
> *…now let's move on to discuss…*
>
> To make your notes short, simple, and clear:
> - use key words, abbreviations, numerals, and symbols to keep them short.
> - use bullets to keep them organized.
> - underline or circle the main ideas to keep them clear.
>
> This will help you follow the speaker and understand your notes later.
>
> Include:
> - main points and examples.
> - questions, names, and references to research later.
>
> Review your notes when you finish listening to revise and reorganize them as needed. A diagram could be helpful with this revision.

3 IDENTIFY Look at the notes a student made on the first part of the lecture. (Some words are missing.) Identify the following.
1. features that make the notes short and clear
2. main points
3. examples
4. a question for later research

4 ▶ INTEGRATE Watch the first part of the lecture, and complete the notes in Exercise 3 with one or two words in each blank.

5 IDENTIFY Match the key ideas from the next part of the lecture to the definitions.
___ roles and responsibilities
___ busyness
___ communication
___ schedule
___ efficiency

a the quality of doing something well with no waste of time or money
b the feeling of always being busy
c a list of things you have to do and the time to do them
d the activity of expressing ideas and giving information
e the position and jobs a person has

6 INTERACT What do you think the lecturer might say about each key idea? Discuss each one with a partner.

U.S. changing work patterns

Big research questions:
1 People working more now?
OR
2 ¹_____ helping us work less?

²_____ answer from research! e.g., people say/think they work more hours, but ³_____ show this not true

??? Does this apply to all types of jobs?

7 ▶ **IDENTIFY** Watch the next part of the interview. Number the key ideas in Exercise 5 in the order they are mentioned. Did the lecturer include any of your suggestions from Exercise 6?

8 **VOCABULARY** Read the sentences. Choose the best definition for the words in bold.

1 Many companies recognize the importance of equal opportunities in the **workplace**.
   a a place where people work
   b a group of people available for work

2 My sister is worried about the **pressure** to perform well at her new job.
   a feeling sadness about an event
   b feeling stress when you have too much to do

3 Couples who divide **household** responsibilities get a lot more done.
   a a group or family living together in one place
   b work to keep the house clean

4 Our team worked at a good **pace** and finished the assignment early.
   a speed at which something happens
   b the quality of work being done

5 The new conference room was built **for the benefit of** the sales department.
   a to bring something new
   b to be useful for

6 If he quits his job now, he will receive his **pension** right away.
   a payment to someone who no longer works
   b an increase in the amount paid to a person

7 I want to **retire** in five years and travel the world.
   a to stop working because of illness
   b to leave a job because you have reached the appropriate age to do so

🔑 Oxford 3000™

9 **USE** Complete the sentences with the words from Exercise 8.

1 I don't want to _____ early. I will be bored at home.
2 If I improve my _____, I will be able to complete the project by the end of the week.
3 My boss changed the meeting time _____ the team.
4 One of the best benefits that my company offers is its _____.
5 He left his job because he didn't like the environment in the _____.
6 The _____ chores should be done by the entire family, not just one person.
7 My co-worker was under so much _____ that he ended up getting sick.

10 **PREPARE** Work with a partner. Plan how to organize your notes for part of the lecture about busyness and people's work schedules.

1 Where are you going to write them?
2 Are you going to use different colors, styles (e.g., underlining)? What for?
3 Will you use a diagram?

11 ▶ **WRITE** Watch this part of the lecture again, and take notes. For each key idea, add a question that you could research later.

12 **IMPROVE** Compare your notes with your partner.

1 Do you have the same information?
2 Are your main points and examples clear?

13 ▶ **EXPAND** Watch the final part of the lecture, and take notes. Add a question to each key idea.

14 **IMPROVE** Review, revise, and reorganize your notes. Then compare your notes in a group. Discuss the questions you added to the notes on the lecture. Can anyone answer them?

15 **WHAT'S YOUR ANGLE?** Discuss these questions in your group.

1 How do you think work will change in the future?
2 Will these be positive or negative changes?

6.3 Quick Fixes

1 ACTIVATE Preview the images, and complete the ad for the podcast series with the words in the box.

| grapefruit | cookie | cabbage | sleeping |
| vinegar | TV | high-protein | burger |

Can you complete the information about these famous diets?

1820
Lord Byron, the English poet, makes drinking ¹_____ and water popular.

1930s
The Hollywood Diet—the low-calorie diet suggests eating a ²_____ with every meal.

1950s
The ³_____ Soup Diet—this diet promises you will lose about 11 pounds a week by eating less and having this soup every day.

1970
The ⁴_____ Beauty Diet suggests losing weight by taking medication to sleep.

1975
The ⁵_____ Diet—a Florida doctor creates a special cookie to help people lose weight.

1991
Low-Fat—with this trend, people started cutting fat from their diet (McDonald's even introduced a low-fat ⁶_____).

1992
The Atkins Diet—eating only ⁷_____, low-carb food is made popular in a new book.

2004
The Biggest Loser first appears on ⁸_____, and taking part in reality shows becomes a way to lose weight.

2 WHAT'S YOUR ANGLE? Answer these questions.
1. Which of the diets in the ad had you heard of before?
2. What other diet trends have you heard of?
3. Do you know anyone who has tried any of the diet trends? What was their experience?

LISTENING SKILL Previewing using images

Previewing pictures before listening will help you understand the speakers more easily.

The images will indicate what the topic is. You can then:
- think about what you already know about the topic.
- predict information which might be included
- check key vocabulary before you listen

3 PREPARE You are going to listen to the introduction to a podcast. Review the information below and in Exercise 1, and answer the questions.
1. What points do you think Dr. Costello will make in the podcast?
2. What key words do you think you will hear?

Diet Trends

the podcast that follows the latest fashions in food and health

On the menu: cabbage soup, low-fat burger, vinegar water, and grapefruit

Dr. Costello, food and health expert, shares her views on diet trends.

Call in | Favorite | Share

4 🔊 **IDENTIFY** Listen to the podcast. Answer the questions.
1 Which familiar information did you hear?
2 Which key words did you hear?

5 🔊 **INTEGRATE** Listen again. Choose the main points Dr. Costello makes.

☐ a New diets come along frequently.
☐ b Men prefer diets that promise fast weight loss to traditional diets.
☐ c Studies show that diets that promise fast weight loss don't work.
☐ d People don't like making changes forever.
☐ e Some doctors support diets that promise fast weight loss.
☐ f It is important who gives the diet message.
☐ g There is too much information about healthy eating.
☐ h The way to lose weight is to control food and exercise.
☐ i The important thing is to eat at certain times of day.

6 **INTERACT** Which of Dr. Costello's ideas do you agree with? Discuss them with a partner.

> **VOCABULARY DEVELOPMENT**
> **Adverbs and phrases for emphasis**
>
> We can use adverbs and phrases to emphasize points. This makes our message clearer to other people. Adverbs and phrases are usually stressed in speech.
>
> Some phrases are usually placed at the beginning of the sentences.
> *In fact*,...   More *importantly*,...   To tell you the *truth*,...
> *In fact*, many can have the reverse effect.
> And, **more importantly**, can they keep the weight off?
>
> The adverbs are normally placed before the word to be emphasized.
> *actually   clearly   honestly*   simply   just   (not) even
> People **clearly** confused by a lot of the diet information they read.
> People **actually** put on weight.

🔑 Oxford 3000™

7 **INTEGRATE** Can you remember which adverbs and phrases were used to emphasize each point in the podcast? Complete the sentences.

clearly	even	more importantly	not even
just	to tell you the truth	simply	honestly

1 And, perhaps _____, why do some people follow one fashionable diet after another, _____ when they know the last one failed?
2 These kinds of fashionable diets are _____ not successful in the long term.
3 Many of us don't want to make long-term changes in our lifestyle, _____ if it makes us overweight.
4 They are connected to people who are _____ beautiful, or charming, or both.
5 It _____ doesn't matter.
6 People _____ don't know what to think.
7 _____, as someone who has to watch her weight, I understand the appeal of these diets.

8 🔊 **IDENTIFY** Listen and check. Underline the main point of emphasis in each sentence in Exercise 7.

9 **WHAT'S YOUR ANGLE?** Choose the words that make these points show your opinions. Which of the points do you feel strongly about? Practice making the points with words or phrases to emphasize them. Add one or two more points of your own about diets, food, and health.

1 Diet trends are **bad** / **not bad** for your health.
2 **Most** / **Few** people put on weight when they stop following a fashionable diet.
3 Diet trends are **fine if** / **no good even if** carefully controlled.
4 The **best** / **worst** way to control weight is to exercise.
5 We need **more** / **less** information about healthy eating.

> **GRAMMAR IN CONTEXT**
> **used to and be / get used to**
>
> To talk about situations or regular actions in the past that don't happen anymore, we use a form of *used to* + infinitive.
> We **used to eat** low-fat food and lots of carbs.
> We **didn't use to think** about diets so much.
> Where **did you use to get** information about diets from?
>
> To talk about regular activities being or becoming easy or familiar, we use a form of *be / get used to* + *-ing* form.
> We **are used to following** our life choices.
> We need to **get used to accepting** the fact.
> I'**m not used to exercising** so much.
> How did you **get used to eating** those types of food?

See Grammar focus on page 164.

10 🔊 **IDENTIFY** Complete the sentences from the podcast with the correct form of *used to* or *be / get used to*. Then listen and check.

1 And just when we _____ doing all this, food bloggers started telling us something different.
2 And then we can go back to what we _____ do.
3 Maybe these famous people _____ be fat, maybe they _____ be.
4 In comparison, we _____ getting colder, harder messages from doctors.

11 **IDENTIFY** Correct the errors in the *used to* and *be / get used to* forms.

1 I use to be a vegetarian, but I'm not anymore.
_____
2 I'm used to cook for myself now.
_____
3 I getting used to being careful about what I eat.
_____
4 I used try all sorts of diets when I was younger.
_____
5 I'm not really used buying groceries online.
_____

🎯 PRONUNCIATION SKILL *used to*

Note the correct pronunciation of *used to* in spoken English:

- *used* has one syllable. The *s* is pronounced /s/ (not /z/); the *-ed* is not pronounced.
- *to* is usually stronger when at the end of a sentence.
  /juːs tu/
  I **used** *to*.
- *to* is usually weaker when followed by another word.
  /juːs tə/
  I **used to** *do* more exercise.
  I'm **used to** *having* that.
- when the next word starts with a vowel sound, a short /w/ sound is often added.
  I **used to** *(w)eat* meat.
  I got **used to** *(w)exercising* more.

12 🔊 **NOTICE** Read the following sentences. Predict the pronunciation of "used to". Then listen and check.

1 A: Liz, do you do yoga in the morning?
  B: I used to. Now I do yoga in the afternoon.
2 A: Do you enjoy chocolate as much as your sister does?
  B: I used to eat it often. I'm trying to eat healthier now.
3 A: David, do you like to do any water sports?
  B: I used to waterski. Now I just like to swim.
4 A: Does it bother you that your husband doesn't eat meat?
  B: Not anymore. I'm used to it now.
5 A: What do you do to stay active?
  B: I used to bike to work every day. I had to stop after I injured my knee.

13 **APPLY** Practice saying the sentences from Exercise 12 with the correct pronunciation of *used to*.

14 **INTEGRATE** Which sentences in Exercise 11 are true for you? Change the others, so they are true, too.

15 **WHAT'S YOUR ANGLE?** Answer the questions.

1 What quick fixes do people usually want in these areas of life?
_____
   exercise   education   fashion/appearance

2 Have you ever tried a quick fix? Did it work? Why or why not?

6.4 Your Honest Opinion

1 ACTIVATE Look at the pictures, and discuss the questions.

1 What do you think Kevin and Max might be talking about?
2 What do you think Andy and Max might be talking about?

2 ▶ IDENTIFY Watch the first part of the video. Did you predict correctly?

3 ▶ ANALYZE Answer the questions. Then watch the first part of the video again to check.

1 Did Max ask for Kevin's opinion?
2 How happy is Max to hear Kevin's opinion? How can you tell?
3 What could Kevin do better next time?

> **REAL-WORLD ENGLISH Asking for and giving opinions**
>
> When you ask a friend or someone you know well for their opinion, you can use these phrases:
>
> *In your honest opinion,…?*
> *What do you think?*
>
> When you give your opinion, you need to judge how much information to give and how direct you should be. Think about these questions:
>
> - Has the other person asked for your opinion?
> - How honest do you want to be?
> - How honest does the other person want you to be?
> - How will your opinion affect the other person?
>
> You can use these phrases to give opinions.
>
> *In my opinion,…*
> *The way I see it,…*
> *I think…*
> *Don't get me wrong,…*

ENGLISH FOR REAL

4 ▶ **ANALYZE** Watch the second part of the video. How is it different from the first with regard to asking for and giving opinions?

5 ▶ **IDENTIFY** Watch the second part of the video again. In each pair, choose the phrase used by Max and Andy. Then decide if each phrase is asking for (A) or giving (G) an opinion.

1. ☐ a Give me your honest opinion. Do I look like a clown? ___
   ☐ b What's your opinion? Do you think I look like a clown? ___
2. ☐ a No, I don't think you look like a clown. ___
   ☐ b What? No, of course not. ___
3. ☐ a Tell me the truth. ___
   ☐ b Tell me honestly. ___
4. ☐ a Well, since you're asking… OK, maybe you do look a bit…strange. ___
   ☐ b Well, since you want to know…maybe there is some truth in what he said. ___
5. ☐ a Does Kevin actually have a point? ___
   ☐ b Is Kevin really right? ___
6. ☐ a You're not wrong—you just have your own style. ___
   ☐ b Don't get me wrong—you have your own style, but… ___

6 INTERACT Work in pairs. Choose situation 1 or 2, and prepare what you will say. Then role-play the situation. Discuss what worked well in your role play. Then swap roles and repeat.

Situation 1: You are not sure about whether to change your college major. You have been taking classes for a semester, and you have enjoyed them. However, you don't like your teachers, and you think they don't like you. You got feedback from them that you don't participate enough. You ask the opinion of your good friend and classmate on your participation and on the teachers. You have known each other for a long time and like each other a lot.

Situation 2: You are unhappy because your boss criticized a report you wrote. You have only had the job for three months, and you have been trying really hard to impress your boss. You tell your colleague about the situation and ask for their opinion on the report. You don't know your colleague very well, but they are a very respected and experienced member of the team.

7 ANALYZE Work with another pair who role-played a different situation. Act out your role plays for each other, and then compare how and why the language you used was different.

8 WHAT'S YOUR ANGLE? When was the last time you were asked for your opinion? Who asked you, and what was it about? Think about what you said. Did you follow the advice in this lesson?

GO ONLINE to create your own version of the English For Real video.

6.5 Fashion Victim

1 **ACTIVATE** Think about the trends in the box. Then discuss the questions.

| big eyebrows | big beard | vintage clothes | toe shoes |

1 Which of these fashion and beauty trends have you seen?
2 How fashionable are they now?
3 What other trends have there been in the past few years?

2 **IDENTIFY** Listen to James and Dena talking about fashion trends. Which trends did they used to follow?

> **SPEAKING Talking about past habits**
>
> When talking about past habits:
>
> Use *used to* to talk about a general past habit.
> I **used to** walk to school.
>
> Use past tenses to talk about specific examples.
> I actually **went** the long way to school that day.
>
> In a conversation, when talking about past shared experiences, use questions to involve the other person in what you are saying.
>
> Do you remember the day when…?
> What was the name of the place where we went?

3 **INTEGRATE** Listen again and answer the questions.
1 What is James wearing now?
2 Why did he stop wearing them in the past?
3 What does Dena think about them?
4 What kind of jeans did James have?
5 Did he enjoy wearing them?
6 What was the problem with them?
7 What did Dena use to have that she saw in some photos recently?
8 Does Dena have a tattoo?

> **GRAMMAR IN CONTEXT *do* for emphasis**
>
> To emphasize an action, we can add *do / does* or *did* before a simple present or simple past verb. Notice that we use the base form of the verb after the emphatic *do*, *does*, or *did*.
>
> I **do** like beards.
> She **does** like jeans.
>
> We can show contrast with *do / does* or *did*.
>
> I **didn't** get a real tattoo, but I **did** have fake ones.
>
> We can also use *do* before an imperative, especially for offers.
>
> **Do** try the shoes on before you buy them.

See Grammar focus on page 164.

4 **IDENTIFY** Listen and add *do*, *does*, or *did* to the extracts from James and Dena's conversation.
1 I _____ like those jeans.
2 I _____ have those, but I never wore them much.
3 You _____ look trendy with your big beard.
4 I _____ have very big eyebrows for a while.
5 I don't have any, but I _____ think about it…

5 **INTEGRATE** Add *do*, *does*, or *did* for emphasis or contrast to the correct place in the sentences below. Make changes to the verb if necessary. Listen and check, and then repeat.
1 I want a new hairstyle.
2 We didn't have dyed hair, but we had very long hair.
3 I don't have any jeans these days, but I used to own five pairs.
4 He doesn't like sports clothes, but he likes sneakers.
5 You wear vintage clothes.
6 They didn't use to buy a lot of clothes, but they used to make them.

6 **PREPARE** Think of two fashion and beauty trends you have followed and make some notes.

7 **INTERACT** In a group, share your experiences of following fashion trends.

8 **WHAT'S YOUR ANGLE?** Discuss your group conversation with a different partner.
1 Who followed similar fashion trends to you in the past?
2 Who would you like to go shopping for clothes with? Why?

Now go to page 152 for the Unit 6 Review.

Unit Reviews

Unit 1

VOCABULARY

1 Choose the correct word to complete the collocations in the questions.

Which buildings in your country...
1. are *beautifully / absolutely* designed?
2. are *differently / widely* recognized?
3. do people think *simply / highly* of?

What is the best way for people to...
4. *guarantee / make* success?
5. *make / acquire* knowledge?
6. *take / live* simply?

2 Complete the statements with the words in the box.

| risks | a difference | |
| an opportunity | my best | the most |

1. I don't like taking _____ and doing new things.
2. I make _____ of my free time.
3. I never miss _____ to see friends.
4. I want to make _____ in the world.
5. I always try to do _____, whatever I am doing.

GO ONLINE to play the vocabulary game.

GRAMMAR

3 Complete the extract with the verbs in the correct tense.

> **Pyramids of Giza**
>
> Of the Seven Wonders of the World, only the pyramids of Giza [1] **remain / are remaining** nearly intact. They [2] **interest / have interested** amateur Egyptologists for many years, and these people [3] **have given / are giving** many explanations for how and why the pyramids exist. Yet, after nearly 200 years of scientific study, it is clear to archaeologists that the pyramids of Giza [4] **are / are being** part of an ancient building tradition and were a very important part of Egyptian culture.
>
> The three pyramid complexes at Giza were built by kings Khufu, Khafre, and Menkare of the Fourth Dynasty (2613 BC–2494 BC) as their tombs and places of eternal worship after their deaths. Significant finds within the pyramids include several coffins of kings from thousands of years ago. One of these [5] **has now resided / is now residing** in the British Museum.
>
> —adapted from *The Oxford Companion to Archaeology*, 2nd ed., edited by Neil Asher Silberman

4 Choose the correct words to complete the sentences.
1. Visitors pay individually to go up *each / each of* tower.
2. *Every of / Every* window is cleaned three times a year.
3. From the top you can see each *sides / side* of the city.
4. Every one of the *buildings / building* in the complex is more than 200 meters high.
5. *Each of / Each* the towers is home to more than 500 companies.

5 Find the four sentences with verb tense errors and rewrite them.
1. I am knowing lots of very successful people.
2. I don't have the skills I need to be successful.
3. I am not believing good organization is necessary for success.
4. I am agreeing that it's OK to use other people's ideas.
5. I feel that I'm having enough confidence to be successful.

GO ONLINE to play the grammar game.

DISCUSSION POINT

6 Read the quote. What are the positive and negative effects of success? Share your ideas with the class.

"Success makes life easier. It doesn't make living easier."
—Bruce Springsteen, selected from *Oxford Essential Quotations*, 5th ed., edited by Susan Ratcliffe

GO ONLINE and listen to a podcast. Then add your comments to the discussion board.

ZOOM IN

7 What about you?

Task 1 Talk about one goal you want to achieve in the coming year.

Task 2 Write about three of your achievements. Choose a different area of life for each.

Task 3 Find a picture of a great human achievement. Share your opinion on it.

8 Complete the table.

	I did this well	I need more practice
Task 1		
Task 2		
Task 3		

Unit 2

VOCABULARY

1 Complete the statements with the verbs in the boxes.

| lead | distract | bring | launch |

Newspapers can…
1 _____ down governments.
2 _____ people's celebrity careers.
3 _____ to a more educated society.
4 _____ readers with sections that don't focus on serious news.

| announce | realize | attempt | prevent |

People…
sometimes 5 _____ when news is false.
usually 6 _____ to see all sides of a story by reading news from different sources.
often 7 _____ special personal events in newspapers.
especially famous people, sometimes try to 8 _____ stories from getting into the newspapers.

2 Read the statements. Do they represent your view? If not, choose an adverb from the box that more closely shows your opinion.

| unfortunately | luckily | naturally | curiously |
| surprisingly | obviously | fortunately | sadly |

1 Curiously, we are more interested in news from closer to where we live.
2 Luckily, we now have TV channels broadcasting news 24/7.
3 Naturally, people prefer to read news on small phone screens.
4 Surprisingly, most major news stories are about bad rather than good news.

GO ONLINE to play the vocabulary game.

GRAMMAR

3 Choose the correct word to complete each sentence.
1 *Either / Neither / All* of the two reports had much information.
2 I studied *both / neither / all* subjects, but I enjoyed Journalism more than History.
3 Many online newspapers don't give free access to *all / either / both* the content.
4 Online news sites and newspapers are popular. I read *either / neither / all* type since the information is the same.

4 Choose the best verb forms to complete the text.

> The first actual radio news program ¹*was / had been* broadcast on August 31, 1920 by the 8MK station in Detroit, Michigan. Radio ²*was being / had been* around for a number of years before this but was not widely listened to. At the start of the 1920s, however, this ³*was changing / had changed*. The Scripps family, which owned the newspaper *The Detroit News*, was exploring the idea of expanding into radio, and by this time, it ⁴*was hiring / had hired* teenage Michael Lyons to get permission from the government to broadcast a news program. Once Lyons had permission, it ⁵*was taking / took* ten more days to work out how to broadcast the news. There ⁶*had been / were being* local elections in the area, and the very first broadcast news on the evening of the August 31 ⁷*was reporting / reported* the results, making history.

5 Think about the past and your plans. What were you never going to do? What were you going to do but then you did something else instead? Write sentences.

GO ONLINE to play the grammar game.

DISCUSSION POINT

6 Read the quote. Was there more good or more bad news today? Do you think everything published as news is news?

"Ever noticed that no matter what happens in one day, it exactly fits in the newspaper?"
—Jerry Seinfeld, selected from *Oxford Essential Quotations*, 5th ed., edited by Susan Ratcliffe

GO ONLINE and listen to a podcast. Then add your comments to the discussion board.

ZOOM IN

7 What about you?
Task 1 Talk about a news story that was important to you.
Task 2 Write a report about some news from your community.
Task 3 Find a powerful photo from a news story. Share the information about what happened.

8 Complete the table.

	I did this well	I need more practice
Task 1		
Task 2		
Task 3		

Unit 3

VOCABULARY

1 Complete the statements with a noun formed by the word in parentheses and one of the suffixes in the box.

-ship	-tion	-ness	-ment	-ence	-ity

1. Most of us want _____ (recognize) for the good things we do.
2. One of the most difficult things to do is make a _____ (commit).
3. _____ (intelligent) is much more important than hard work.
4. Our own _____ (happy) is the most important thing in life.
5. A successful _____ (friend) is more important than a successful professional life.
6. You need the right _____ (personal) to succeed in life.

2 Match the words to the definitions.

keep going	independent	explore
quit	survive	flexible

1. travel through an area you don't know to learn about it: _____
2. ready and able to change in different situations: _____
3. continue to do something despite the difficulties: _____
4. continue to live, especially in a difficult or dangerous situation: _____
5. confident and free to do things without other people's help: _____
6. stop doing something: _____

GO ONLINE to play the vocabulary game

GRAMMAR

3 Complete the sentences with the correct forms of the verbs in parentheses. Which sentences do you agree with?

1. Too many people forget _____ (enjoy) where they are—they are too busy thinking about where they want to go.
2. Governments should stop _____ (spend) money on space exploration and use it for problems in their own countries instead.
3. We need to remember _____ (congratulate) everyone on a team, not only the leader.

4 Choose four items you think are useful for exploration and write sentences using *so* and *such*.

5 Complete the text with the correct form of the verbs in parentheses. (Sometimes two forms are possible.)

World-changing inventions

In the past, most people could not imagine [1] _____ (leave) the earth and going into space. However, after some successful experiments with large rockets, in 1926, scientists began [2] _____ (see) the possibilities. Nowadays several companies have started [3] _____ (plan) for a future of space tourism.

In the past, people attempted [4] _____ (keep) food fresh for longer by salting, smoking, or pickling it. However, in the 1850s, mechanical refrigeration arrived. With this technology, people stopped [5] _____ (get) sick so often from bad food.

Many of us remember [6] _____ (have) our first vaccination—mostly the tears and pain. Vaccinations were first invented in 1796, but it wasn't until 1885 and Louis Pasteur's rabies vaccine that people started [7] _____ (believe) that making people ill could actually help them.

GO ONLINE to play the grammar game

DISCUSSION POINT

6 Read the poem. Do you agree with it? What do you think are the most important benefits of exploration?

"We shall not cease from exploration
And the end of all our exploring
Will be to arrive where we started
And know the place for the first time."
—T.S. Eliot, *Four Quartets*, selected from *Oxford Essential Quotations*, 5th ed., edited by Susan Ratcliffe

GO ONLINE and listen to a podcast. Then add your comments to the discussion board.

ZOOM IN

7 What about you?

Task 1 Talk about a discovery that interests you.
Task 2 Find a photo of a place you would like to explore. Tell your group about it.
Task 3 Write a list of pros and cons of exploring the place you talked about.

8 Complete the table.

	I did this well	I need more practice
Task 1		
Task 2		
Task 3		

Unit 4

VOCABULARY

1 Put the words in order to make sentences. Add a capital letter and period.

___ a you need to / following that, / the main characters / decide on
___ b a story / is to think of / the first stage
___ c and comment / finally, / before / ask a friend to read it / you share it with the world
___ d start writing / then / you can / the first draft
___ e once / read it and / you have finished / improve it / the first draft,
___ f is to / the last step / cutting out any unnecessary parts / rewrite the story,
___ g think of / during this stage, / will feel about the story / how the reader

2 Number the sentences in Exercise 1 in order to make instructions. What are the instructions for? Have you ever done this?

3 Complete the text about the production of a very famous movie with the correct verbs.

The movie *Titanic* was expensive to [1] **solve / revise / film**; it actually cost more than building the original ship. The results, however, were amazing, both on-screen and in the bank. The movie was written and [2] **produced / solved / promoted** by James Cameron, and he [3] **created / edited / selected** the main actors, Kate Winslet and Leonardo DiCaprio, very carefully. One difficulty was to have so many actors in the right costumes. Deborah Scott [4] **filmed / promoted / designed** the clothes, and she had to [5] **solve / revise / select** many problems to do this. Interestingly, during the stage when the movie was [6] **filmed / promoted / edited**, Cameron revised the ending to avoid it being too happy. A 3D version was [7] **developed / solved / selected** later to promote the film to 21st-century audiences.

GO ONLINE to play the vocabulary game.

GRAMMAR

4 Correct the grammar errors in the passive sentences with modals.

1 Plans must always be make before starting work.
2 The correct process must followed to get the correct result.
3 It could said that the result is more important than the process.
4 Writing can always improved by editing.
5 A traditional meal should be making according to the proper recipe.

5 Choose the correct preposition. Then complete the sentence so it is true for you.

1 I am never surprised *with / by / in* _____.
2 I am pretty bad *by / at / about* _____.
3 I am very interested *with / at / in* _____.
4 I am really good *about / in / at* _____.
5 I am most pleased *about / at / in* _____.

GO ONLINE to play the grammar game.

DISCUSSION POINT

6 Read the quote. What kinds of things do artists produce? Why does an artist produce art? Why do people buy art? Share your ideas with the class.

"An artist is someone who produces things that people don't need to have but that he—for some reason—thinks it would be a good idea to give them."
—Andy Warhol, selected from *Oxford Essential Quotations*, 5th ed., edited by Susan Ratcliffe

GO ONLINE and listen to a podcast. Then add your comments to the discussion board.

ZOOM IN

7 What about you?

Task 1 Talk about one thing you want to learn to make.
Task 2 Write about two things you have made. Compare and contrast the experience of making them.
Task 3 Find an interesting diagram. Share it with the class.

8 Complete the table.

	I did this well	I need more practice
Task 1		
Task 2		
Task 3		

150

Unit 5

VOCABULARY

1 Match the nouns to the phrasal verbs. Then add one more noun for each verb.

1. look forward to ___
2. look ___ up
3. look into ___
4. look up to ___
5. look around ___
6. look up from ___
7. look through ___

a a vacation / _____
b a problem / _____
c a word / _____
d a house / _____
e a magazine / _____
f a colleague / _____
g a computer / _____

2 Complete the questions with the correct words.

1. Do governments *prepare / destroy / forecast* enough for natural disasters?
2. Can we *react / destroy / protect* ourselves from all natural disasters?
3. How can a natural disaster *react / forecast / affect* people who were not where it happened?
4. Will we be able to *forecast / react / destroy* all natural disasters one day?
5. How do we usually *protect / prepare / react* when we see natural disasters on the news?

GO ONLINE to play the vocabulary game.

GRAMMAR

3 Match the advice to the problem.

1. A: There is a very bad storm coming. ___
2. A: We're going to get a new sofa. ___
3. A: I am really late with a project for work. ___
4. A: My child said something awful to the teacher. ___

a B: You'd better talk to your boss about it.
b B: He ought to say sorry immediately.
c B: You should check that the windows are closed.
d B: You shouldn't get a white one if you have children.

4 Complete the rules for when the fire alarm goes off in an office. Use each verb only once.

don't have to	must	can't	have to

You ¹_____ leave the building immediately.
You ²_____ use the stairs and not the elevator.
You ³_____ spend time turning off computers.
You ⁴_____ return if it is the end of the workday.

5 Make the sentences stronger or weaker by changing the intensifier and the adjective. Use the adjectives and intensifiers in the box to help.

afraid	freezing	small	exhausted
important	awful	hardly	absolutely
fairly	a little	really	extremely

1. The last movie I saw was fairly bad.
2. I'm absolutely terrified of one type of animal.
3. It was extremely cold last winter.
4. The work I do is absolutely essential.
5. When I get home from work, I'm often really tired.
6. The place where I live is absolutely tiny.

GO ONLINE to play the grammar game.

DISCUSSION POINT

6 Read the quote. What have humans done over history to survive? What different ways do individual people have of surviving modern life? Would the modern-day person survive living 500 years ago, or have we changed too much?

"If we assume that mankind has a right to survive, then we must find an alternative to war and destruction."
    Martin Luther King, selected from *Oxford Dictionary of Political Quotations*, 4th ed., edited by Antony Jay

GO ONLINE and listen to a podcast. Then add your comments to the discussion board.

ZOOM IN

7 What about you?

Task 1 Talk about some really important advice somebody has given you.
Task 2 Write instructions for what to do in an everyday disaster.
Task 3 Find a photo of a natural disaster. Tell your group about it.

8 Complete the table.

	I did this well	I need more practice
Task 1		
Task 2		
Task 3		

Unit 6

VOCABULARY

1 Write at least five sentences about your clothes and fashion sense using the words in the box.

collar	heel	leg	pants	sleeve
top	casual	classic	formal	loose
stylish	tight	trendy	unfashionable	

2 Rewrite the sentences with the word or phrase for emphasis in parentheses in the best place.

1 Diets that promise fast weight loss never work. (clearly)
   _____

2 Most people believe anything a famous person says. (honestly)
   _____

3 Most people have at least one pair of jeans. (in fact)
   _____

4 Most people have terrible fashion sense. (to tell you the truth)
   _____

5 People should check work emails at home. (not even)
   _____

> GO ONLINE to play the vocabulary game.

GRAMMAR

3 Complete the text with the present perfect or simple past of the verbs in parentheses.

> Work places ¹_____ (improve) a lot in recent years. In the past, most work ²_____ (happen) within the four walls of the office from 9 to 5. The landline telephone ³_____ (be) the only way to connect with the outside world. Then the Internet and mobile technology ⁴_____ (arrive), and since then, we ⁵_____ (not look) back. In the modern workplace, many people carry work cell phones, and many of us ⁶_____ (have) video conferences with people around the country or even the world. The downside is that since this change happened, many of us ⁷_____ also _____ (start) taking our work home with us.

4 Add *do*, *does*, or *did* to the sentences to emphasize or contrast. Change the main verbs if necessary.

1 The modern workplace looks very different from the old one.
   _____

2 Workplaces didn't have mobile technology, but they used landline phones.
   _____

3 The Internet changed everything at work.
   _____

4 Lots of people have work cell phones nowadays.
   _____

5 We didn't use to work at home in the evening, but we work at home now.
   _____

5 Complete the sentences, so they are true for you.

1 I used to _____, but now _____.

2 I never used to _____, but now _____.

3 I'm getting used to _____.

4 I'm used to _____ because _____.

> GO ONLINE to play the grammar game.

DISCUSSION POINT

6 Read the quote. How does something become fashionable or unfashionable? How many people need to like or do something for it to become a trend?

"Fashion is made to become unfashionable."
—Coco Chanel, selected from *Oxford Essential Quotations*, 5th ed., edited by Susan Ratcliffe

> GO ONLINE and listen to a podcast. Then add your comments to the discussion board.

ZOOM IN

7 What about you?

Task 1 Talk about something you used to do but no longer do.

Task 2 Watch a video about a trend and write notes. Discuss the ideas with a group.

Task 3 Find a photo of one of your favorite fashion trends. Share it with your class.

8 Complete the table.

	I did this well	I need more practice
Task 1		
Task 2		
Task 3		

Grammar focus

Unit 1

Simple present, present continuous, and present perfect

USE

We use the simple present to talk about facts.
> The sun **sets** in the west.
> I **live** in Paris.

We also use the simple present to talk about things that happen regularly or repeatedly.
> We **play** tennis every Tuesday.

We use the present continuous to talk about things happening now or around now.
> What **are** you **looking** at?
> Dave**'s teaching** me to play the guitar.

We also use the present continuous to talk about trends and things that are changing.
> Prices **are rising** all the time.
> The Earth's temperature **is increasing**.

We use the present perfect to talk about experiences up to now.
> I**'ve lived** here all my life.
> I**'ve never met** a movie star.

We also use the present perfect to talk about things that have already or just happened.
> Max **has** already **left**.
> I'm not hungry. I**'ve** just **eaten**.

State verbs

USE

Most verbs express actions, and we can use them in simple tenses…
> I **use** the Internet all the time.

… and in continuous tenses.
> I**'m using** the Internet at the moment.

Some verbs usually express states, such as thoughts, feelings, possessions, and things we experience. We usually use these verbs in simple tenses, even if we mean "just now."
> Do you **believe** me? (NOT ~~Are you believing me?~~)

How we think: *agree*, *believe*, *forget*, *imagine*, *know*, *prefer*, *realize*, *recognize*, *remember*, *think*, *understand*
> Do you **believe** me?
> I don't **agree**.
> I **think** it's a great idea!

What we feel: *appear*, *dislike*, *feel*, *hate*, *like*, *look*, *love*, *need*, *seem*, *sound*, *want*
> How do you **feel** about the news.
> He didn't **sound** upset.
> She **seems** nervous.

What we possess: *belong*, *have*, *own*
> Do you **have** any money on you?
> My family **owns** the café in town.
> It doesn't **belong** to me.

What we experience: *be*, *hear*, *look*, *see*, *smell*, *taste*
> Can you **hear** the phone?
> The soup **tastes** delicious.
> The flowers **smell** really nice.

Some state verbs are used in both simple and continuous tenses with different meanings.
> I **have** a headache. (illness)
> I**'m having** lunch. (action)
> I **think** it's a great idea. (opinion)
> I**'m thinking** of getting a new phone. (consider)

Each and *every*

USE

We can use *every* + singular noun or to talk about all the people or things in a group.
> **Every person** in the photo is smiling!

We use *each* + singular noun to talk about every individual person or thing in a group.
> **Each child** is different and has different needs.

We can also use *each* + *of the* + plural noun or pronoun with the same meaning. Use a singular verb.
> **Each of the** places looks wonderful.

We can also use *every* + *one of* + plural noun or pronoun with the same meaning as *each*.
> **Every one of them** is smiling!

GO ONLINE for the complete grammar reference.

Unit 2

Narrative tenses—simple past, past continuous, and past perfect

USE

When we describe events or tell a story in the past, we use the narrative tenses: simple past, past continuous, and past perfect. We use the simple past to describe the main events in the story.

*It **was** a warm summer evening when Jack **left** work.*

We form negatives and questions with *did* and the infinitive without *to*.

*We **didn't recognize** the stranger who was standing outside the house.*

*What **did** he **want** with us?*

We use the past continuous for background events or longer actions which are interrupted by shorter actions. We use the simple past for the shorter actions.

*He **was walking** along the road when suddenly he heard a loud noise.*

We use the past perfect to talk about an action or event that happened before something else in the past.

*Suddenly, he heard a loud noise. A large stone **had fallen** from the sky.*

We also use the past perfect to look back to the past before the events of the story.

*He'd **never seen** a meteorite before!*

All, both, either, neither

BOTH

We use *both* + plural noun to talk about two people or things. We can use *both* without a following noun when it is obvious what we are talking about.

***Both** photos show forms of travel.*

*Photo A is similar to photo B because they **both** show people who are smiling and happy.*

We can also use *both* + *(of) the* + plural noun or pronoun with the same meaning.

***Both of the** photos show forms of travel.*

EITHER AND NEITHER

We use *either* + singular noun to talk about one of two people, things, or groups.

*You can describe **either** photo.*

We use *neither* + singular noun to talk about none of a group of two people, things, or groups.

***Neither** form of transport is very fast.*

We can also use *either/neither* + *of the/these/those/them* + plural noun with the same meaning. Use a singular verb.

*You can describe **either of the** photos.*

***Neither of these** forms of transport is very fast.* (NOT *Neither of these forms of transport are very fast.*)

If *neither* is the object of the sentence, not the subject, use *not…either* instead.

*I d**on't** recognize **either** of these places.*

ALL

We use *all* with a plural noun to talk about all the people or things in a group.

Use *all* + *(of) the/them* to talk about a particular group of people or things.

***All the children** are playing.*

***All of them** look happy.*

Use *all* + noun, without *(of) the* to talk about people or things in general.

***All children** enjoy playing games.*

Was / were going to

USE

We use *was/were going to* + infinitive to talk about intentions in the past. The action may or may not happen.

*I **was going to do** some homework, but I'm too tired.*

We use *was/were going to* + infinitive + *but* to give reasons why an action does/did not happen.

*We **were going to go** to Canada, **but** it's too expensive.*

We can use *was/were going to…* when we refuse an invitation and give a reason.

"Do you want to come to the movies?"

*"No, I **was going to call** Dad. Have a nice time!"*

We can use *was/were going to…* followed by a question when we offer something.

*I **was going to make** some coffee. Would you like some?*

We also use *was/were going to…* to talk about predictions in the past.

*I thought we **were going to be** late, but we weren't.*

For past predictions with *would*, see here.

GO ONLINE for the complete grammar reference.

Unit 3

Verbs + *to* infinitive or *-ing* form

-ING FORM OR *TO* INFINITIVE?
Some verbs can take either the *-ing* form or the *to* infinitive, with little or no change in the meaning: *attempt, begin, can't stand, continue, hate, like, love, prefer,* and *start*.
> I **started playing** the guitar when I was ten.
> I **started to play** the guitar when I was ten.

We don't usually use two *-ing* forms next to each other.
> I'm **starting to feel** better. (NOT ~~I'm starting feeling better.~~)

Some verbs can take either the *-ing* form or the *to* infinitive, but with a difference in the meaning or use: *stop, forget, remember*.
> I've **stopped buying** CDs. (I no longer buy CDs.)
> I **stopped** on the way **to buy** you a gift. (I stopped (at a store). I bought a gift.)
> Grandma **remembers dancing** when she was a girl. (She remembers an activity that she did regularly in the past.)
> Grandma **remembered to send** me a card. (She remembered to do an action.)

Verbs + *-ing* form and verbs + *to* infinitive

-ING FORM
We use the *-ing* form after the following verbs: *admit, avoid, consider, deny, finish, imagine, practice, recommend, stop,* and *suggest*.
> Dave **recommended seeing** the latest Bond movie.

We use the *-ing* form after verbs that express likes and dislikes: *can't stand, enjoy, feel like, hate, like, love, (don't/doesn't) mind,* and *prefer*.
> I really **enjoy going** to the theater.

We can also use the *-ing* form after the prepositions *about, at, before, in, of, on, to,* and *without*.
> Dad insisted **on paying** for the meal.

TO INFINITIVE
We use the *to* infinitive after the following verbs: *afford, agree, aim, appear, arrange, choose, decide, demand, expect, fail, forget, hope, manage, need, offer, plan, seem,* and *want*.
> Emma **offered to give** me a lift to work.

To form the negative, we put *not* between the two verbs.
> I **promise not to tell** anyone.

So and *such*

FORM

	so/such	(article)	adjective	(noun)
It's	so		exciting!	
I'm			excited!	
It's	such	a	beautiful	day!
			wonderful	weather!
		a		nuisance!

USE
We use *so* and *such* to say that people or things are very happy, exciting, beautiful, terrible, etc.

We use *so* + adjective, without a noun.
> She's **so kind**. (NOT ~~She's a so kind person.~~)
> The tennis match was **so exciting**!

We use *such* + adjective + noun.
> Maya is **such** a **kind** person. She helps everyone.
> It's **such** a **beautiful** day. I think I'll go to the beach.

We can also use *such* + noun (without an adjective) when the noun is something that is always beautiful, exciting, terrible, etc.
> "The train was three hours late." "Oh, that's **such a nuisance**!"

GO ONLINE for the complete grammar reference.

Unit 4

Present passive

FORM

We form the passive with *be* + past participle.

		be	past participle	
present	Our pizza	is	baked	in a special oven.
	The objects	are	displayed	in a museum.

USE

We use the active form when we focus on the person or thing that does the action.

> Shah Jahan **commissioned** the Taj Mahal in 1631.

We use the passive form when we focus on what happens to someone or something. The person who does the action is less important.

> The Taj Mahal **is considered** one of the wonders of the world.

We use *by* + noun if we want to say who or what did the action.

> It **is visited by** about 7 million people every year.

We often use the passive form to continue talking about the same thing or person.

> Shale gas is an important source of energy in the United States. It **is extracted** by a process of "fracking."

Past passive

FORM

We form the passive with *be* + past participle.

		be	past participle	
past	Stonehenge	was	built	5,000 years ago.
	All the documents	were	destroyed	in a fire.

USE

We use the active form when we focus on the person or thing that does the action.

> Shah Jahan **commissioned** the Taj Mahal in 1631.

We use the passive form when we focus on what happens to someone or something. The person who does the action is less important.

> The main buildings **were completed** in 1643.

We use *by* + noun if we want to say who or what did the action.

> They **were built** by workers from nearby towns.

We often use the passive form to continue talking about the same thing or person.

> Kickstarter is a crowd-funding platform. It **was launched** in 2009.

Present passive with modal verbs

FORM

We form the present passive with modal verbs with:

Subject + modal verb + *be* + past participle.

Subject	modal verb	be	past participle	
Calculators	can	be	used	on the exam.
Valuables	should	be	left	in the hotel safe.
Loud music	shouldn't	be	played	after 11 p.m.

USE

We can use the passive with modal verbs, such as *can*, *could*, *might*, *should*, *must*, etc.

We use the passive when we focus on what happens to something or someone. The person or thing that does the action is less important or not known.

> Microchips **can be manufactured** quite cheaply.
> Triathlons **should not be attempted** without a lot of training.

Adjectives with prepositions

FORM

Some adjectives are used with particular prepositions.

	adjective	preposition	
She's	good / terrible	at	math.
Sam was	shocked / surprised	at/by	their behavior.
I'm	fed up / bored	with	my job.
They were	pleased / worried	about	the result.

USE

We use prepositions after adjectives to talk about feelings, abilities, etc.

> She's **good at** languages.
> We're **fed up with** the constant delays.

We can use an *-ing* form after some prepositions.

> I'm **interested in** hearing all about your vacation.
> He isn't **happy about** people smoking in his car.

GO ONLINE for the complete grammar reference.

Unit 5

Advice and warning with *should*, *ought to*, *had better*

FORM

We use *should*, *ought to,* and *had better* with an infinitive without *to*. The form of each of these expressions is the same for every subject. We don't use *oughtn't to*.

Subject + *should/shouldn't* + infinitive without *to*.
Subject + *ought to* + infinitive.
Subject + *had better* + infinitive without *to*.

> I **should get** the flu vaccination.
> You **ought to apologize** to him.
> They **had better clean up** the mess.
> You **shouldn't worry** so much.
> We **had better not be** late.

We usually use *should/shouldn't* in questions and answers.

Should + subject + infinitive without *to*?
Question word + *should* + subject + infinitive without *to*?

> **Should** I **call** the police?
> What **should** we **do**?

We use short answers with questions that begin with *should*.

> "**Should** I **call** the police?"
> "Yes, you **should**."/"No, you **shouldn't**."

USE

We use *should*, *ought to*, and *had better* to give and ask for advice. *Ought to* is more formal than *should*, and *had better* is a stronger expression.

> You **should** always **wear** a helmet when you ride a bike.
> We **ought to get** more sleep before the journey.
> He'd **better not wear** that horrible old jacket to the theater!

We don't use *ought to* or *had better* in questions. We use *should* instead, or start the sentence with *Do you think…*?

> **Should** I **show** them my poems?
> Do you think I **ought to show** them my poems?

Obligation with *must* and *have to*

PRESENT

We use *must* or *have to* to say that something is necessary. We often use *must* to talk about the feelings and wishes of the speaker.

> We **must improve** conditions in the zoo.

We usually use *have to* to talk about rules or obligations that come from someone or somewhere else.

> The government **has to announce** the date for the next elections.

We use *can't* to say it is necessary NOT to do something.

> You **can't be** late for school.

We use *don't have to* to say that something isn't necessary.

> You **don't have to eat** with us if it doesn't suit you.

We usually ask questions with *have to*.

> "**Do** I **have to apply** online?" "No, you **don't**."

PAST

Must doesn't have a past tense form. We use *had to* to say something was necessary in the past.

> They **had to land** at a different airport because of the strike at Heathrow. (NOT *They did must to land…*)

We use *didn't have to* to say something wasn't necessary in the past.

> We **didn't have to wear** a uniform when I was in school. (NOT *We didn't must to wear…*)

Intensifiers

USE

We can use an adverb before an adjective to say "to what extent" or "how much." The adverb makes the adjective stronger or weaker.

to a very low degree: *hardly*
to a low degree: *slightly*, *a bit*, *a little*
to some degree: *fairly*
to a high degree: *extremely*, *really*, *quite*
to the highest degree (with ungradable adjectives only): *absolutely*, *completely*

> The book is **slightly damaged**. I can offer you a discount.
> Car racing is **extremely dangerous**. (It is one of the most dangerous activities.)

The adverbs *slightly*, *a bit,* and *a little* usually describe bad qualities.

> The book's **a bit boring**. (NOT *The book's a bit exciting.*)

However, we can also use *slightly*, *a bit,* and *somewhat* before comparative adjectives, including adjectives that describe good qualities.

> The table is **a bit higher** than the desk.

Some adjectives are "ungradable." They express qualities that cannot exist in different degrees. They often express perfection or its opposite.

> That's a **brilliant** idea! I can't think of a better one.

With ungradable adjectives, we cannot use adverbs like *very*, *extremely*, *fairly*, or *really*. But we can use *absolutely*.

> That's an **absolutely brilliant** idea! (NOT *That's an extremely brilliant idea.*)

We can only use *absolutely* with ungradable adjectives. We cannot use it with other adjectives.

> That book's **interesting**. (NOT *That book's absolutely interesting.*)

GO ONLINE for the complete grammar reference.

Unit 6

Time expressions with the present perfect and simple past

USE

We can think of time periods as being unfinished (e.g., *this week, since 2013*) or finished (e.g., *yesterday, in 2014*). We usually use the present perfect to talk about unfinished time periods.

I've sent a lot of emails today.
Have you already eaten?

We usually use the simple past to talk about finished time periods.

I got my first computer when I was eight.
Did you see Cathy last week?

Some time expressions can refer to either unfinished or finished time.

Have you seen Sarah this morning? (It is still this morning.)
Did you see Sarah this morning? (The morning is finished—it is now afternoon or evening.)

Used to and *be/get used to*

FORM

We use *used to* with an infinitive.

used to				
	subject (+ auxiliary)	used to/ use to	infinitive	
+	I	used to	like	listening to stories.
-	I didn't	use to	like	classical music.
?	Did you	use to	play	sports in school?

We use *be used to* with an -ing form.

be used to				
	subject + be	used to	-ing form	
+	I'm	used to	bicycling	to school.
-	I'm not	used to	speaking	in public.
?	Are you	used to	getting up	early?

USE

Used to and *be used to* are different expressions with different meanings.

USED TO

We use *used to* with an infinitive to talk about regular actions that we did in the past but don't do now, or about situations that were true in the past but are not true now.

We used to live in Minneapolis. (but now we don't)
There used to be an office park here. (but now there isn't)

Note that there is no final '*d*' in negatives and questions.

I didn't use to drink tea. (NOT *I didn't used to drink tea.*)
Did you use to play sports at school? (NOT *Did you used to play sports at school?*)

BE/GET USED TO

We use *be used to* with an -ing form to talk about activities that we do regularly and find easy or familiar.

We're used to working hard.

We use *get used to* to talk about activities that we started doing recently. We often use it in the present continuous tense, and it means that the activity is becoming easier or more familiar.

We're getting used to speaking over the Internet.

We can also use *be/get used to* with a noun.

I'm used to hard work.
I'm still getting used to my new phone.

We can also use *be/get used to* in other tenses to talk about activities or situations that were familiar in the past, have become familiar now, or will become familiar in the future.

I found the work tiring at first, but I soon got used to it.

Do for emphasis

FORM

	do/does/did	verb	
I	do	like	your new shoes.
We	did	enjoy	the party.
	Do	help yourself	to a drink.
	Do	take	a seat.

USE

We use *do, does,* or *did* before a simple present or simple past verb for emphasis.

"Have you seen Emma?" "Yes. I *do like* her new hairstyle."
"Meetings with Tom always take a long time." "He *does talk* a lot."

We can use *do, does,* or *did* to show a contrast.

That job wasn't easy, but he did finish it on time.

We can use *do* before an imperative especially for offers.

Do help yourself to some food.

GO ONLINE for the complete grammar reference.

Wide Angle

4A

WORKBOOK

MARI VARGO

OXFORD
UNIVERSITY PRESS

Contents

UNIT	GRAMMAR	VOCABULARY	REAL-WORLD READING	ENGLISH FOR REAL	UNIT REVIEW PODCAST
1 Achievements Page 1	Simple present, present continuous, and present perfect State verbs *Each* and *every*	Personal development Collocations	Why People Do What They Do Skimming and scanning	Making inquiries	Interview: Making it Recognizing sentence stress and word boundaries
2 News Page 8	Narrative tenses: Simple past, past continuous, and past perfect *All, both, either,* and *neither* *Was / were going to*	Taking action (verbs) Comment adverbs	From Books to the Internet: The Progress of Mass Media Identifying topic sentences	Giving and reacting to news	Interview: You're joking, right? Recognizing linkers in fast speech
3 Frontiers Page 15	Verbs + *to* infinitive or *-ing* form Verbs + *-ing* form and verbs + *to* infinitive *So* and *such*	Exploration Suffixes for nouns	Gertrude Bell: Daughter of the Desert Working out meaning from context	Interrupting and resuming	Interview: Guardians of the planet Recognizing rephrasing in a talk
4 Processes Page 22	Present passive and past passive Present passive with modal verbs Adjectives with prepositions	Explaining a process Production (verbs)	The Process of Crowdfunding Classifying information from a text	Asking for and giving clarification	Interview: How to do anything Using visual information while listening
5 Survival Page 29	Advice and warning with *should, ought to,* and *had better* Obligation with *must* and *have to* Intensifiers	Phrasal verbs with *look* Natural disasters Extreme adjectives	The Eruptions of Tambora and Krakatoa Recognizing and understanding exemplification	Asking for and giving advice	Interview: Life through the ages Interpreting changes in volume, speed, and pitch
6 Trends Page 36	Time expressions with the present perfect and simple past *Used to* and *be / get used to* *Do* for emphasis	Fashion (adjectives) Adverbs and phrases for emphasis	A Trendy Problem Using questions when reading	Asking for and giving opinions	Interview: Trend talk Previewing using images

1 Achievements

Simple present, present continuous, and present perfect ▶ 1.1

1 Choose the correct word or words for each sentence.

1. Ch'oe Yun is an important South Korean writer. She *writes / has written* several books about Korean politics and history.
2. Her novel *Mannequin tells / is telling* the story of a young girl.
3. She *have / has* a Ph.D from Seoul's Sogang University.
4. Ch'oe currently *teaches / has taught* French literature at Sogang University.
5. Right now, she *doesn't work / isn't working* on a new book.

2 Correct the sentences.

1. The Royal Swedish Academy of Sciences been giving Nobel prizes since 1901.
   _____
2. The Academy is choosing winners every October.
   _____
3. The winners are receiving their awards in December.
   _____
4. Since 1901, the Academy giving over 580 prizes.
   _____
5. Several young people win scientific Nobel prizes over the years.
   _____
6. Right now, many young scientists work hard to make new scientific discoveries.
   _____

State verbs ▶ 1.2

3 Choose the state verbs.

☐ have   ☐ belong   ☐ design
☐ see   ☐ want   ☐ change
☐ believe   ☐ be   ☐ like
☐ live   ☐ plan   ☐ look

4 Choose the correct verb form for each sentence.

1. Most people *are hearing / have heard* about the Eiffel Tower in Paris.
2. It *was being / was* the tallest structure in France until 1973.
3. About 7 million visitors *are seeing / see* the tower every year.
4. In 1909, some city officials *wanted / have wanted* to destroy the tower.
5. However, many Parisians *were not agreeing / didn't agree*.
6. They said that the Eiffel Tower *belongs / was belonging* in Paris.
7. Today many people *are believing / believe* the Eiffel Tower is the most beautiful structure in Paris.

Each and every ▶ 1.3

5 Use the words in the box to complete the chart.

every	every one of	each	each of

Singular	Plural
1 _____ job	3 _____ my jobs
2 _____ project	4 _____ my projects

6 Use the correct word or phrase to complete each sentence.

1. I have taken *each / every* business course that my college offers.
2. The school offers ten businesses classes *every one of / each* semester.
3. I've learned something new and interesting in *every one / each of* the courses.
4. *Every one / Every* of my professors has been great.
5. I've done well in *each of / every* course.

Unit 1   Achievements

VOCABULARY

Personal development ▶ 1.1

1 Choose the correct verb to complete each phrase.

1 ____ advantage of
   a do   b miss   c take

2 ____ a difference
   a do   b make   c take

3 ____ an opportunity
   a do   b make   c miss

4 ____ your best
   a do   b make   c take

5 ____ risks
   a do   b miss   c take

6 ____ the most of
   a do   b make   c miss

2 Complete each sentence with a phrase from Exercise 1.

1 I don't like to _____. That's why I don't ski or go rock climbing.

2 Anyone can help people, animals, and the environment and _____ in the world.

3 I always try to _____ every situation. When I lost my job, I took the time to go back to school and learn new skills.

4 This is a difficult project. Just _____. Don't worry about being perfect.

5 You should _____ this opportunity. This is a great job offer!

6 I look at the new job postings every day because I don't want to _____.

VOCABULARY DEVELOPMENT: Collocations ▶ 1.2

3 Match the beginning of the collocation in A with the ending in B.

A		B
1 make	____	a success
2 live	____	b pleased
3 heavily	____	c guarded
4 think	____	d simply
5 guarantee	____	e real progress
6 secretly	____	f highly of

4 Write the collocation type for the collocations in Exercise 3: *verb + noun*, *verb + adverb*, or *adverb + adjective*.

1 _____
2 _____
3 _____
4 _____
5 _____
6 _____

5 Use the correct word to complete each sentence.

1 You can *do / make* contact with me by email.
2 Skydivers live *dangerously / riskily*.
3 My office is in a *beautiful / beautifully* designed building.
4 My co-workers don't take their work *heavily / seriously*.
5 There are a lot of different ways to *acquire / take* knowledge.
6 You can *avoid / stop* trouble by completing applications accurately.
7 The company is widely *considered / recognized* for its excellent customer service.
8 People have strong opinions when they are young, but they often think *simply / differently* about things when they get older.

Unit 1 Achievements

READING SKILL: Skimming and scanning ▶ 1.1

1 Skim the article to understand the gist of it. Then choose the correct topic.

☐ How to improve motivation   ☐ Why people are motivated
☐ Why motivation is important   ☐ How to find motivated employees

2 Scan the article. Match the questions to the answers.

____ 1 What does *intrinsic* mean?   a food, clothing, and a home
____ 2 What does *extrinsic* mean?   b inside factors
____ 3 What is self-actualization?   c being the best you can be
____ 4 What are some physiological needs?   d a psychologist
____ 5 Who was Abraham Maslow?   e outside factors

3 Read the textbook article.

Why People Do What They Do

Types of Motivation

What motivates people to achieve their goals? According to experts, both extrinsic (outside) and intrinsic (inside) factors motivate people. Extrinsic factors are things like rewards or punishments. We all understand that people like to get rewards. For example, more pay might motivate an employee to complete a project. Other times, people are motivated *not* to do things so that they don't get punished. People follow the law, for instance, to avoid trouble with the police. Intrinsic factors come from a person's desire to do something for themselves. Someone might work hard to become a doctor in order to make a difference in the world, for example. A big factor in motivation is the desire to become the best person you can be. This is called "self-actualization."

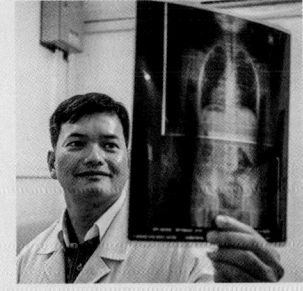

Meeting Human Needs First

The desire for self-actualization can be very powerful. However, according to one theory, people cannot achieve self-actualization until they have taken care of each of several more basic needs. Psychologist Abraham Maslow developed an ordered list, or hierarchy, of these needs called "Maslow's hierarchy of needs":

1 physiological—air, food, water, sleep, clothing, a home
2 health and safety—personal safety, exercise, a healthful diet
3 social—friendships, family
4 esteem—respect from others, having others think highly of you
5 self-actualization—being the best person you can be

Once people have achieved each need on the list, they can be motivated to achieve the next. In other words, a person must have air, food, and water before that person can feel safe and healthy.

Maslow's hierarchy of needs has become widely recognized in the workplace and in education. Many employers are taking advantage of Maslow's ideas to motivate workers. They understand that when employees feel respect from others, they are motivated to do their best. Schools have also learned from Maslow's hierarchy of needs. Some schools are providing breakfast and lunch for every student because they believe that children are more likely to make real progress in school if they have eaten healthy meals and do not feel hungry.

—adapted from *A Dictionary of Business and Management*, 6th ed., edited by Jonathan Law, and *A Dictionary of Human Resource Management*, 3rd ed., edited by Edmund Heery and Mike Noon

Unit 1 Achievements

READING: Practice

4 What do people need before they can achieve self-actualization?

☐ They need extrinsic motivation.
☐ They need to take more risks.
☐ They need to understand Maslow's hierarchy of needs.
☐ They need to be healthy and have respect from others.

5 Read each situation. Which kind of motivation does it describe? Write *I* (intrinsic) or *E* (extrinsic).

1 A student studies for a test all night because he wants to get an A in the class. ____
2 An employee doesn't miss any opportunity to do extra work because she wants to get a raise. ____
3 A man exercises after work every day because it makes him feel good. ____
4 A woman studies old manuscripts because she is interested in learning about ancient cultures. ____
5 A college student cleans his room when he finds out that his mother is coming to visit. ____

6 Match each need in Maslow's list with an example of how a person might be motivated to satisfy it.

____ 1 physiological   a A person works hard to become successful in a new field.
____ 2 health and safety   b A person works two jobs, so she can buy food and pay her rent.
____ 3 social   c A person joins a gym to get exercise to improve his health.
____ 4 esteem   d A person asks for feedback on her writing.
____ 5 self-actualization   e A person joins a club to make contact with people.

REAL-WORLD ENGLISH: Making inquiries ▶1.4

1 Complete the conversation from Scene 1 of the video with words from the box.

| could the person | I wonder if | for your time | sorry to trouble you | do I apply |

Company Rep: Hello!
Kevin: Hi. ¹_____ you could help me?
Company Rep: Sure.
Kevin: Thanks. Does your company hire part time? I'm a student, so I can only work evenings and weekends.
Company Rep: Yes, we do. Are you interested in forensic technology?
Kevin: Yes, I am! So, how ²_____?
Company Rep: Fill out this application, and then we'll call you tomorrow to set up an interview.
Kevin: Right. Uh, ³_____ text me instead? I'm in classes all day.
Company Rep: I'm sorry, but that's not possible. We call first, and then interviewees come into the office.
Kevin: I see. Thanks ⁴_____!
Company Rep: Thanks for stopping by!
Kevin: Oh, ⁵_____, but...where is your office?
Company Rep: Our office is on Main Street. Next to the law office.
Kevin: Really? Great! Thanks!

2 Match the expression type with the example.

____ 1 making an inquiry   a I wonder if you could help me.
____ 2 asking for help   b I'm in classes all day.
____ 3 giving information   c Does your company hire part time?
____ 4 thanking   d Thanks for stopping by!

3 Complete the conversation with expressions from the box. Two expressions are not needed.

| can I apply | can you tell me | help me, please |
| thank you for your time | wonder if you could help me | wonder if you could tell me |

You: Can you ¹_____?
Company Rep: Sure, what can I help you with?
You: I'm interested in a position with your company. How ²_____?
Company Rep: You can pick up an application in the administrator's office.
You: I see. I ³_____ where that is.
Company Rep: Of course! Just go down the hall. It's the first door on the right.
You: ⁴_____.
Company Rep: You're welcome. Good luck!

Unit 1   Achievements   5

UNIT REVIEW PODCAST

UNIT REVIEW: Podcast

GO ONLINE to listen to the podcast from the Unit Review.

1. Read the sentences from a podcast. Predict the main stressed words. Then listen and check.
   1. Thanks for listening to *Making It*, the podcast about finding the perfect job for you.
   2. I live in a college town.
   3. Well, I've wanted to own a restaurant since I was a little girl. I love to cook.
   4. I hear that your restaurant is doing very well.

2. Listen to the Unit Review Podcast. Choose *True*, *False*, or *Not Given*.

	True	False	Not Given
1 Annie Santos was a lawyer.	☐	☐	☐
2 Annie was happy as a lawyer.	☐	☐	☐
3 Her restaurant serves pizza and burgers.	☐	☐	☐
4 Annie's family members work with her.	☐	☐	☐
5 Her business is closed on weekends.	☐	☐	☐

LISTENING SKILL: Recognizing sentence stress and word boundaries ▶1.2

3. Listen again and complete the conversation.

   Annie: …When I'm cooking, I feel really happy, and people ¹_____ me that they love my food. I wanted to make the most of my natural talent as a chef. So I decided to ²_____ and open a restaurant.

   Mike: How did you decide what type of restaurant you wanted to have?

   Annie: …There are burger and pizza places ³_____ corner near the college. I wanted ⁴_____ differently.…

   Mike: I ⁵_____ that idea.

   Annie: Me, too! ⁶_____ breakfast all day—eggs, pancakes, French toast.

   Mike: I ⁷_____ that your restaurant ⁸_____ very well. Do you spend a lot of time there?

   Annie: Yes, I do, but the restaurant is closed every Monday and Tuesday. Also, I get to see my family all the time because I decided to ⁹_____ their natural talents, too! My husband is very organized, so he's my restaurant manager. And my children love working with people, so they are my servers. I ¹⁰_____ we're successful because we ¹¹_____ as a team.

DISCUSSION BOARD PREPARATION

4. Look at the Unit 1 Review Discussion Point. Read the questions in the prompt. Then read the reply. Does the writer agree with the quote? Explain your answer.

_____

5. Label the part of the reply that answers question 1 from the prompt. Then label the parts that answer questions 2 and 3.

Unit 1 Achievements

UNIT REVIEW PODCAST

Unit 1 Review Discussion Point

Answer the questions in a post.
1. Read the quote. What are the positive and negative effects of success?
   "Success makes life easier. It doesn't make living easier."
   —Bruce Springsteen, selected from *Oxford Essential Quotations*, 5th ed., edited by Susan Ratcliffe
2. Is there any part of life that success does not affect?
3. Do you think this quote is correct? Explain.

Latest: Mia Ryan
I think there are both positive and negative effects of success. For example, if you are successful, you have a good salary and people think highly of you. If you have money, you can have a nice house in a safe neighborhood and buy good food to eat. You can also afford a good education and take nice vacations. However, success can make life complicated. For instance, I've been a successful doctor for 20 years. During the first few years, work was the most important thing in my life. I always had to compete with other people to keep my success. I owned two houses and four cars, so I had a lot to take care of. Things are different now. I'm still successful, but work isn't so important. In fact, these days, I'm taking dancing classes with my husband, and my daughter and I are learning how to paint.

I think success can affect every part of a person's life. However, you can make sure that success doesn't affect your life in a negative way. For example, you can make sure that you continue to do the things that you liked before you became successful. Or you can make sure that you always have time for your family and friends.

I think this quote is correct. Successful people can do or have almost anything they want, but having and doing so much might make life more complicated.

6 According to the writer, what is one negative effect of success?

7 Does the writer think that there's any part of life that success does not affect? Explain.

8 Did the writer answer all the questions? If yes, explain. If no, what can the writer change?

_____

_____

9 Review the rubric. Use the rubric to give a score for the reply.
Give points: 0 (not successful)–10 (successful).

Writing a Discussion Board Post	Points
The post answers the questions clearly and completely.	
The post has clear explanations and examples.	
The post shows careful thinking about the topic.	
The post uses simple present, present continuous, and present perfect verbs correctly.	
The post is long enough (200–250 words).	
Total	

WRITE YOUR POST

10 Read the quote. What does it mean? What are the positive and negative effects of success? Is there any part of life that success does not affect? Do you think this quote is correct? Explain. Write a draft of your post for the Unit 1 Review Discussion Point.

"Success makes life easier. It doesn't make living easier."
Bruce Springsteen, selected from *Oxford Essential Quotations,* 5th ed., edited by Susan Ratcliffe

11 Use the rubric from Exercise 9 to score your post. Then improve your post.

GO ONLINE to add your comments to the discussion board.

Unit 1 Achievements

2 News

Narrative tenses: Simple past, past continuous, and past perfect ▶2.1

1 Write the correct forms of the verbs in the chart.

| become | see | start | crash |
| fall | begin | spill | leave |

Simple Past: Main events

_____
_____

Past Continuous: Background events / longer actions

was/were becoming
_____
_____

Past Perfect: Events earlier than main events

_____
_____
_____

2 Complete the paragraph with the correct forms of the verbs in Exercise 1.

Last night, a gas truck ¹_____ on the highway. The driver ²_____ asleep after 14 hours on the road. Thousands of gallons of gas ³_____ to spill on the road, causing a major traffic jam. When people realized that gas ⁴_____, they started to get out of their cars. By midnight, everyone ⁵_____ their cars on the highway. When I ⁶_____ the story on the news the next day, the police chief said no one was injured. He also said situations like this ⁷_____ more and more common because of the shortage in truck drivers.

All, both, either, and neither ▶2.2

3 Complete the rules with *all*, *both*, *either*, or *neither*.

1 _____ one or the other in a pair
2 _____ not one and not the other in a pair
3 _____ two things in a pair
4 _____ everything in a group of three or more

4 Complete the sentences with *all*, *both*, *either*, or *neither*.

1 The fire quickly spread over the whole school. One firefighter thinks the fire started in the cafeteria. Another believes it started in a science classroom on the other side of campus. _____ could be correct.

2 The school principal disagrees. She believes that _____ firefighter is right. She thinks the fire started in the gym.

3 The fire department will investigate _____ the possibilities.

4 Luckily, _____ of the students and teachers got out of the school safely.

5 One student ran back inside to help a student who had fallen. _____ are OK.

Was / were going to ▶2.3

5 Read each sentence. Write *but* where it is appropriate or – (nothing).

1 She was going to leave work early, _____ she stayed late to finish her project.

2 I was going to change lanes _____ because the car in front of me was going so slowly.

3 The police were going to talk to everyone _____ at the police station.

4 The reporters were going to interview everyone, _____ half of the people had already left.

5 She was going to fly to Portland to spend the holiday with her family, _____ all flights were canceled because of bad weather.

Taking action (verbs) ▶2.1

1 Complete the definitions with the words from the box.

attention	aware	begin	cause
direct	doesn't	happen	make
power	sure	tell	try

1 **attempt**: to _____ to do something
2 **announce**: to _____ people about something
3 **bring down**: to _____ somebody lose _____
4 **distract**: to _____ somebody's _____ to something different
5 **launch**: to _____ an activity
6 **lead to**: to _____ something to _____
7 **prevent**: to make _____ something _____ happen
8 **realize**: to become _____ of something

2 Complete the sentences with the correct form of the bold words from Exercise 1.

1 The reporter _____ that all local airports are closed until tomorrow.
2 People _____ that something was wrong when they saw police cars on their street.
3 After the accident, the road was still dangerous. The police closed the road to _____ more accidents.
4 We're asking people not to _____ to go out tonight because we're expecting a very strong storm.
5 News about strange events can _____ people from more serious news.
6 Some believe that lower rents will _____ more new businesses in the area.

3 Choose the word or phrase that is different.

1	attempt	do	wait	make an effort
2	announce	say	state	keep secret
3	bring down	stop	help	destroy
4	distract	open	interest	entertain
5	launch	start	close	open
6	lead to	create	ask	result in
7	prevent	become	stop	slow
8	realize	forget	see	understand

VOCABULARY DEVELOPMENT:
Comment adverbs ▶2.3

4 Which adverbs have positive or negative meanings? Which can be either positive or negative? Write the adverbs in the correct column.

apparently	curiously	luckily	naturally
obviously	sadly	surprisingly	unfortunately

Positive	Negative	Positive or negative

5 Match the sentences in A with the correct comment adverbs in B.

A

1 There was juice on the carpet, and the girl was crying. ____ the girl spilled her juice.
2 ____ all of the employees were able to get out of the burning building.
3 ____, there was a snow storm in the middle of the summer.
4 ____, it rained during the baseball game.
5 ____ 150 of the company's employees have lost their jobs.

B

a Apparently
b Unfortunately
c Luckily
d Surprisingly
e Sadly

Unit 2 News

REAL-WORLD READING

READING: Practice

1 Read the article. According to the article, what has helped mass media progress?

☐ books ☐ radio waves ☐ technology

From Books to the Internet: The Progress of Mass Media

We all rely on mass media such as newspapers, magazines, radio, television, and the Internet. However, we wouldn't have much access to information without technology.

Johannes Gutenberg invented the printing press in the fifteenth century. The printing press allowed publishers to print books, and improvements to the press led to more affordable books. By the 1700s, publishers had launched the first newspapers and magazines. Unfortunately, though, magazines were expensive to print. Newspapers and magazines became more widely used when the price of printing decreased in the early 1800s.

While millions of people were reading their newspapers, others were working on new ways to spread information. By the early twentieth century, sending electronic signals either through wires or through radio waves had made it possible to spread information instantly. With the invention of radio and television, media producers no longer had to deliver a physical product. Neither did the public have to travel to buy it. Anyone with a radio or a TV could receive information, and both television and radio became very popular.

Technological innovations in the late twentieth century completely changed the face of media. Satellites, computers, and the Internet led to new products and formats. Information spread through websites, blogs, and podcasts. People realized that they could quickly access information about almost anything. They could also produce information and comment on it. Because most people have their smartphones with them all the time, they can share information in seconds. All these advances have had an enormous impact on communication. What changes might we see in the future?

—adapted from *Oxford Encyclopedia of the Modern World* edited by Peter N. Stearns

2 Which types of mass media were the results of…?

1 satellites and Internet

_____

2 sending electronic signals

_____

3 improvements to the printing press

_____

Unit 2 News

3 Read each statement. Write *T* (true), *F* (false), or *NG* (not given).

___ 1 The first magazines were available in the 1800s.

___ 2 The first magazines looked like books.

___ 3 Information could be shared quickly with the use of electronic signals.

___ 4 TV and radio allowed the public to create and share information.

___ 5 The Internet cannot be owned or controlled by governments or corporations.

READING SKILL: Identifying topic sentences ▶2.1

4 Choose the correct topic sentences.

1 Paragraph 2
   a The printing press allowed publishers to print books, and improvements to the press led to more affordable books.
   b Newspapers and magazines became more widely used when the price of printing decreased in the early 1800s.

2 Paragraph 3
   a While millions of people were reading their newspapers, others were working on new ways to spread information.
   b Naturally, both television and radio became very popular.

3 Paragraph 4
   a Because most people have their smartphones with them all the time, they can share information in seconds.
   b Technological innovations in the late twentieth century completely changed the face of media.

5 Read the headings. Which paragraph does each heading support?

	Paragraph 2	Paragraph 3	Paragraph 4
1 The Introduction of Radio and TV	☐	☐	☐
2 Introducing the Printing Press	☐	☐	☐
3 Media Through Electronic Signals	☐	☐	☐
4 The First Form of Mass Media	☐	☐	☐
5 The Impact of the Internet	☐	☐	☐
6 Today's Media Revolution	☐	☐	☐

6 Read the details from the article. Which paragraph does each detail belong in? Write *2*, *3*, *4*, or write *X* if not in the article.

___ 1 Information was available through radio and television.

___ 2 Technology created new ways of sharing information, such as websites and podcasts.

___ 3 Before the printing press, books took a very long time to make.

___ 4 Books became less expensive.

___ 5 For the first time, people could spread information instantly.

___ 6 Newspapers became available in the 1700s.

___ 7 It became difficult to determine whether information was true.

___ 8 Individuals were able to create information themselves.

Unit 2 News

ENGLISH FOR REAL

REAL-WORLD ENGLISH: Giving and reacting to news ▶2.4

1 Complete the conversation from Scene 1 of the video with words from the box.

| I'm afraid | some bad | don't believe | exciting |
| great news | Guess what | Really | |

Anna: Andy!? Hey bro…I was just going to call you.

Andy: Beat you to it! ¹_____…I have some ²_____.

Anna: ³_____? What? Tell me!

Andy: I was chosen to go to the pre-law student conference in LA!

Anna: Good job, bro! LA? That's ⁴_____. When is it?

Andy: Two weeks from now. Uh, it starts on the 21st.

Anna: Wow! Great! So, I guess I'll see you the following weekend, and I can still stay with you, right?

Andy: Oh…Uh. Well, ⁵_____ I've got ⁶_____ news about that.

Anna: What?

Andy: Uh, Max's parents are visiting from England…so they'll be staying in Max's room, and Max will have to sleep in the living room. So…we won't have room.

Anna: The same weekend? I ⁷_____ it. Well, I guess I should cancel my ticket.

Andy: No! I'll find you a place to stay. I'll check with my colleagues at the office.

2 Match the sentence or phrase in A with the sentence or phrase in B.

A

1 Something amazing has happened! I

2 I'm afraid I've got some bad news.

3 I don't know how to say this, but

4 Have you heard the good news?

B

a the company is going to close in two weeks.

b got the job that I applied for!

c We're all going to get raises next week!

d Sales are down, and 15 employees are going to lose their jobs.

3 Choose the best responses to the news in Exercise 2 from the box. Different answers and more than one answer are possible.

| Really? That's great! | I don't believe it. How awful. | That's terrible. |
| How exciting! | I'm so pleased for you. | I'm so sorry. |

1 _____

2 _____

3 _____

4 _____

UNIT REVIEW: Podcast

 GO ONLINE to listen to the podcast from the Unit Review.

1 🔊 Listen to the Unit 2 Review Podcast. Match the beginning of the sentences in A with the endings in B.

A	B
1 Nigel Richards learned to play Scrabble ____	a English-language competitions.
2 Richards won his first competition ____	b when he was 28.
3 Until 2015, he had only entered ____	c French World Scrabble championship.
4 In 2015, Richards won the ____	d a French dictionary.
5 He memorized words in ____	e in 1997.

2 🔊 Listen again and complete the conversation.

Louisa: …Before he ¹_____ Scrabble, he ²_____ interested in words at all. In fact, he still doesn't talk a lot. His mom thought she would finally be able to beat him at a game, but he got really good at Scrabble, and in 1997, ³_____ his first Scrabble competition.

Carrie: Wow, just a couple of years after ⁴_____ to play?

Louisa: …I know. But wait, it gets better. Since then, Richards has won ⁵_____ of the competitions that he has entered, including the World Scrabble Championship, which he has won at least three times. Now, ⁶_____, these have all been English-language Scrabble competitions since Richards is from New Zealand.

LISTENING SKILL: Recognizing linkers in fast speech ▶2.3

3 🔊 Read the sentences. Predict which linkers (*and, but, or, so*) are used. Listen and check.

1 I'm Carrie Lang, _____ you're listening to *You're Joking, Right?*…
2 I was going to tell you guys about this next week, _____ I can't wait!
3 I think our show schedule is on Facebook, _____ maybe it's on our website.
4 Each player gets seven game pieces with letters on them, _____ players take turns spelling out words on a board.
5 His mother taught him to play the game when he was 28, _____ that was probably around 1994 or 1995.

DISCUSSION BOARD PREPARATION

4 Look at the Unit 2 Review Discussion Point. Read the questions in the prompt. Then read the reply. Where does his real-life example come from?

5 Label the part of the reply that answers question 1 from the prompt. Then label the parts that answer questions 2 and 3.

Unit 2 News

UNIT REVIEW PODCAST

Unit 2 Review Discussion Point

Answer the questions in a post.
1. Read the quote. Was there more good or more bad news today?
   "Ever noticed that no matter what happens in one day, it exactly fits in the newspaper?"
   —Jerry Seinfeld, selected from *Oxford Essential Quotations*, 5th ed., edited by Susan Ratcliffe
2. Do you think everything published as news is news?
3. Why do you think people like to read bad news?

Latest: Peter Wong
Unfortunately, most of the news today is bad news. The news is often about war or accidents. I try to avoid reading bad news.

I don't think everything published is real news. Real news is important information that people should know about. Sadly, I think lots of news stories are not really news. People just read the stories because they are interesting. For example, many people like to read about famous people. I don't think that's important. I think people like to read about surprising events, too—even when they aren't important news

There was a surprising event in my local online newspaper last week. A woman was working in her garden one morning when she found a kitten. She had never seen this kitten in her garden before. She was going to pick the kitten up, but she decided not to move it in case it was injured. Instead, she called animal control. Twenty minutes later, a man from animal control arrived. He carefully picked the kitten up, stared at it for a few seconds, and started laughing. The woman asked why he was laughing, so he put the kitten in her hands. Then the woman laughed, too! She hadn't had her glasses on when she had first seen the kitten, so she hadn't realized that it was a toy! Apparently, her granddaughter had left it in the garden.

6 According to the writer, what makes an event news?

7 Does the writer think the story about the kitten is real news? Why or why not? Why does the writer tell the story?

8 Overall, did the writer answer all the questions? If yes, explain. If no, what can the writer change?

9 Review the rubric. Use the rubric to give a score for the reply.
Give points: 0 (not successful)–10 (successful).

Writing a Discussion Board Post	Points
The post answers the questions clearly and completely.	
The writer explains each point with clear examples.	
The post shows careful thinking about the topic.	
The post uses simple past, past continuous, and past perfect verbs correctly.	
The post is long enough (200–250 words).	
Total	

WRITE YOUR POST

10 Read the quote. Was there more good or more bad news today? Do you think everything published as news is news? Why do people like to read bad news? Write a draft of your post for the Unit 2 Review Discussion Point.

"Ever noticed that no matter what happens in one day, it exactly fits in the newspaper?"
—Jerry Seinfeld, selected from *Oxford Essential Quotations,* 5th ed., edited by Susan Ratcliffe

11 Use the rubric from Exercise 9 to score your post. Then improve your post.

Go ONLINE to add your comments to the discussion board.

3 Frontiers

Verbs + *to* infinitive or *-ing* form ▶ 3.1

1 Write the words in the correct order to make sentences and questions.

1 was / began / exploring / I / 15 / when / I
   _____

2 prefer / Do / traveling / you / alone
   _____

3 to / countries / like / visit / I / new
   _____

4 remember / here / Do / you / coming / year / last
   _____

5 stopped / ago / two / three / exploring / He / or / years
   _____

2 Match each sentence with the correct meaning.

1 I don't remember going to that place. ____
2 Let's remember to go to that place. ____
3 You should stop to look at the map. ____
4 You should stop looking at the map. ____
5 I forgot to read the guidebook. ____
6 I don't remember reading the guidebook. ____

a I want us to go to that place.
b I went to that place, but I don't have a memory of going there.
c I didn't read the guidebook because I forgot to.
d You should stop driving, so you can look at the map.
e I forgot I had read the guidebook.
f You should not look at the map anymore.

Verbs + *-ing* form and verbs + *to* infinitive ▶ 3.2

3 Choose the correct verb form.

1 Can we afford *to stay / staying* for two weeks?
2 Do you enjoy *to travel / traveling*?
3 What do you plan *to do / doing* on your trip?
4 We chose *to go / going* to Vietnam.
5 You should consider *to come / coming* with me.
6 I usually practice *to speak / speaking* Japanese on Tuesdays.

4 Write each verb under the correct rule that describes the form of the verb that follows.

| avoid | decide | hate | hope | like |
| love | plan | practice | suggest | |

Use *-ing* form only	Use *to* infinitive only	Use either *-ing* form or *to* infinitive

So and *such* ▶ 3.3

5 Choose the correct word or phrase to complete each sentence.

1 It's ____ important for people to explore.
   a so   b such   c such an

2 Exploring new places is ____ way to learn about the world and yourself.
   a so   b such a   c such a great

3 Some people have ____ fear about going to unknown places.
   a so   b such   c such a

4 I think it is ____ exciting to hear a new language and meet new people.
   a so   b such an   c such a fun

5 Being an explorer can be ____ experience.
   a so   b such an   c such an amazing

6 Correct the incorrect sentences.

1 This is so beautiful city.
   _____

2 I'm having such a great time.
   _____

3 It's such a hard to learn Hungarian.
   _____

4 Everyone is filled with so excitement.
   _____

5 The buildings here are so old.
   _____

Unit 3 Frontiers

VOCABULARY

VOCABULARY: Exploration ▶3.1

1 Write each word in the correct column.

| explore | flexible | independent | keep going |
| practical | quit | set off | survive |

Adjectives	Verbs

2 Complete the sentences with the words from the boxes.

| keep going | independent | quit | practical |

1 Young explorers look forward to growing up and becoming _____.
2 _____ knowledge can be as important as academic knowledge.
3 Good explorers don't usually _____ when things are difficult.
4 For an explorer, it can be hard to _____ without support from other team members.

| explore | flexible | set off | survive |

5 Being _____ is an important quality for explorers because plans often have to change.
6 Humans will continue to _____ the planet until we know everything about it.
7 We all need food, water, and shelter to _____.
8 Being prepared before you _____ will help your trip to be a success.

3 Match the word with its synonym.

____ 1 quit   a live
____ 2 set off   b continue
____ 3 survive   c stop
____ 4 explore   d start
____ 5 keep going   e discover

VOCABULARY DEVELOPMENT: Suffixes for nouns ▶3.2

4 Complete the chart with nouns, verbs, and adjectives.

Adjectives	Nouns	Verbs
ill	1 _____	
2 _____	friendship	
committed	3 _____	commit
4 _____	personality	personalize
confident	5 _____	
	contribution	6 _____
	recognition	7 _____

5 Use the suffixes in the box to change each word to a noun.

| -tion | -ment | -ness | -ence | -ity | -ship |

1 different _____   5 explain _____
2 member _____   6 encourage _____
3 secure _____   7 organize _____
4 happy _____   8 willing _____

6 Complete the sentences with nouns from Exercise 5.
1 He told me which way we're going to go, but I didn't understand his _____.
2 _____ can make travel easy. Keep all your travel information and your passport in one place, so you can find them easily.
3 You can communicate with the locals if you have the _____ to learn the language.
4 There's a _____ between taking a vacation and exploring. You take a vacation to relax, but you explore to learn new things.
5 Young explorers can get _____ from people who have explored a lot. Experienced explorers can help young people keep going when things get difficult.
6 _____ is very important, especially for people traveling alone. Stay in hotels in safe neighborhoods, and don't stay out late if you are by yourself.

READING: Practice

1 Read the article. Where did Gertrude Bell do most of her work?

☐ Oxford University and other areas of England   ☐ Arabia and surrounding areas

Gertrude Bell: Daughter of the Desert

Home | About | **Articles**

Gertrude Bell was born on July 14, 1868, in Durham, England. She was one of the first women admitted to Oxford University, where she studied history. When she was 37, she began exploring Arabia. She set off on an expedition to Syria and surrounding areas. Her explorations brought her such happiness that she decided to continue living in the Arab world.

The Arabs called Gertrude Bell a "daughter of the desert." This is because Bell liked traveling throughout Arabia, Syria, and Asia Minor. She chose to travel in the area for about a decade. From 1905 to 1914, she studied ancient sites and artifacts used by people thousands of years before. She also mapped the sites of wells. The location of these springs was important because water is so hard to find in the desert. Perhaps most importantly, however, she established ties with people in Arabia. Many of these relationships were with the highest-ranking leaders of the Arab world. As Bell traveled, she took photographs, kept detailed notes and a diary, and wrote long letters. She used this material to write and publish a number of books and articles.

Bell had become such an authority on the languages, history, culture, and politics of Persia and Mesopotamia that she was asked to work as an expert for the British government. She worked in Egypt and Iraq. While in Iraq, she composed laws designed to protect Iraq's many ancient artifacts. She also founded the country's archaeological museum. In 1921, Prime Minister Winston Churchill invited her to participate in the Cairo Conference where Iraq's boundaries would be determined.

Bell died on July 12, 1926. In recognition of her achievements and contributions, the British government gave her a full military funeral. She was buried in Baghdad, the city she had loved and lived in until the end.

—Adapted from *The Oxford Companion to World Exploration* edited by David Buisseret

2 Choose the things that Gertrude Bell was involved in.

☐ writing map books   ☐ finding water in the desert   ☐ the British government
☐ exploration   ☐ teaching in Durham England   ☐ building relationships
☐ studying the culture of Persia   ☐ the ancient history of Britain   ☐ military groups in Arabia

3 Complete the sentence with the correct years for the events.

1   Gertrude Bell first set off for Arabia in _____.

2   Bell traveled in Arabia, Syria, and Asia Minor until _____.

3   Gertrude Bell was born in Durham, England, in _____.

4   After she died in _____, Bell was buried in Baghdad.

5   In _____, Winston Churchill asked Bell to attend a conference in Cairo, Egypt.

Unit 3   Frontiers

REAL-WORLD READING

READING SKILL: Working out meaning from context ▶ 3.2

4 Read the sentences. Choose the words or phrases that best describe the words in **bold**.

1 From 1905 to 1914, she studied ancient sites and **artifacts** used by people thousands of years before.
   a From 1905 to 1914, she studied   b used by people thousands of years before

2 She also mapped the sites of **wells**. The location of these springs was important because water is so hard to find in the desert.
   a mapped the sites   b The location of these springs

3 She established **ties** with people in Arabia. Many of these relationships were with the highest-ranking leaders of the Arab world.
   a these relationships   b highest-ranking

4 As Bell traveled, she took photographs, kept detailed notes and a diary, and wrote long letters. She used this **material** to write and publish a number of books and articles.
   a As Bell traveled   b took photographs, kept detailed notes and a diary, and wrote long letters

5 Bell had become such an **authority** on the languages, history, culture, and politics of Persia and Mesopotamia that she was asked to work as an expert for the British government.
   a work as an expert   b the British government

6 In recognition of her achievements and contributions, the British government gave her a full military **funeral**. She was buried in Baghdad, the city she had loved and lived in until the end.
   a buried in Baghdad   b she had loved

5 Match each word to its definition. Use the sentences in Exercise 4 to help.

____ 1 artifacts   a an event to remember someone after they die
____ 2 wells   b objects that were made and used by people a long time ago
____ 3 ties   c a person with special knowledge
____ 4 material   d something that connects you with a particular group of people
____ 5 authority   e places where you can access water from underground
____ 6 funeral   f information that you collect before you write a book or an article

6 Read the sentences. Then write each word's suffix and part of speech in the chart.

Her **explorations** brought her such **happiness** that she decided to continue living in the Arab world.

	Suffix	Part of speech (adjective, adverb, noun, or verb)
1 exploration	-tion	noun
2 happiness	-	

Perhaps most **importantly**, however, she **established** ties with people in Arabia.

	Suffix	Part of speech (adjective, adverb, noun, or verb)
3 importantly	-	
4 established	-	

18   Unit 3 Frontiers

REAL-WORLD ENGLISH: Interrupting and resuming ▶ 3.4

1 Number the lines from Scene 1 of the video in order.

___ Max: Well, I was wondering if maybe we should pay more attention to our Earth instead of exploring space?

___ Dr. Bronson: Exploration! As well as going out into outer space, we can also go inwards to…

___ Dr. Bronson: Of course, uh, go ahead.

___ Dr. Bronson: That's a very good point. But I'm talking about inward exploration… the way the brain…

___ Max: Excuse me for interrupting. Could I ask a question?

2 Number the lines from Scene 2 of the video in order.

___ Andy: Yeah, right? What was all that about the brain and looking inwards?

___ Andy: Well, that wasn't what I expected.

___ Kevin / Andy: Huh? / No wonder!

___ Kevin: Where was I? Oh. Space travel! And every time someone asked a question about space, he kept talking about the brain!

___ Kevin: Modern-day exploration! Right! I thought he was going to talk about…

___ Max: Yeah, I know what you mean. I thought the whole thing was about…

___ Phil: Oh, can I just interrupt here? Guys? Um, the title of the lecture was "Inner Space Exploration"! And that was Dr. Bronson, not Branson!

___ Max: Space! Yeah. But, as I was saying, some of it just didn't make sense. I mean…

3 Match the expression type with the example.

___ 1 an informal interruption   a Oh, can I just interrupt here?

___ 2 a formal interruption   b That's a very good point. But I'm talking about inward exploration

___ 3 resuming formally   c Where was I?

___ 4 resuming informally   d Excuse me for interrupting. Could I ask a question?

4 Should you use formal or informal phrases to interrupt people in the following situations? For each situation, write *F* (formal) or *I* (informal).

___ 1 A person who you don't know is giving you directions to a place.

___ 2 Your good friend is telling you what she did over the weekend.

___ 3 Your friend's friend, whom you just met, is telling you about his new job.

___ 4 Your brother or sister is complaining that your room is messy.

___ 5 Your professor is explaining a project to you.

___ 6 Your boss is telling you what happened at an important meeting.

___ 7 A person on the phone is giving you technical help.

___ 8 A server in a restaurant is explaining a menu item.

UNIT REVIEW PODCAST

UNIT REVIEW: Podcast

GO ONLINE to listen to the podcast from the Unit Review.

1 🔊 Listen to the Unit Review Podcast. Are the statements T (true), F (false), or NG (not given)?

____ 1 The podcast is about a group of artists.
____ 2 Zaria Forman is an explorer, environmentalist, and artist.
____ 3 She sells her photographs of places that are affected by climate change.
____ 4 She made an expedition to the Arctic in 2012.
____ 5 Her art focuses on the destruction of the environment.

2 🔊 Listen again, and complete the conversation.

Andrew: The person we're talking about today is protecting ¹_____ in an unusual way—she's using her artwork to raise our ²_____ of climate change.

Maggie: That's right. We're talking about artist and explorer Zaria Forman. Forman found ³_____ her art when she was very young. Her mother was a photographer who took photos of remote areas of the world...One place that Forman's mother ⁴_____ was the Arctic, and that's where Forman led her first expedition.

Andrew: Yes, in 2012, Forman took a group of artists and scholars to icy Greenland, which is in the Arctic. Forman's process starts with ⁵_____...

LISTENING SKILL: Recognizing rephrasing in a talk ▶ 3.1

3 🔊 Read the sentences from the podcast. Add the expressions in parenthesis. Listen and check.

1 Her mother was a photographer _____ who took photos of remote areas of the world, _____ faraway places where there are very few people _____ or no people at all. (that is)

2 When you hear that, _____ you might imagine that her drawings are difficult to look at, _____ but that's not the case. _____ her drawings are beautiful. (By that I mean)

3 Forman doesn't like to focus _____ on the destruction of the environment. _____ Forman prefers to draw the beauty of the environment. (To put it another way,)

DISCUSSION BOARD PREPARATION

4 Look at the Unit 3 Review Discussion Point. Read the questions in the prompt. Then read the reply. Does the writer agree with the poem?

5 Label the part of the reply that answers question 1 from the prompt. Then label the parts that answer questions 2 and 3.

UNIT REVIEW PODCAST

Unit 3 Review Discussion Point

Answer the questions in a post.
1. Read the poem. Do you agree with it?
   "We shall not cease from exploration   Will be to arrive where we started
   And the end of all our exploring   And know the place for the first time."
   —T. S. Eliot, *Four Quartets*, selected from *Oxford Essential Quotations*, 5th ed., edited by Susan Ratcliffe
2. What do you think are the most important benefits of exploration?
3. What personal benefits do you think explorers get from their explorations?

Latest: Carlos Ruiz
I agree with the first part of the poem. I think we will continue to explore forever. First, I think we naturally want to know as much as we can about our planet. Second, I think individuals like to explore, so even if someone has already learned everything about a place, other people will want to explore it again themselves. Third, we have been working on space exploration for a long time, but we haven't really seen much of space. I think that we will never stop wondering what is out there. The reason that I don't agree with the whole poem is I don't think we will always arrive where we started. I think that we will continue finding new places to explore, such as other planets.

I think there is one main important benefit of exploration—it teaches us about the place where we live. Exploration of our own planet is practical. I think we need to know what is out there. Exploration can teach us about new plants and animals, and it can show us the places on Earth that need to be protected.

Explorers probably get a lot of personal benefits from their explorations. Most importantly, I think they enjoy exploring. It seems exciting to go to a remote place and possibly see things that no one has ever seen before. I think explorers also become very independent because they have to take care of themselves in remote areas.

6 What does the writer think are some important benefits of exploration in general?

7 What personal benefits does the writer think explorers get from exploring?

8 Overall, did the writer answer all the questions? If yes, explain. If no, what can the writer change?

9 Review the rubric. Use the rubric to give a score for the reply.
Give points: 0 (not successful)–10 (successful).

Writing a Discussion Board Post	Points
The post answers the questions clearly and completely.	
The post has clear explanations and examples.	
The post shows careful thinking about the topic.	
The post uses verbs + infinitive and *-ing* forms correctly.	
The post is long enough (200–250 words).	
Total	

WRITE YOUR POST

10 Read the poem. Do you agree with it? What do you think are the most important benefits of exploration? What personal benefits do you think explorers get from their explorations? Write a draft of your post for the Unit 3 Review Discussion Point.

"We shall not cease from exploration   Will be to arrive where we started
And the end of all our exploring   And know the place for the first time"
—T. S. Eliot, *Four Quartets*, selected from *Oxford Essential Quotations*, 5th ed., edited by Susan Ratcliffe

11 Use the rubric from Exercise 9 to score your post. Then improve your post.

Go ONLINE to add your comments to the discussion board.

Unit 3   Frontiers

4 Processes

Present passive and past passive ▶4.1

1 Read the sentences about creating a canvas for painting. Write *A* (active) or *P* (passive).

___ 1 To make a painting, the painter first staples a type of cloth on a wooden frame.
___ 2 This cloth is called a canvas.
___ 3 Liquid called gesso is applied to the canvas.
___ 4 Then the gesso is left alone to dry.
___ 5 Once the gesso dries, the painter might draw a picture on the canvas.
___ 6 Finally, the painter can begin painting.

2 Use the information in the box to complete sentences in the present passive and past passive.

> Seventeenth century: invention of denim in Europe
> 1871: first pair of jeans made in the United States
> Process of making blue jeans:
> 1: clean and process cotton
> 2: color cotton blue
> 3: cut layers of denim with machines
> 4: sew pieces of denim together

1 Denim _____ in Europe in the seventeenth century.
2 The first pair of jeans _____ in the United States in 1871.
3 To make blue jeans, first, cotton _____ and processed.
4 Secondly, the cotton _____ blue.
5 Following that, layers of denim _____ with machines.
6 Finally, the pieces of denim _____ together.

Present passive with modal verbs ▶4.2

3 Complete the sentences with the passive form of a phrase from the box.

| can place | can slice | must allow |
| should bake | should clean | |

1 The pie crust _____ first in a 350° oven.
2 The crust _____ to cool.
3 Then the strawberries _____ with a wet towel.
4 The berries _____ if you like smaller pieces in your pie.
5 Finally, the strawberries _____ inside the pie crust with cream.

4 Rewrite the active sentences as present passive sentences with modal verbs.

1 A person can make paper with cloth.
   Paper can be made with cloth.
2 A person should cut the cloth into very small pieces.
   _____
3 A person must boil the cloth in water for an hour.
   _____
4 A person should put the cloth in a blender to make a paste.
   _____
5 A person can spread the paste out to dry.
   _____

Adjectives with prepositions ▶4.3

5 Write the correct preposition (*about, at, by, in,* or *with*) after each adjective.

1 I'm bad _____ sports.
2 I get bored _____ video games quickly.
3 Robert is excellent _____ cooking.
4 Are you good _____ math?
5 We're interested _____ this movie.
6 I was pleased _____ my teacher's comments.
7 Was he surprised to hear _____ your visit?

6 Choose the correct prepostions.

1 Tsutomu has a test tomorrow, and he is worried *about / with* it.
2 Yasuko is interested *by / in* Tsutomu's notes.
3 Stephanie has been waiting a long time. She is fed up *at / with* the long wait.
4 Stephanie is not pleased *by / with* her friends.

VOCABULARY DEVELOPMENT: Explaining a process ▶4.1

1 Select the correct choices to complete the instructions.

1. *The first step / Firstly,* for baking a cake is turning the oven on to the correct temperature.
2. *The second step / Second step* is gathering the ingredients.
3. *Then / Once* you have all the ingredients, you can mix the dry ingredients, such as flour and salt, together.
4. *The last step, / Following that,* mix the wet ingredients, like butter and eggs, together.
5. *After that, / Once* pour the dry ingredients into the bowl with the wet ingredients.
6. *The last / Finally,* bake the cake.

2 Complete the sentences with a word or phrase from the box to explain the process for folding a paper airplane.

| The last step | Secondly | Once |
| The first stage | After that | |

1. _____ is to fold the paper in half across the long way.
2. _____, unfold the paper and fold the top corners so that they meet on the folded line.
3. _____, fold the top edges, so they meet on the folded line in the center.
4. _____ you've done this, fold the plane in half along the first fold in the center.
5. _____ is to fold the wings down.

Production (verbs) ▶4.2

3 Use the words in the box to complete the chart.

| create | design | film | produce (a film) |
| promote | revise | select | solve |

Verb only	Noun or verb

4 Unscramble the words to complete the sentences.

1. The I L M F was three hours long. _____
2. Ramya D L O S E V her problem. _____
3. Tom G I S E D E N D the poster. _____
4. We will T O P O R E M the event. _____
5. They T R A C E D E a new product? _____
6. The author will S I R E V E her book. _____

5 Are these sentences correct? Choose *Yes* or *No*.

		Yes	No
1	The author promoted her book.	☐	☐
2	The actor revised his hairdo.	☐	☐
3	The musician designed a song.	☐	☐
4	The girl solved a puzzle.	☐	☐
5	The chef produced a cake.	☐	☐
6	The mechanic selected the problem.	☐	☐
7	My mother filmed the event.	☐	☐

READING: Practice

1 Read the article. What is crowdfunding?

☐ donating money to a group of people on the Internet
☐ funding a project with money from donors on the Internet

The Process of Crowdfunding

One way to fund a project is through crowdfunding. Crowdfunding is financing a project by giving rewards to small private investors on the Internet. Artists frequently use crowdfunding. These artists include painters, musicians, filmmakers, and writers. A lot of wonderful art is paid for by crowdfunding, but it should be noted that not everyone is good at raising money for themselves. Follow this process to launch a campaign that will help you get the money you need.

The first step you should take is to start promoting your project six months before you start crowdfunding. This will get people interested and ready to donate. Share short clips of your film or a chapter from your book. Post these samples on social media, and share them with friends and family.

Secondly, look at past crowdfunding campaigns for projects that are similar to yours to see what was done by other crowdfunders. Select a few of the most successful campaigns, and review them carefully. Don't copy them, but use them as a guide. Was video included on their pages? What kinds of rewards were offered? Examine some unsuccessful campaigns as well, and avoid making the mistakes those crowdfunders made.

Once you've done some research, it's time to design your own campaign. Figure out exactly how much money you need to complete your project. Then decide what you can afford to give out as a reward to people who donate money. If you're a musician, for example, you could offer free downloads of your songs before your CD comes out. Create a video if it will help donors understand your project better, and if you don't already have a website, build one and link it to your campaign.

Finally, when your campaign has been accepted by a fundraising website, it's time to promote your project again. Let everyone who is interested in your art know that they can start donating to your project. And, of course, after your project is well funded, you can go to work creating your masterpiece.

—featuring content from *A Dictionary of Finance and Banking*, 5th ed., edited by Jonathan Law

2 Complete the sentences with words from the box.

| design | donating | rewards | similar campaigns |
| six months | social media | unsuccessful | website |

1 Start promoting your project _____ early to build interest in your project.

2 You can promote your project by posting samples of your work on _____.

3 Research _____ to find out what was done well.

4 Avoid mistakes made by _____ campaigns.

5 As you _____ your campaign, figure out how much money you will need to complete your project.

6 Decide what _____ to give to people who donate.

7 Your _____ should be linked to your crowdfunding campaign.

8 Let people know that they can start _____.

3 According to the article, which activities are involved in designing a crowdfunding campaign?

☐ deciding how much money to ask for
☐ raising money to design the campaign
☐ downloading songs from other campaigns
☐ determining what to give to donors
☐ creating a video
☐ linking the campaign to friends' websites
☐ building a website and connecting it to the crowdfunding campaign

READING SKILL: Classifying information from a text ▶ 4.2

4 Choose the best type of diagram for taking notes about the information in the article.

☐ a flow chart

Step 1 → Step 2 → Step 3

☐ a mindmap

☐ a timeline

1850 1900 1950 2000

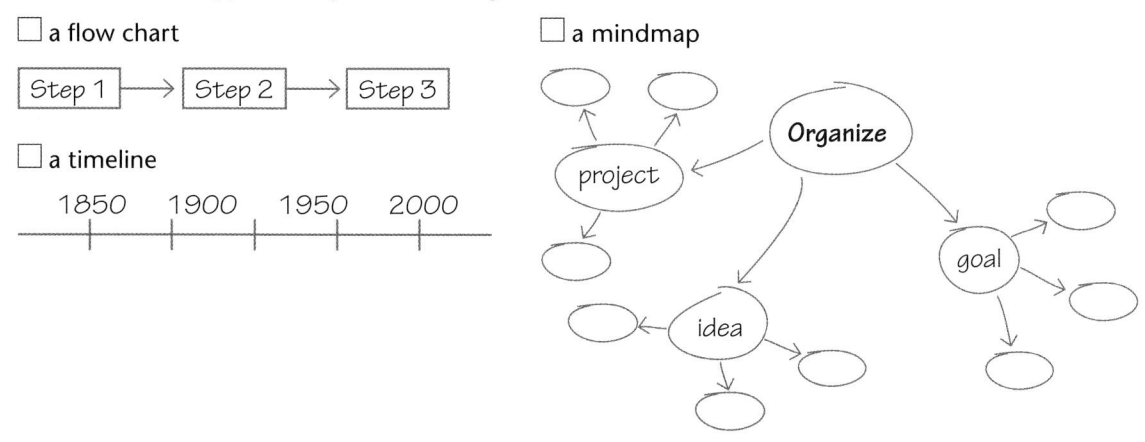

5 Use the steps in the box to complete the the diagram.

Design your campaign.	Promote your project again.
Review similar crowdfunding campaigns.	~~Start creating your masterpiece.~~
Start promoting your project six months early.	~~You have an idea for a project.~~

You have an idea for a project. →

Start creating your masterpiece ←

Unit 4 Processes

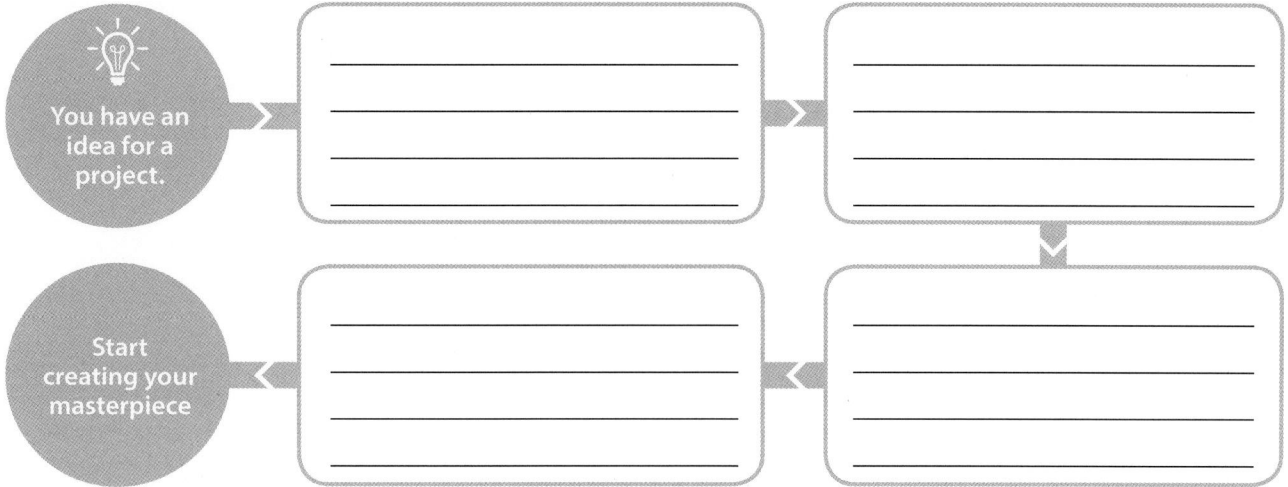

ENGLISH FOR REAL

REAL-WORLD ENGLISH: Asking for and giving clarification ▶ 4.4

1 Complete the conversation from Scene 1 of the video with words from the box.

| another thing | let me explain | I didn't get | I get it now | Why is that funny | Why was he |

Max: Well, we just saw that film about the guys who made the first science fiction film.
Sarah: Oh…I loved that movie!
Andy: It was really funny.
Max: ¹_____ some of the jokes.
Sarah: Such as?
Max: They kept making jokes about the Best Boy. ²_____ the best?
Sarah: OK, ³_____. First, the "best boy" is the guy on the movie set who uses tape to mark places for actors. And it was funny because he was so good at it.
Max: Oh! ⁴_____. How do you know so much about film?
Sarah: I went to film school.
Andy: I didn't know that.
Max: So…⁵_____. They kept complaining about a lost muffler. I never saw a scarf!
Sara: Oh…No!
Max: ⁶_____?
Sarah: A muffler is part of a car. It keeps the engine quiet.

2 Match the situation with the correct phrase.

___ 1 You cannot hear a person clearly.   a OK, that makes sense.
___ 2 You want to indicate that you understood.   b When I said…I meant that…
___ 3 You don't understand a word that someone said.   c To give you an example…
___ 4 You want to use an example to explain something.   d Could you say that again?
___ 5 You want to explain an idea using different words.   e What exactly does…mean?

3 Complete the conversation using phrases for asking for and giving clarification.

| What exactly | I didn't understand the part about | I get it | Could you say that again | Let me explain |

A: Thanks for the directions. So I turn left here. Then I go down Miller Road, right?
B: Yes, until you get to Parkmead Drive.
A: Parkneed Drive? ¹_____?
B: Sure, sorry. It's Parkmead, with an *m*.
A: OK, thanks. ²_____ the highway. Where do I get on the highway?
B: ³_____. After you pass the bus depot, the highway is on your right.
A: ⁴_____ is a bus depot?
B: It's the place where the buses are parked when they aren't in use.
A: OK. ⁵_____ now.

Unit 4 Processes

UNIT REVIEW: Podcast

GO ONLINE to listen to the podcast from the Unit Review.

1 Listen to the Unit Review Podcast, and number the steps in the correct order.

____ Record—do the first recording for practice, listen, have a friend listen, and revise your notes

____ Select your equipment

____ Plan—decide what it's going to be about, what the name of it is, and who the listeners are

____ Prepare your first episode—decide what it's going to be about, do research if you have to, and make notes

____ Choose a format—decide if you will you host it alone or with another person

2 Listen again, and complete the conversation.

Susanna: Hello, friends! Welcome to the ¹_____ episode of "How to Do ²_____"! I feel like we can call our listeners "friends" now, after 100 weeks of podcasting. Don't you think, John?

John: Absolutely, Susanna! Especially since when we started, it was only our friends who were listening!

Susanna: That's true, but now we have thousands of listeners! Thanks to all of you for listening, and thanks for the ³_____ and tweets supporting us. We love hearing from you.

John: And we love meeting you at our live shows. One thing that ⁴_____ a lot at our live show last week is that you want to learn ⁵_____ a podcast. So, that's what we're going to talk about.

LISTENING SKILL: Using visual information while listening ▶4.1

3 Look at the pictures. What kind of podcast does each picture represent? Listen again to check your answer, and number the pictures in the order that they are mentioned.

This image represents a podcast about:

1 _____ 2 _____ 3 _____ 4 _____

DISCUSSION BOARD PREPARATION

4 Look at the Unit 4 Review Discussion Point. Read the questions in the prompt. Then read the reply. Does this writer think that society needs art? Why or why not?

5 Label the part of the reply that answers question 1 from the prompt. Then label the parts that answer questions 2, 3, and 4.

Unit 4   Processes

UNIT REVIEW PODCAST

Unit 4 Review Discussion Point

Answer the questions in a post.
1. Read the quote. What kinds of things do artists produce?
   "An artist is someone who produces things that people don't need to have but that he—for some reason—thinks it would be a good idea to give them."
   —Andy Warhol, selected from *Oxford Essential Quotations*, 5th ed., edited by Susan Ratcliffe
2. Why does an artist produce art?
3. Why do people buy art?
4. Do you think a society needs art? Why or why not?

Latest: Anita Bernhart
Artists produce things like paintings, drawings, sculptures, music, and stories. Art is also created by dancers and actors. I think artists create art because they have ideas in their minds, and they want to make the ideas reality. For example, a musician might have a tune in her mind, and she might want to hear it for real, so she writes a song. I also think making art makes artists happy.

I think people buy art because they feel emotions when they look at it, listen to it, or read it. For example, I buy a lot of music because listening to music can make me feel relaxed or it can give me energy, depending on how it sounds. It can also make me feel happy or sad. I go to museums because paintings can make me feel emotions, too. In addition, I just like to see art that is made by people who are excellent at painting, especially because I'm really bad at it.

I do think society needs art. Art was created even before written language, so I think it's natural for humans to make art. Without art, life would be pretty boring. We wouldn't have music or paintings. We also wouldn't have movies to watch or books to read. We all spend so much time reading books, listening to music, and watching films and television. What would we do if all of that didn't exist?

6 Why does the writer think artists create art?

7 Why does the writer think people buy art?

8 Overall, did the writer answer all the questions? If yes, explain. If no, what can the writer change?

9 Review the rubric. Use the rubric to give a score for the reply.
Give points: 0 (not successful)–10 (successful).

Writing a Discussion Board Post	Points
The post answers the questions clearly and completely.	
The post has clear explanations and examples.	
The post shows careful thinking about the topic.	
The post uses passive verbs and adjectives with prepositions correctly.	
The post is long enough (200–250 words).	
Total	

WRITE YOUR POST

10 Read the quote. What kinds of things do artists produce? Why does an artist produce art? Why do people buy art? Do you think a society needs art? Why or why not? Write a draft of your post for the Unit 4 Review Discussion Point.

"An artist is someone who produces things that people don't need to have but that he—for some reason—thinks it would be a good idea to give them."
—Andy Warhol, selected from *Oxford Essential Quotations*, 5th ed., edited by Susan Ratcliffe

11 Use the rubric from Exercise 10 to score your post. Then improve your post.

Go ONLINE to add your comments to the discussion board.

5 Survival

Advice and warning with *should*, *ought to*, and *had better* ▶5.1

1 Write the words in the correct order to make sentences and questions.

1 her / ought / talk / to / to / you
   _____

2 not / had / he / job / quit / better / his
   _____

3 ask / I / again / him / should
   _____

4 better / stay / today / you / had / home
   _____

5 buy / car / should / new / a / we
   _____

2 Match the sentences to make conversations.

____ 1 Should I let Andy use my car?
____ 2 I have to tell Eric that I crashed his car.
____ 3 My paper is due on Friday, but I have to work all week.
____ 4 Should I take time off from work to help Sara?
____ 5 I lost my credit card.

a You shouldn't tell him on the phone.
b You'd better call your bank.
c Yes, you should. She really needs your help.
d No, you'd better not. He's a bad driver.
e You ought to ask your professor for more time.

Obligation with *must* and *have to* ▶5.2

3 Write the words in the correct column.

| can't | don't have to | have to | must |

It's necessary to do something	It's NOT necessary to do something	It's necessary NOT to do something

4 Choose the best answer.

1 To survive an earthquake, you *can't / have to* have a plan and a survival bag.
2 You *can't / must* wait for someone else to make a survival bag for you.
3 You *don't have to / have to* put a lot of things in the bag. You only need a few things.
4 You *can't / must* have a plan for finding family members if you get separated from each other.
5 You *have to / can't* stay in your home after it is badly damaged by an earthquake.

Intensifiers ▶5.3

5 Choose four adjectives that you can use with *absolutely* to intensify the meaning to the highest or lowest degree.

☐ difficult   ☐ exhausted   ☐ pleased
☐ important   ☐ amazing   ☐ awful
☐ good   ☐ essential   ☐ busy

6 Complete the sentences with an intensifier from the box. Different answers may be possible.

| absolutely | extremely | fairly | hardly |
| a little | really | pretty | |

1 To some degree:
   I'm _____ busy at my job this week.

2 To a very low degree:
   I had meetings in town all day. I _____ spent any time in the office.

3 To a high degree:
   We're _____ pleased about the news.

4 To the highest degree:
   These three tasks are _____ essential.

5 To a low degree:
   My job is _____ difficult.

VOCABULARY

VOCABULARY DEVELOPMENT: Phrasal verbs with *look* ▶5.1

1 Match each word with its definition.

___ 1 look into   a examine
___ 2 look up   b be careful
___ 3 look up to   c take care of
___ 4 look after   d look for information
___ 5 look out   e respect

2 Choose the best answer.

1 Look *up / out*! There's a person standing in the street!
2 I need to look *up to / into* getting a new laptop.
3 Can you look *out / after* my plants while I'm away?
4 I look *up to / up* my older sister. She's amazing.
5 Will you look *up / after* this word for me? I don't know what it means.

Natural disasters ▶5.2

3 Complete the definitions with a word from the box.

| change | damage | future | get ready | happened | safe |

1 If you destroy something, you _____ it so badly that it doesn't work or exist anymore.
2 If you affect something, you produce a _____ in it.
3 When you react, you do or say something because of something that _____.
4 If you forecast something, you use information that you have to say that something will happen in the _____.
5 If you prepare, you _____ for something.
6 If you protect something, you make sure that it is _____.

4 Match the beginning of the sentence in A with the ending in B.

A
1 The weather forecast says that ___
2 Extremely strong storms ___
3 You should cover your windows with wooden boards ___
4 We're buying food and water to ___
5 The storm is going to affect the roads ___
6 Some animals don't ___

B
a and cause a lot of traffic.
b there is going to be a huge storm tomorrow.
c prepare for the storm.
d react well to loud storms.
e can destroy houses.
f to protect them from the storm.

Extreme adjectives ▶5.3

5 Choose the words with a different meaning.

1	**amazing**	great / bad / awesome
2	**awful**	excellent / horrible / unpleasant
3	**delighted**	sad / happy / pleased
4	**essential**	necessary / main / unimportant
5	**exhausted**	tired / sleepy / excited
6	**extraordinary**	small / great / special
7	**freezing**	cold / warm / icy
8	**huge**	big / large / little
9	**ridiculous**	silly / smart / funny
10	**terrible**	bad / great / horrible
11	**terrified**	scared / safe / afraid
12	**tiny**	huge / small / little

6 Complete the sentences with the bold words from Exercise 5.

1 Don't go out in the snow. It's _____.
2 I have an _____ headache. I feel sick.
3 You did an _____ job on the project. It's perfect!
4 I was _____ during the storm. It was so scary.
5 Some rain is coming through the ceiling. There's a hole. You can't see it because it's _____.
6 I'm _____. I didn't fall asleep until 3 a.m., and I had to get up at 6.
7 Candles are _____ in a storm. You have to have them in case the lights go out.
8 I was _____ when I found out that no homes were damaged in the storm.

Unit 5 Survival

READING: Practice

1 Read the article. What are Tambora and Krakatoa?

☐ deadly volcanoes ☐ strong earthquakes ☐ huge waves

The Eruptions of Tambora and Krakatoa

Volcanic eruptions can be extremely deadly. Two of the world's deadliest were in Indonesia. Together, the eruptions of Mount Tambora and Krakatoa were responsible for the deaths of hundreds of thousands of people.

Mount Tambora erupted in 1815. It was the deadliest volcanic eruption in modern history. It killed about one hundred thousand people. Over five days, Tambora spewed fiery ash, rock, and lava into the air and onto the ground. The actual eruption was really terrible, but the ash continued the destruction well after Tambora stopped erupting. Ash covered everything and destroyed all the plants on the island. The resulting starvation and disease caused an additional eighty thousand deaths. The ash affected other parts of the globe, too. It caused crops to die as far away as Europe and the United States.

The 1883 eruption of Krakatoa was the largest and most famous in recorded history. After months of fairly small rumblings, there was a very loud eruption. In fact, it was so loud that people heard it from more than 2,500 miles away.

When survivors looked up after the eruption, they could no longer see Krakatoa because it had blown itself up. It blew debris an amazing fifty miles into the air, and ash spread across the globe. On the island, the ash filled the air in such a thick fog that it blocked out the sun for two days. But people didn't have to feel the shaking or see the ash to be affected by the eruption. The volcano crashed into the sea, causing tsunamis. These huge waves killed more than thirty-five thousand people.

The late nineteenth century saw a growth in the study of weather and natural disasters. Technologies such as the telephone and telegraph let individuals across the globe study the eruption and share their information with extraordinary speed. These technologies made Krakatoa one of the best understood natural disasters of its time. In the past, people hardly knew what to expect, but in the future, scientists might have the technology to forecast exactly when a volcano will erupt. They might even be able to predict which way lava will flow. Scientists must continue to study volcanoes so that people will be able to prepare. Until volcanoes can be absolutely understood, people should plan an escape route and leave the area if they ever see a volcano start to rumble and spit out ash.

—adapted from *Oxford Encyclopedia of the Modern World* edited by Peter N. Stearns

2 Match the numbers with what they represent.

___ 1 5   a the number of miles from which Krakatoa could be heard
___ 2 2,500   b the year that Tambora erupted
___ 3 100,000   c the number of deaths from tsunamis after Krakatoa crashed into the sea
___ 4 35,000   d the number of people killed by the eruption of Tambora
___ 5 1815   e the number of days that Tambora erupted

3 What did technology allow people to do in the past? What might it allow people to do in the future? Write *P* (past) or *F* (future) next to each item.

___ 1 learn from past eruptions
___ 2 forecast the exact time of the next eruption
___ 3 leave the area before a volcano erupts
___ 4 share information about eruptions quickly
___ 5 predict the direction of lava flow

REAL-WORLD READING

4 Complete the diagram with the words in the box.

| Indonesia | eruption | tsunamis | destroyed | all plants |
| deadliest | loud | five days | two days | around the world |

Tambora
_____ eruption
ash destroyed _____
erupted for _____

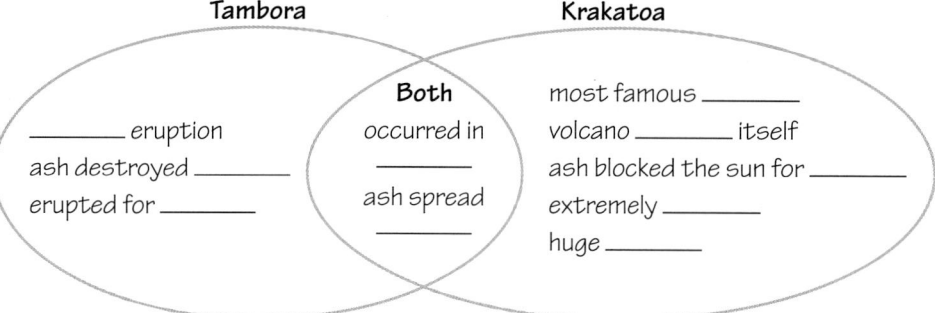

Both
occurred in _____
ash spread _____

Krakatoa
most famous _____
volcano _____ itself
ash blocked the sun for _____
extremely _____
huge _____

READING SKILL: Recognizing and understanding exemplification ▶5.2

5 Reread the first and second paragraphs of the article. Complete the sentences with an example from the box.

| 100,000 people died | ash continued the destruction | other parts of the world |
| starvation and disease | Tambora and Krakatoa | |

1 According to the article, _____ are examples of deadly volcanic eruptions.
2 To show that the eruption of Tambora was deadly, the writer explains that _____.
3 The fact that all the plants on the island died explains how _____.
4 The writer explains that _____ were results of dead plants.
5 The article mentions the United States and Europe to explain how _____ were affected by the eruption.

6 Reread paragraphs 3 and 4 of the article. Match the points in A with their examples in B.

A
1 The fact that Krakatoa blew debris five miles into the air explains ____
2 The eruption of Krakatoa was so loud that ____
3 People were affected by more than the shaking and the ash; ____
4 The article explains that a tsunami is ____
5 The telephone and the telegraph are examples of ____

B
a that it was the largest eruption.
b technologies that allowed people to share information quickly.
c a huge wave.
d Tsunamis also killed thousands of people.
e people heard it from 2,500 miles away.

REAL-WORLD ENGLISH: Asking for and giving advice ▶5.4

1 Number the lines from Scene 1 of the video in order.

____ Kevin: The bus stop. Could I come over?

____ Andy: Oh no! What happened?

____ Andy: Hey Kevin…what's up?

____ Kevin: Uh, I left my coat on the bus, and everything's in it. My keys, my ID, my credit card…I just have my phone!

____ Andy: Uh…sure. See you.

____ Kevin: Hey Andy?

____ Kevin: Andy, uh, there's a storm coming, and I'm in a bit of trouble.

____ Andy: Oh no…that's awful. Where are you?

2 Complete the conversation from Scene 2 of the video with words from the box.

| better | have to | I'd | should | think | would |

Max: Was that Kevin?

Andy: Yeah. He left his coat and keys…on the bus…unbelievable!

Max: Oh no! What's he going to do?

Andy: He's coming over. What ¹_____ I do? Should I invite him to stay?

Max: Well, I ²_____ study! I ³_____ you should call Phil.

Andy: But he's one of my oldest friends. What ⁴_____ you do if you were me?

Max: Well, of course ⁵_____ invite him. But Kevin is never quiet. You'd ⁶_____ call Phil. Please.

3 Complete the conversation using phrases for asking for and giving advice from the box.

| I think you should | What do you think | I'd recommend | It might be | If I were you |

A: Doctor, I get awful stomachaches sometimes after I eat. ¹_____ I should do?

B: ²_____, I would keep a food diary. ³_____ write down everything you eat and how you feel afterward.

A: OK, that's a good idea.

B: ⁴_____ a good idea to keep the diary on your phone since you always have it with you.

A: All right.

B: ⁵_____ that you start out eating very simple foods without a lot of ingredients. That will make it easier for you to figure out what is causing the problem.

A: Thank you, Doctor.

Unit 5 Survival

UNIT REVIEW PODCAST

UNIT REVIEW: Podcast

GO ONLINE to listen to the podcast from the Unit Review.

1. Listen to the Unit Review Podcast. What is it about?

   ☐ dangers in the past   ☐ history of travel   ☐ how to protect your teeth

2. Listen again. Are the sentences True or False?

	True	False
1 Traveling was fairly safe 500 years ago.	☐	☐
2 There were a lot of inns for travelers to stay in 500 years ago.	☐	☐
3 Doctors didn't know sugar was bad for people's teeth.	☐	☐
4 People sometimes brushed their teeth with sugary toothpaste.	☐	☐
5 In the 1600s, bad teeth often led to death.	☐	☐

3. Listen again, and complete the conversation.

   Ken: I ¹_____ information about dangers that people faced around 500 years ago. ²_____, one of the most dangerous things that people could do at that time was travel.

   Lina: Really? Why was traveling ³_____?

   Ken: Well, it was dangerous for a few different reasons. First of all, travelers back then couldn't always find a ⁴_____ on their journeys. Occasionally, travelers might find an inn—a kind of small hotel—to sleep in, but most of the time, they ⁵_____. One of the dangers of sleeping outside was ⁶_____. Travelers could actually freeze to death in their sleep.

   Lina: ⁷_____. They ⁸_____ traveled only in warm weather.

LISTENING SKILL: Interpreting changes in volume, speed, and pitch ▶5.1

4. Listen again. Match each sentence with a reason for the speaker's change in volume, speed, or pitch.

   ___ 1 They should have traveled only in warm weather.
   ___ 2 But wait, that probably wasn't always possible, was it?
   ___ 3 Oh wow, a couple of days?
   ___ 4 People, if you don't brush your teeth, you're going to lose them.

   a She was expressing surprise.
   b He was giving a warning.
   c She was giving advice.
   d She realized something as she said it.

DISCUSSION BOARD PREPARATION

5. Look at the Unit 5 Review Discussion Point. Read the questions in the prompt. Then read the reply. What does the writer think are two important things that humans have done to survive?

6. Label the part of the reply that answers question 1 from the prompt. Then label the parts that answer questions 2, 3, and 4.

UNIT REVIEW PODCAST

Unit 5 Review Discussion Point

Answer the questions in a post.
1. Read the quote. What have humans done over history to survive?
   "If we assume that mankind has a right to survive, then we must find an alternative to war and destruction."
   —Martin Luther King, selected from *Oxford Dictionary of Political Quotations*, 4th ed., edited by Anthony Jay
2. What different ways do individual people have of surviving modern life?
3. Would the modern-day person survive living 500 years ago, or have we changed too much?
4. Do you think a person from 500 years ago would survive in today's world? Why or why not?

Latest: **Eric Johnson**
Two of the most important things that humans have done to survive are discovering fire and building houses. People have to have fire to cook healthy food and to stay warm. Without fire, people could freeze to death in cold weather. Also, without fire, we would eat uncooked meat, and that could be very dangerous. Houses keep people safe, too. In the past, there were a lot of wild animals around. Houses protected people from these animals. Houses also protected, and continue to protect, people from extremely hot and cold weather.

One way that people survive modern life is by finding time to relax. Most people I know spend a lot of time working or studying and are really stressed. Stress is bad for your health, so you'd better find ways to avoid stress.

I don't think that the modern-day person would survive living 500 years ago. First of all, we wouldn't know how to look after ourselves. We wouldn't know how to grow our own food, and we wouldn't know what to do if we got sick. Second, we rely on modern technology so much that I don't think we know how to live without it. Any time we want to know something, we look it up online. If we went back in time 500 years and wanted to know if a certain type of plant was poisonous, for example, we would have no way of knowing unless we could ask a neighbor or a friend.

7 According to the writer, what is one way that people survive modern life?

8 Does he think that modern-day people would survive living 500 years ago? Why or why not?

9 Overall, did the writer answer all the questions? If yes, explain. If no, what can the writer change?

10 Review the rubric. Use the rubric to give a score for the reply.
Give points: 0 (not successful)–10 (successful).

Writing a Discussion Board Post	Points
The post answers the questions clearly and completely.	
The post has clear explanations and examples.	
The post shows careful thinking about the topic.	
The post uses *should, ought to, had better, must, have to,* and intensifiers correctly.	
The post is long enough (200–250 words).	
Total	

WRITE YOUR POST

11 Read the quote. What have humans done over history to survive? What different ways do individual people have of surviving modern life? Would the modern-day person survive living 500 years ago, or have we changed too much? Do you think a person from 500 years ago would survive in today's world? Why or why not? Write a draft of your post for the Unit 5 Review Discussion Point.

"If we assume that mankind has a right to survive, then we must find an alternative to war and destruction."
—Martin Luther King, selected from *Oxford Dictionary of Political Quotations*, 4th ed., edited by Anthony Jay

12 Use the rubric from Exercise 10 to score your post. Then improve your post.

Go ONLINE to add your comments to the discussion board.

6 Trends

Time expressions with the present perfect and simple past ▶6.1

1 Choose the correct verb forms. Then underline the time expressions.

1. Levi Strauss & Co. *was / has been* one of the best-selling brands of jeans since the 1800s.
2. In 2016, Levis *was / has been* at the top of the list of best-selling jeans brands.
3. Wrangler *took / has taken* the second spot on the list of best-selling jeans in 2016.
4. The Wrangler company *began / has begun* over 100 years ago.
5. Over the past century, both Levi and Wrangler jeans *were / have been* top sellers.
6. Some brand-new jeans companies *started / have started* in the past few years.
7. The brand AMO *launched / have launched* in 2015.
8. Two South Korean designers *created / have created* their company, Steve J and Yoni P, in 2008.

2 Complete the sentences with one of the phrases from the box.

for almost	in the 1950s
in the early	in the early
over the	

1. Jeans have been an important clothing item _____ 200 years.
2. _____ days, only men wore jeans.
3. Strength was the most important feature of jeans _____ 1900s.
4. _____, jeans became fashionable.
5. _____ past decades, more and more companies have started selling jeans.

Used to and be / get used to ▶6.3

3 Complete each sentence with the correct form of the verb in parentheses.

1. I didn't use to _____ when I was in my twenties. (exercise)
2. I can't get used to _____ to the gym before I go to work in the morning. (go)
3. What types of exercise _____ you use to _____? (do)
4. What kinds of food are you used to _____? (eat)
5. I got used to _____ for myself when I moved out on my own. (cook)

4 Choose the best answer.

1. *Are you used to / Did you use to* cooking all your meals yet?
2. *I didn't use to / I'm not used to* using this exercise machine.
3. *We are used to / We used to* run in the park every morning.
4. *I didn't use to / I'm not used to* like vegetables.
5. *Are you used to / Did you use to* go to this gym?

Do for emphasis ▶6.5

5 Complete the sentences with *do*, *does*, or *did* for emphasis or contrast.

1. We _____ buy a lot of clothes when we were younger.
2. People _____ wear jeans to work these days.
3. She _____ like to follow current fashion trends.
4. I didn't think we would ever see trends of the 1970s again, but some of them _____ come back.
5. _____ try out new trends if you like them.

6 Correct the incorrect sentences with *do*, *does*, and *did* for emphasis or contrast.

1. I did spent a lot of money on clothes this month.
   _____
2. Shaun does goes shopping a lot.
   _____
3. I didn't read fashion magazines when I was in school, but I do reading them now.
   _____
4. Trends do coming and going quickly.
   _____

Fashion (adjectives) ▶6.1

1 Choose the word that is the opposite.

1 **casual**   trendy ./ loose / cheap / formal
2 **classic**   formal / trendy / old / traditional
3 **stylish**   easy / tight / unfashionable / formal
4 **loose**   tight / easy / casual / classic

2 Read the descriptions. Then choose two adjectives that match each description.

1 a big old sweatshirt
    ☐ tight   ☐ formal
    ☐ loose   ☐ unfashionable

2 a pair of Levi's jeans
    ☐ formal   ☐ classic
    ☐ unfashionable   ☐ casual

3 a pair of bicycling shorts
    ☐ loose   ☐ tight
    ☐ fashionable   ☐ casual

4 a well-fitting men's business suit by a new designer
    ☐ stylish   ☐ loose
    ☐ classic   ☐ tight

5 a denim jacket style that all the clothing stores are selling right now
    ☐ unfashionable   ☐ trendy
    ☐ stylish   ☐ formal

3 Complete the sentences with an adjective from the box.

| casual | formal | loose | tight | unfashionable |

1 I like watching awards shows like the Oscars and seeing all the _____ suits and dresses.

2 I can't wear this dress anymore. It's from seven years ago. It looks so _____ now.

3 These jeans are too _____. I can't breathe!

4 I like _____ shirts because it's easier to move around in them.

5 We don't have to wear suits to work. We can wear _____ clothes.

VOCABULARY DEVELOPMENT: Adverbs and phrases for emphasis ▶6.3

4 Write the words in the correct order to make sentences.

1 these / truth, / I've / most of / To / the / diets / tell you / tried
_____

2 don't / make / clearly / lose / weight / They / people
_____

3 weight / I / fact, / every / after / gained / diet / In
_____

4 and / cook / I'll stop / foods / just / dieting / healthy
_____

5 last week / signed up / actually / a / cooking / I / class / for
_____

5 Correct five incorrect sentences.

1 In the early 1800s, Lord Byron actually made it popular to drink vinegar and water.
_____

2 To tell you truth, Lord Byron tried many strange diets.
_____

3 When he was in fact, in college, he sometimes ate only potatoes soaked in vinegar.
_____

4 He clearly wanted to lose weight.
_____

5 We can see that he thought that honestly these diets would help.
_____

6 However, actually the diets were very unhealthy.
_____

7 In fact, eating only potatoes and vinegar can make you really weak.
_____

8 More important, not getting enough vitamins and minerals can damage your body.
_____

Unit 6   Trends

READING SKILL: Using questions when reading ▶6.1

1 Look at the title and the headers. What do you think this article is about? Choose the correct answer.

☐ food and fashion   ☐ food and health   ☐ food and the environment

2 Read the first paragraph. Then check the questions that you think the article might answer.

☐ Can you save money if you eat less meat?
☐ What are some plants that are bad for the environment?
☐ What are some "green" ways to produce clothing?
☐ How can you grow your own food?
☐ Why are some plants bad for the environment?

3 Read the article. Write the questions you selected in Exercise 2. Then check the paragraphs where you found the answers.

Questions	Answers				
	1	2	3	4	5
1	☐	☐	☐	☐	☐
2	☐	☐	☐	☐	☐

A Trendy Problem

Home | About | **Articles**

Over the past few years, being "green," or environmentally conscious, has become trendy. People who used to eat a lot of meat and dairy are feeling the pressure to eat more fruits and vegetables instead. This is because raising animals for food uses a lot of land and resources and creates a large amount of greenhouse gases. Eating more vegetables and less meat and dairy for the benefit of the environment sounds like a great idea, but some plants may actually be harmful to the environment.

Soy Products

As it has become unfashionable to eat meat and dairy, soy products have become very trendy. The most common soy products are soy milk, tofu, and tempeh—a popular meat replacement. It might take some people a little while to get used to eating tofu and tempeh instead of meat, but soy manufacturers are working hard to create new meat-like products. In fact, in Japan, you can even find soy "steaks," which are shaped, flavored, and colored to look like meat.

The Need for Land

The problem with soy is that it needs a lot of land to grow. This means less land is available for other crops. More importantly, delicate environments, like rain forests, are being destroyed so that farmers can grow soybeans. This is really harmful to the environment because rain forests help clean dangerous gases out of our air, and plants and animals that can only be found in rain forests will disappear if the rain forests are gone.

Almonds, Avocados, and the Need for Water

Soy products are not the only trendy foods that can harm the environment. In the past several years, almond milk has become popular. What people might not realize is it takes a gallon of water to grow a single almond. The avocado is another popular food that uses a lot of water. It takes 72 gallons of water to grow a pound of avocados. Crops that need a lot of water might not be problematic in places with a lot of rainfall, but they make a big impact in places that are experiencing drought.

Protecting the environment is always a good idea. After all, Earth is our home. Just make sure that your efforts to protect the environment don't actually damage it.

—featuring content from *The Oxford Companion to Food*, 3rd ed., edited by Alan Davidson and Tom Jaine

READING: Practice

4 Write the name of the foods in the pictures. Then choose the pictures of foods that were mentioned in the article.

1 ☐ _____
2 ☐ _____
3 ☐ _____
4 ☐ _____

5 Read the statements. Choose *True, False,* or *Not Given*.

		True	False	Not Given
1	People eat and drink soy products in place of meat and dairy products.	☐	☐	☐
2	The first time people try tempeh they think it tastes just like meat.	☐	☐	☐
3	Soy milk is more popular than cow's milk.	☐	☐	☐
4	Someone in Japan created a soy product that looks like a steak.	☐	☐	☐
5	Soybeans create a lot of dangerous gases.	☐	☐	☐
6	Each year, thousands of miles of rain forests are destroyed to plant almonds.	☐	☐	☐
7	Almond milk tastes more like cow's milk than soy milk does.	☐	☐	☐

6 Complete the sentences with a phrase from the box.

soy products	soybean farming	a pound of avocados
rain forests	the environment	clean the air
an almond	land to grow	meat and dairy products

1 Being "green" means not harming _____.
2 People who are environmentally conscious often stop eating _____.
3 There is less land to grow other types of food because of _____.
4 Soybean plants need a lot of _____.
5 Tofu and tempeh are popular _____.
6 Rain forests _____.
7 Some animals live only in _____.
8 It takes over 72 gallons of water to grow _____.
9 It takes a gallon of water to grow _____.

Unit 6 Trends

ENGLISH FOR REAL

REAL-WORLD ENGLISH: Asking for and giving opinions ▶ 6.4

1 Number the lines from Scene 1 of the video in order.

____ Max: Why would you ask me that?

____ Kevin: Hey…Max! Oh wow…what are you doing in *that*?

____ Kevin: Sorry, Max, I'm just being honest. See ya later.

____ Kevin: No, I mean, are you going to a costume party?

____ Max: I'm not dressed like a clown. What's wrong with…?

____ Max: Uh…these are TROUSERS!

____ Max: Hi, Kevin. Just doing some sketching.

____ Kevin: Well, you're dressed like a clown!

____ Kevin: Personally, I think you look silly. Those pants, for one thing!

2 Complete the conversation from Scene 2 of the video with words from the box.

actually	asking	do look	honest	give
of course	Really	Right	the truth	wrong

Andy: Hey Max! You're home early.

Max: Yeah…

Andy: What's wrong?

Max: OK, ¹_____ me your ²_____ opinion. Do I look like a clown?

Andy: What? No, ³_____ not.

Max: Come on, tell me ⁴_____. Kevin said I looked like a clown.

Andy: Well, since you're ⁵_____…OK, maybe you ⁶_____ a bit…strange.

Max: ⁷_____? Does Kevin ⁸_____ have a point?

Andy: Don't get me ⁹_____—you have your own style, but…but please, take those pants over to Tina in the costume department at the theater!

Max: They're TROUSERS!

Andy: ¹⁰_____.

Max: Fine. But I'm keeping the hat.

3 Listen to Scene 2 again. Choose *True*, *False*, or *Not Given*.

		True	False	Not Given
1	Max wants Andy to give him an honest opinion.	☐	☐	☐
2	Andy's first response is honest.	☐	☐	☐
3	Andy changes his response.	☐	☐	☐
4	Max is angry with Kevin.	☐	☐	☐
5	Andy's final answer is polite.	☐	☐	☐
6	Max is pleased with Andy's answer.	☐	☐	☐
7	Max is planning to take his clothing to the theater.	☐	☐	☐

LISTENING SKILL: Previewing using images ▶6.3

1 Look at the pictures. Then choose the topics that you think the speakers are going to talk about.

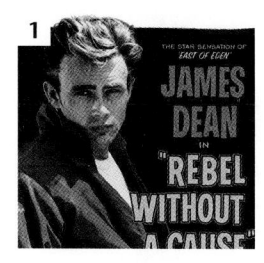

☐ sports ☐ trends ☐ old movies ☐ technology
☐ fashion ☐ cowboy boots ☐ celebrities ☐ blue jeans

UNIT REVIEW: Podcast

> GO ONLINE to listen to the podcast from the Unit Review.

2 Listen to the Unit Review Podcast. Who is the guest speaker?

☐ a fashion designer ☐ someone who creates trends ☐ someone who predicts trends

3 Listen again. Read the statements. Match each group of people with the correct description.

____ 1 innovators   a people who want to be stylish but don't want to be the first to try something new
____ 2 early adopters   b people who create new looks and don't care about being trendy
____ 3 the early majority c people who copy things that they like and create trends
____ 4 the late majority   d people who like traditional clothes and won't wear things that are trendy
____ 5 laggards   e people who won't try a trend until they are used to it

4 Listen again, and complete the conversation.

Lisa: For ¹_____ my listeners, can you give us an example?

Brian: Of course. Let's look at blue jeans. The innovators were film actors, like James Dean, who wore them in movies ²_____. Wearing blue jeans showed that a movie character ³_____ other people. Early adopters were the young people who liked the way blue jeans looked and, ⁴_____, what they meant...

Lisa: OK, that makes sense. So, we have ⁵_____ and early adopters. What is the third group?

DISCUSSION BOARD PREPARATION

5 Look at the Unit 6 Review Discussion Point. Read the questions in the prompt. Then read the reply. Does the writer like to follow fashion trends?

6 Label the part of the reply that answers question 1 from the prompt. Then label the parts that answer questions 2 and 3.

UNIT REVIEW PODCAST

Unit 6 Review Discussion Point

Answer the questions in a post.
1. Read the quote. How does something become fashionable or unfashionable?
   "Fashion is made to become unfashionable."
   —Coco Chanel, selected from *Oxford Essential Quotations,* 5th ed., edited by Susan Ratcliffe
2. How many people need to like or do something for it to become a trend?
3. Do you like to follow fashion trends? Why or why not?

Latest: Michelle Park
I think something becomes fashionable when a small group of people that others look up to start to wear it. For example, if actors or musicians start wearing something, it often becomes popular with people who watch their movies or listen to their music. For me personally, I think about a quarter of the people who I know have to start doing something before I think it is a trend. If only a few people start doing or wearing something, it seems like it's their own individual style, and I think it would be strange to copy it.

I used to follow fashion trends, but I don't now. Over the past few years, I've become less interested in fashion. I think it's because I'm so busy with school. Also, I can't afford to keep up with new trends.

As I mentioned, I'm not really interested in fashion, but I do notice trends. I think my favorite fashion trend is graphic T-shirts—T-shirts with pictures and writing on them. I actually wear those all the time, so I guess I'm a little stylish. I like them because they're fun and they're comfortable.

7 According to the writer, when does something become fashionable?

8 Does she like to follow trends? Why or why not?

9 Overall, did the writer answer all the questions? If yes, explain. If no, what can the writer change?

10 Review the rubric. Use the rubric to give a score for the reply.
Give points: 0 (not successful)–10 (successful).

Writing a Discussion Board Post	Points
The post answers the questions clearly and completely.	
The post has clear explanations and examples.	
The post shows careful thinking about the topic.	
The post uses time expressions and *used to* and *be/get used to* correctly.	
The post is long enough (200–250 words).	
Total	

WRITE YOUR POST

11 Read the quote. How does something become fashionable or unfashionable? How many people need to like or do something for it to become a trend? Do you like to follow fashion trends? Why or why not? What is your favorite and least favorite recent fashion trend? Why? Write a draft of your post for the Unit 6 Review Discussion Point.

"Fashion is made to become unfashionable."
—Coco Chanel, selected from *Oxford Essential Quotations,* 5th ed., edited by Susan Ratcliffe

12 Use the rubric from Exercise 10 to score your post. Then improve your post.

Go ONLINE to add your comments to the discussion board.

WORKBOOK ACKNOWLEDGMENTS

Back cover photograph: Oxford University Press building/David Fisher
Illustration: A. Richard Allen/Morgan Gaynin Inc, pp. 46.
Video: Mannic Productions, pp. 5, 26, 47.

The Publishers would like the thank the following for their kind permission to reproduce photographs and other copyright material: **123rf:** pp. 41 (jeans patch/Thodsapol Thongdeekhieo). **Alamy:** pp. 4 (woman w/ manuscript/dpa picture alliance archive), 23 (watching a film/EditorialByDarrellYoung), 27 (outdoor restaurant/ Bruce yuanyue Bi), 31 (volcano/tom pfeiffer), 69 (Voynich manuscript/GL Archive). **Blink:** pp. Cover: Quinn Ryan Mattingly, 3 (xray/Quinn Ryan Mattingly), 10 (satellite dishes/Nadia Shira Cohen), 37(women reading notes/Gianni Cipriano), 53(laptop & monitors/ Edu Bayer), 59 (man in theatre/Gianni Cipriano). **Bridgeman:** pp. 17 (Gertrude Bell/Pictures from History). Getty: pp. 1 (Eiffel Tower/Elena Segatini), 27 (people in theatre/John Eder), 52 (man, baby, laptop/KidStock). **OUP:** pp. 8 (firefighter/Shutterstock /Toa55),17 (Mesopotamian men/Kamira/Shutterstock), 27 (palm trees/Shutterstock/Maria Dryfhout), 39 (almonds/Sinelyov/Shutterstock), 39 (apple/Valentina Razumova/Shutterstock), (grapes/R. Gino Santa Maria/Shutterstock), 39 (avocados/Anna Kucherova/Sbytterstock) 39, (soy products/ Getty/photodisc) 51 (drone/Shutterstock/Maria Dryfhout), 66 (ship/Getty/Flickr), 73 (cars in flood/ 123rf / federicofoto), 80 (stack of money/Shutterstock/Lendy16). **Rex:** pp. 41(James Dean/Warner Bros/Kobal/REX/Shutterstock). **Shutterstock:** pp. 2 (rockclimbing/Vixt), 2 (skydiving/Germanskydiver), 10 (smartphone/ leungchopan), 23 (paper airplane/MicrostockStudi), 24 (laptop/Andrey Bondarets), 27 (flying car/Peter Albrektsen), 41 (cowboy boots/Evgeniya Porechenskaya), 72 (man on computer/Stokkete).

Authentic Content Provided by Oxford Reference

The author and publisher are grateful to those who have given permission to reproduce the following extracts and adaptations or copyright material:

p.3 Adapted from *A Dictionary of Business and Management* (6th ed.) edited by Jonathan Law. Copyright Oxford University Press 2016.
http://www.oxfordreference.com/view/10.1093/acref/9780199684984.001.0001/acref-9780199684984-e-3516?rskey=vrwMpq&result=3 http://www.oxfordreference.com/view/10.1093/acref/9780199684984.001.0001/acref-9780199684984-e-3425?rskey=2ErVtb&result=3
http://www.oxfordreference.com/view/10.1093/acref/9780199684984.001.0001/acref-9780199684984-e-2403?rskey=OflJkz&result=1
And *A Dictionary of Human Resource Management* (3rd ed.) edited by Edmund Heery and Mike Noon. Copyright Oxford University Press 2017.
http://www.oxfordreference.com/view/10.1093/acref/9780191827822.001.0001/acref-9780191827822-e-1122?rskey=VKf6Wt&result=1
http://www.oxfordreference.com/view/10.1093/acref/9780191827822.001.0001/acref-9780191827822-e-759?rskey=sFux4d&result=3

p.7 Bruce Springsteen, in *Oxford Essential Quotations* (5th ed.), edited by Susan Ratcliffe. Copyright Oxford University Press 2017.
http://www.oxfordreference.com/view/10.1093/acref/9780191843730.001.0001/q-oro-ed5-00010371?rskey=7gCGnS&result=1

p.10 Adapted from *Oxford Encyclopedia of the Modern World*, edited by Peter N. Stearns. Copyright Oxford University Press 2008.
http://www.oxfordreference.com/view/10.1093/acref/9780195176322.001.0001/acref-9780195176322-e-837?rskey=uWU0F1&result=1

p.14 Jerry Seinfeld in *Oxford Essential Quotations* (5th ed.) edited by Susan Ratcliffe. Copyright Oxford University Press 2017.
http://www.oxfordreference.com/view/10.1093/acref/9780191843730.001.0001/q-oro-ed5-00016411?rskey=qKaHYQ&result=1

p.17 Adapted from *The Oxford Companion to World Exploration*, edited by David Buisseret. Copyright Oxford University Press 2007.
http://www.oxfordreference.com/view/10.1093/acref/9780195149227.001.0001/acref-9780195149227-e-0079?rskey=ueBWEu&result=3

p.21 T. S. Eliot, Four Quartets, in *Oxford Essential Quotations* (5th ed.) edited by Susan Ratcliffe. Copyright Oxford University Press 2017.
http://www.oxfordreference.com/view/10.1093/acref/9780191843730.001.0001/q-oro-ed5-00004036?rskey=BP5Fky&result=1

p.24 Featuring content from *A Dictionary of Finance and Banking* (5th ed.) edited by Jonathan Law. Copyright Oxford University Press 2016.
http://www.oxfordreference.com/view/10.1093/acref/9780199664931.001.0001/acref-9780199664931-e-7174?rskey=Q7Nf0l&result=4

p.28 Andy Warhol in *Oxford Essential Quotations* (5th ed.) edited by Susan Ratcliffe. Copyright Oxford University Press 2017.
http://www.oxfordreference.com/view/10.1093/acref/9780191843730.001.0001/q-oro-ed5-00011293?rskey=IxsTon&result=1

p.31 Adapted from *Oxford Encyclopedia of the Modern World*, edited by Peter N. Stearns. Copyright Oxford University Press 2008.
http://www.oxfordreference.com/view/10.1093/acref/9780195176322.001.0001/acref-9780195176322-e-517?rskey=BQFCAR&result=2

p.35 Martin Luther King in *Oxford Dictionary of Political Quotations* (4th ed.) edited by Anthony Jay. Copyright Oxford University Press 2012.
http://www.oxfordreference.com/view/10.1093/acref/9780199572687.001.0001/q-author-00002-00000883?rskey=Mn5BiL&result=1

p.38 Featuring content from *The Oxford Companion to Food* (3rd ed.) edited by Alan Davidson and Tom Jaine. Copyright Oxford University Press 2014.
http://www.oxfordreference.com/view/10.1093/acref/9780199677337.001.0001/acref-9780199677337-e-2295?rskey=722Rd5&result=11
http://www.oxfordreference.com/view/10.1093/acref/9780199677337.001.0001/acref-9780199677337-e-0119?rskey=sVZZmA&result=4
http://www.oxfordreference.com/view/10.1093/acref/9780199677337.001.0001/acref-9780199677337-e-2294?rskey=FjoISU&result=3

p.42 Coco Chanel in *Oxford Essential Quotations* (5th ed.) edited by Susan Ratcliffe. Copyright Oxford University Press 2017.
http://www.oxfordreference.com/view/10.1093/acref/9780191843730.001.0001/q-oro-ed5-00012116?rskey=2Ej0j2&result=1

p.45 Featuring content from *Encyclopedia of Aesthetics* (2nd ed.) edited by Michael Kelly. Copyright Oxford University Press 2014.
http://www.oxfordreference.com/view/10.1093/acref/9780199747108.001.0001/acref-9780199747108-e-535?rskey=sjbhGn&result=1
http://www.oxfordreference.com/view/10.1093/acref/9780199747108.001.0001/acref-9780199747108-e-669?rskey=vHRH4t&result=1

p.49 Anonymous in *Oxford Essential Quotations* (5th ed.) edited by Susan Ratcliffe. Copyright Oxford University Press 2017.
http://www.oxfordreference.com/view/10.1093/acref/9780191843730.001.0001/q-oro-ed5-00000294?rskey=kDtnuW&result=1

p.52 Featuring content from *Oxford Encyclopedia of the Modern World*, edited by Peter N. Stearns. Copyright Oxford University Press 2008.
http://www.oxfordreference.com/view/10.1093/acref/9780195176322.001.0001/acref-9780195176322-e-788?rskey=MAM1OM&result=1

p.56 Andrew Grove in *Oxford Essential Quotations* (5th ed.) edited by Susan Ratcliffe. Copyright Oxford University Press 2017.
http://www.oxfordreference.com/view/10.1093/acref/9780191843730.001.0001/q-oro-ed5-00005087?rskey=pYmzVZ&result=1

p.59 Adapted from *The Oxford Encyclopedia of American Literature*, edited by Jay Parini and Phillip W. Leininger. Copyright Oxford University Press 2005.
http://www.oxfordreference.com/view/10.1093/acref/9780195156539.001.0001/acref-9780195156539-e-0163?rskey=wURxlP&result=8

p.63 W. Somerset Maugham in *Oxford Essential Quotations* (5th ed.) edited by Susan Ratcliffe. Copyright Oxford University Press 2017.
http://www.oxfordreference.com/view/10.1093/acref/9780191843730.001.0001/q-oro-ed5-00007179?rskey=IkcWM7&result=1

p.66 Adapted from *The Oxford Companion to Ships and the Sea* (2nd ed.) edited by I. C. B. Dear and Peter Kemp. Copyright Oxford University Press 2006.
http://www.oxfordreference.com/view/10.1093/acref/9780199205684.001.0001/acref-9780199205684-e-719?rskey=rCnfeJ&result=1

p.70 Rene Magritte in *Oxford Essential Quotations* (5th ed.) edited by Susan Ratcliffe. Copyright Oxford University Press 2017.
http://www.oxfordreference.com/view/10.1093/acref/9780191843730.001.0001/q-oro-ed5-00012502?rskey=apOmI1&result=1

p.73 Featuring content from *A Dictionary of Economics* (5th ed.) edited by John Black, Nigar Hashimzade, and Gareth Myles. Copyright Oxford University Press 2017.
http://www.oxfordreference.com/view/10.1093/acref/9780198759430.001.0001/acref-9780198759430-e-3869?rskey=eOou0h&result=1

p.77 Heraclitus in *Oxford Essential Quotations* (5th ed.) edited by Susan Ratcliffe. Copyright Oxford University Press 2017.
http://www.oxfordreference.com/view/10.1093/acref/9780191843730.001.0001/q-oro-ed5-00005370?rskey=8iZjQL&result=1

p.80 Featuring content from *Oxford Dictionary of Quotations* (8th ed.) edited by Elizabeth Knowles. Copyright Oxford University Press 2014.
http://www.oxfordreference.com/view/10.1093/acref/9780199668700.001.0001/q-author-00010-00002681?rskey=jiiFxO&result=6

p.84 Stephen Vincent Benét in *Oxford Essential Quotations* (5th ed.) edited by Susan Ratcliffe. Copyright Oxford University Press 2017.
http://www.oxfordreference.com/view/10.1093/acref/9780191843730.001.0001/q-oro-ed5-00000888?rskey=cxMZ4S&result=1